BK 663.406 K92M
MAKING FRIENDS IS OUR BUSINESS : ONE HUNDRED YEARS
OF ANHEUSER-BUSCH /KREBS, ROL
1953 4.00 M

3000 357212 40013
St. Louis Community College

400

663.406 K92m   M
KREBS
MAKING FRIENDS IS OUR BUSINESS:
100 YEARS OF ANHEUSER-BUSCH
                                    4.00

WITHDRAWN

JUNIOR COLLEGE DISTRICT
of St. Louis - St. Louis County
LIBRARY
5801 Wilson Ave.
St. Louis, Missouri 63110

D1264769

M   LIBRARY
JUNIOR COLLEGE DISTRICT
ST. LOUIS, MO.

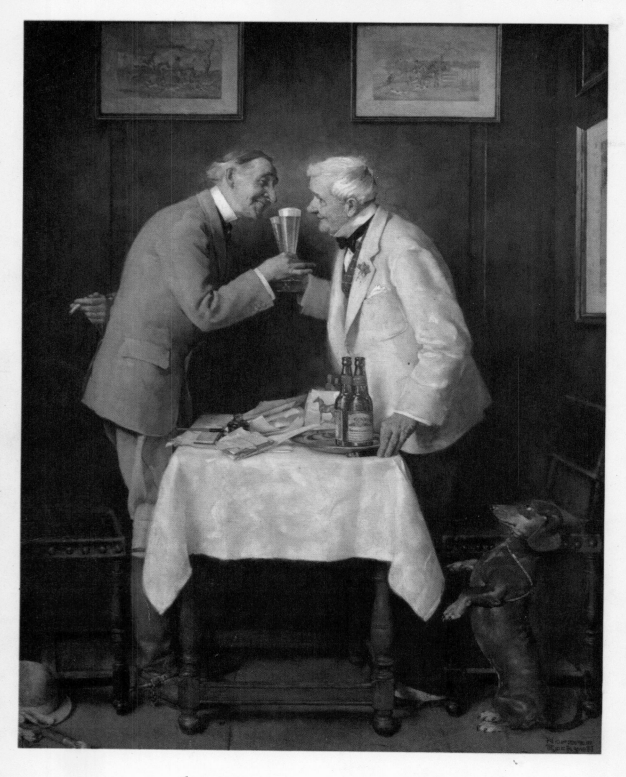

When gentlemen agree

Making Friends Is Our Business

100 YEARS OF

ANHEUSER-BUSCH

Making

Friends

IS OUR BUSINESS

100 Years of Anheuser-Busch

By Roland Krebs in collaboration with Percy J. Orthwein

Copyright, 1953
by Anheuser-Busch, Inc.

REPRODUCTION OF THE CONTENTS HEREOF, IN WHOLE
OR PART, PROHIBITED WITHOUT WRITTEN PERMISSION

Printed in the U.S.A.
The Cuneo Press, Inc.

TABLE OF CONTENTS

This in capsule form is the story of Anheuser-Busch through one hundred years . . . . Its purpose is to vignette the happenings that made movement and drama in the birth and growth of a great American institution . . . . Its purpose is to give you a clue to the colorful incidents, the perplexing problems and the clever and often painful solutions that came to pass in the century . . . The Introduction hopes to provide the incentive for the reader to go through the many pages of detail that follow and depict American workmen at work.

Chapter I

An obscure man starts an obscure brewery in 1852 and brews a failure . . . . Eberhard Anheuser, a creditor, takes over the brewery and its management, but soon finds that guiding his old business and his new business is too much . . . . Eberhard asks his son-in-law, Adolphus Busch, to take over management of The Bavarian Brewery . . . . Adolphus has a job very much to his liking and quickly begins to make things hum . . . . Adolphus revolutionizes his brewery and the whole brewing industry with the perfection of the first successful refrigerator car to ship beer into many regions . . . . He revolutionizes both all over again with the perfection of a method to pasteurize bottled beer . . . . Anheuser-Busch is definitely on its way to greatness.

Chapter II

Anheuser-Busch proudly offers the world Budweiser and the world takes it to its heart . . . . The beer destined to be the most famous beer ever known and destined to be enjoyed by more people than any other beer in history makes a spectacular success of itself over night . . . The brewing industry is troubled by cloudiness in bottled beer and Anheuser-Busch discovers a way to solve the problem.

Chapter III

Budweiser wins laurels the world over and in Bohemia it is declared officially finer than the finest Bohemian beers . . . . Adolphus pins back the ears of a cocky competitor . . . . Anheuser-Busch establishes "pure food laws" long before Uncle Sam does . . . . The famous picture, "Custer's Last Fight," begins

to make its appearance . . . . Young August A. Busch unhorses Adolphus by
deciding to become a cowboy—and quickly gives it up . . . . Young Gussie is
hustled off to Europe to learn brewing techniques . . . . Adolphus gives his son
a job at the brewery—on the bottom rung . . . . The son breaks up his father's
vacation in Europe by "tinkering" with the Budweiser bottling method . . . .
August A., introduces the metal crown cap and Adolphus is delighted upon
his return to St. Louis to see what a great success the 'blunder' has become . . . .

We learn something of the personality and character of Adolphus Busch . . . .
The young German immigrant comes to St. Louis and takes a humble job as a
steamboat clerk . . . . He becomes a salesman of brewers' supplies . . . . Becoming manager of the brewery gives him an opportunity to begin living with the
flair that is to characterize his whole life . . . . At Tony Faust's restaurant and
in his own dining room Adolphus entertains friends and business associates in
the grand manner . . . . A flashback to the marriage of Adolphus and Lilly
and how they began life together.

A newspaper reporter visits No. 1 Busch Place and describes its splendors and
distinguished visitors . . . . Adolphus acquires art treasures for his home . . . .
A granddaughter describes life in the household and preparations at Christmas
time . . . . Easter egg hunts for the neighbors' children become an institution
. . . . A private railroad car waits close to the house . . . . The family buys
a horseless carriage . . . . Adolphus and Lilly acquire homes in California,
New York and Germany . . . . He keeps in touch with the business by Atlantic cable . . . . He presents fine homes to his children . . . . Six thousand
employees celebrate the Golden Wedding.

Adolphus's health begins to fail . . . . Death comes suddenly but peacefully in
Germany in October of 1913 . . . . The story of his passing dominates the
newspapers . . . . There are many stories of his generosity . . . . Hundreds wait
in the rain for the train returning the body . . . . Employees take the casket on
the last inspection trip of the brewery . . . . St. Louis and the world go all out
to pay homage . . . . Crowds line the 20-mile route of the funeral cortege . . . .
Trolley cars stop for five minutes and two hotels extinguish all their lights **for**

five minutes as a tribute . . . . Charles Nagel delivers an inspiring eulogy . . . .
The press publishes many anecdotes about Adolphus.

tising to confidence messages that win wide acclaim . . . . In 1938 the brewery passes the two million barrels per year mark . . . . The Japs strike at Pearl Harbor . . . . Gus goes into the Army.

year . . . . Retirement means that an employee can enjoy a monthly income for the remainder of his lifetime . . . . 'Round-the-clock dispensary service and nursing care are provided . . . . A fine, big cafeteria with delicious food . . . . At the Coronation Ball each year the queen is chosen . . . . Handsome gifts are awarded to old employees.

Introduction

HAD YOU BEEN a visitor in San Francisco on the evening of April 17, 1906, you would have found that city's charm at its best. The traditional fogs were absent. Clean, clear, spring atmosphere let the stars look down on sights that delighted human eyes.

Light, laughter and the aroma of fine foods came from the many restaurants. The Grand Opera House had standing room only, for Caruso with his magnificent voice was the attraction. Market Street was thronged and noisy. The little cable cars scurried up and down the hills as though they were on a lark instead of in a business.

Fun was everywhere. You ended that evening pleasantly weary, and you rested peacefully—until 5:17 o'clock next morning. At that moment you were thrown violently from your bed to a floor that was undulating.

You heard a hideous rumble that could not drown out the crash of bric-a-brac and bulwark alike. That rumble told the story. Earthquake.

Outside was a new and awful world. Sidewalks wrenched up, walls torn down. Dust fouled the air, and in its haze hung a gory disc that was the morning sun. Ruptured water mains brought thirst first and finally fire. Smoke enveloped whole neighborhoods in sudden nightfall.

1

Terror and panic were rampant but matched by coolness and action. Disaster knit instant friendships among utter strangers. The need for a helping hand was everywhere.

Trying to comfort the homeless was a visitor from St. Louis . . . a man who loved the good things of life with great ardor, but loved stability, progress and peace even more.

Eventually, he found the telegraph office and sent a message to his company in St. Louis asking that $100,000 for public relief work be forwarded to him immediately. The telegram was signed, "Adolphus Busch."

That was a sturdy sum, indeed, in those days. If you didn't know him very well, you might have concluded that the president of the great Anheuser-Busch Brewing Association in St. Louis could well afford the gift; he probably inherited barrels of money.

Actually, Adolphus Busch was heir to nothing . . . nothing but character, initiative and a kindly feeling for his fellow men. Half a century earlier, he had gone from the deck of an immigrant ship to the clerk's cubbyhole on a Mississippi steamboat. Later he became a salesman of brewers' supplies and took the peculiar type of pushing around that is the salesman's lot. He learned that a good business head needed an ally in a good heart . . . that if you made friends, business took care of itself and ever so pleasantly.

What Adolphus Busch did in San Francisco seemed on the surface to be a spur-of-the-moment action. And so seemed most of the decisions that he made in his lifetime. On the contrary, those decisions had nothing to do with hunches. They sprang from deep-rooted convictions of what was right and what was wrong, what to do and what to shun. New ideas he explored inwardly and endlessly and when the thought was crystallized, action was trigger-fast.

That Adolphus Busch started from scratch and made a great success of himself is a story as old as is this land of opportunity. That story is relatively unimportant when it stands beside the story of what this one man did to influence the ways of thinking and the way of life of generations of men who were to give greater stature to the institution which he founded. Nor does his personal success come near to matching his success in cutting the pattern for the entire brewing industry.

From the moment that Busch took over a small and not too profitable brewery in St. Louis after the War between the States, there was no quibbling about quality. He proved what he knew—that quality through and through went far and wide. Having got the hoped-for response from St. Louis to his notion of what beer should be, he began thinking of how other communities would respond.

There he came up with a thought that revolutionized not only his own business, but the brewing and other industries as well.

It had to do with what you have looked at dully from train windows many times—the refrigerator railroad car.

Others, too, had thought that a refrigerator car would be a good thing. One Chicago meat packer was induced to send a trainload of his products to the East in what were presumed to be refrigerator cars. The shipment spoiled and the experiment was dropped.

Busch reasoned that if immobile refrigeration were possible, refrigeration on wheels could be perfected. Proper insulation and temperatures as nearly uniform as possible were essential. His idea worked so well that soon he began building ice manufacturing plants along railroad trunks fanning out of St. Louis. Beer that left St. Louis by the refrigerated trainload was re-iced along the way and Adolphus's beloved Budweiser beer was available in Texas and Chicago and east and west of both.

The number of ice plants which the brewery either owned outright or in which it had a half interest increased until there were thirty in operation.

Other brewers followed suit, just as they did when Busch perfected a method for pasteurizing beer. Big production and shipping became a new phase in an industry that, since the days when Washington and Jefferson had done their own brewing, had been confined to local and sectional operations.

In everything that he undertook, Adolphus Busch never feared failure. He believed that the sooner you got it over with the better. How, through this philosophy, he gave industrial reality to vision will be told on pages that follow.

The interesting thing at the moment is what manner of man was this that to this day every problem of corporation policy poses the question, "What would Grandfather have done?" Those problems are thoroughly discussed by "the family." And just who is "the family"?

Well, Anheuser-Busch is pretty much of a closed corporation. Very little of its blue-chip stock has been on the market. The majority is held and treasured by the descendants of Adolphus Busch and Eberhard Anheuser and their kin. So, in a directors' meeting, it is not uncommon to hear someone remark, "This is one of the worst problems the family ever has had to face." But the family goes further.

If you are an Anheuser-Busch department head, you're in "the family." If you work in that chilly place where Budweiser draught beer is kegged, don't bother to take off your fleece-lined rubber boots when your opinion is wanted. March yourself into the directors' room and say what you think. Problems are something for the whole family, you know.

A combination of birthplace and personality made it inevitable that Adolphus Busch would bring into his business a feudal system of sorts—with feudalism's foundations, not its fallacies. No winner-take-all sophistry, for example. If, on your new job, you outlasted your probationary period, you were expected to stay for your lifetime and grow and profit with "the family."

Spellbinders and windjammers were notoriously unwelcome. Men who knew their jobs were respected. Busch didn't take any particular pride in being able to call employees all over the place by their names. He just enjoyed doing so.

The brewmaster, the maltster, the man who bought the cooperage—all these were feudal lords whose word was law. If costs went up, they had a free hand to meet them. Cutting costs was all right, cutting quality was out.

When Busch's son, August Anheuser Busch, reached his maturity, he was

ADOLPHUS BUSCH—Having completed his education in Germany, and become a linguist of considerable skill, he went to America to seek his fortune.

hustled off to Germany to learn the fundamentals of making fine lager beer. Upon August's return to America, he was put through a brewers' school in Chicago so that the American facets of the science were not overlooked. Then he got not a desk, but a pair of all-weather shoes and was put to work at plant maintenance. In that way, the successor to the founder began to learn every phase of the business.

Does this sound as though Adolphus Busch lived for and loved only his business?

He loved life and what gives meaning, depth and color to life—people. Most of all people, he loved his wife, Lilly, and their children. His evenings were for his family and its friends. His mornings and afternoons were for his business and his friends . . . and at luncheon his hospitality had many a grand flourish plus the fact that there never was any four-flushing about who picked up the check. It wasn't swagger. It was the feeling, "You're part of the family . . . and I'm head of the family . . . period."

The combination of affection and acumen that was Adolphus Busch left to his descendants a heritage difficult to describe. That heritage was a flourishing business, yes. It was an institution, yes, but it was something that goes far beyond the meaning of those words.

You might call it a fountainhead of enterprise that pioneered in making science and the laboratory the guardians of beverage and food products, while at the same time giving a helping hand to union labor when workmen took their first steps in collective bargaining . . . and you can correctly call it a factor in bettering human health, nutrition, animal husbandry . . . the first to build an American diesel . . . the last to put self before public service.

In the pages which follow you'll find no statistical saga of corporate greatness content merely to be first in its field, but you will find the living of life by a group of people who found happiness and stimulation in startling innovation and solid achievement.

This is a story that begins most unexcitingly, as has been said, in a small

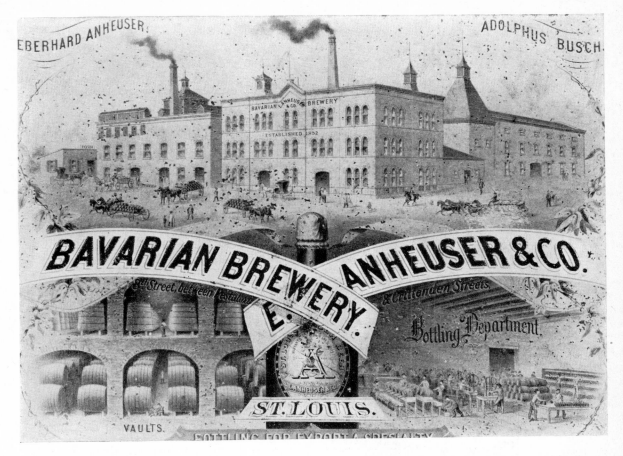

THE BAVARIAN BREWERY—This old tin-
type shows the original Bavarian Brewery. It was a failure until taken over by
Eberhard Anheuser.

EBERHARD ANHEUSER—He chose his
son-in-law, Adolphus Busch, to manage
the brewery he took over.

St. Louis brewery and goes quickly into one hundred years of healthful fermentation, bubbling with results that many have shared.

This brewery found its way into the unwilling hands of Eberhard Anheuser through an unsatisfied loan. It was a development that he had not sought, since he long before had proved his business ability as a manufacturer of good soap, which had produced a comfortable fortune for him.

Eberhard Anheuser was known as a man of the highest integrity, with many warm attributes of character. His son-in-law, Adolphus, always spoke of him with the utmost tenderness and affection and, with great pride, pointed to his father-in-law's great attachment and love for the business.

But Eberhard Anheuser was only too well aware of the fact that his brewery needed the courage and the resourcefulness and virility of a younger man—one to whom he could entrust its management and see it grow from year to year. In this he was not disappointed for, when he died in 1880 at the age of 75, the brewery he had lived to see prosper and on its way to fame, sold 141,163 barrels of beer that year.

When Anheuser was prompted to make a partner of Adolphus Busch and turn active management of the brewery over to him, the brewery soon was buzzing and sales were zooming. Expansion of business was followed by expansion of facilities . . . and again by expansion of business.

Thus it has been for a century . . . expansion of facilities, expansion of business . . . plus expansion of enterprise and activity.

From the small and little-known brewery came a sprawling giant covering 70 city blocks, but it was no longer merely a brewery.

The Home of Budweiser beer became the world's largest single source of natural vitamins of the B complex. With these vitamins, its research staff co-operated with physicians and hospitals in the mass correction of diet deficiencies that whipped pellagra and restored vitality and usefulness to sufferers half blind or otherwise physically handicapped as a result of malnutrition.

The Home of Budweiser beer found itself so allied with the sciences of

ADOLPHUS TASTES SUCCESS—His urbanity and business sagacity win him friends and advancement in St. Louis.

medicine and nutrition that it made and continues to make substantial financial grants to universities and hospitals. Its pharmaceutical yeasts are of such quality that if the quantity could be doubled or even tripled the market for them would be there.

In the Home of Budweiser beer was installed the first diesel engine built in America under patent rights acquired by Adolphus Busch, who formed a separate corporation to manufacture these wonder-engines for stationary and marine use. Fortunately, Anheuser-Busch was in a position to supply diesel engines in imposing numbers for Navy submarines in World War I.

In World War II, the skill that had produced diesel after diesel turned to the production of an intricate robot masquerading under the unimpressive name of "ammunition hoist." Actually, it brought up from the magazine of a warship a high-explosive shell whose firing time was electronically controlled on the way up by the gunnery officer mathematically calculating ranges and trajectories high above deck.

A wartime visitor to the diesel plant once remarked, "Why, these things work like a fine watch."

The answer given him was, "If this equipment had the magnified tolerances of a fine watch, it wouldn't work; these are *close* tolerances."

At about the time that these ammunition hoists were being made, Anheuser-Busch sacrificed its profitable refrigerator manufacturing department in order to concentrate upon production of military glider fuselages and wing assemblies. And, at the same time, it gave up its flourishing Budweiser beer business on the Pacific coast by voluntarily withdrawing from that market so that more freight cars would be available to the government to ship the essentials of war to embarkation points. It was the only brewery to make such a contribution.

Of course, everyone in wartime is eager to exhibit resourcefulness and make a contribution. The House of Anheuser-Busch always has been on the move in times of peace, too.

For example, it long had been the custom of brewers to dump their spent grains and residual yeast into the most convenient river. The men of Anheuser-Busch followed the common practice for a time, but searched diligently for ways to avoid this waste and eventually discovered how to make excellent use of these residuals.

The spent grains, richer in protein than they were at the harvest, were dried and processed and sold to farmers as stock and poultry food. The yeast residues were dried and processed and made available to the pharmaceutical industry.

At the time that this is written—in 1952—Anheuser-Busch is looking with satisfaction back to the summer of 1950, which brought a most unusual tribute to an American corporation. The city of Newark, New Jersey, declared a public holiday on the occasion of the ground-breaking ceremonies that marked the beginning of a new Home of Budweiser beer far from St. Louis. State, municipal and civic leaders tendered a luncheon to the Anheuser-Busch management and then went in a body to the site of the new plant.

The celebration was attended by big newspaper headlines, radio broadcasts and newsreel cameras.

Thus, as Anheuser-Busch approached its one hundredth birthday, in 1952, it could well afford to look back with pride upon its achievements—and its adversities. In a sense, Anheuser-Busch was "founded" three times. When prohibition scuttled its business overnight, a new kind of Anheuser-Busch had to be created quickly. In the thirteen years of prohibition, the company brought itself back to prosperity, gradually at first, but steadily.

The once great brewery became the manufactory of soft drinks, bakers' and pharmaceutical yeasts, refrigerator cabinets for the ice cream industry, table syrups and syrups for medicines, and corn products. A giant suddenly appeared in the form of hopped malt syrup sold in one-pound cans.

The demand for this syrup, as well as competitive brands, reached enormous proportions, thanks to the determination of millions of Americans to make "home-brew," a poor substitute for beer. For that they required malt syrup. The sale of it was legal to begin with and, besides, the federal government, already sick of its prohibition law, made no attempt to interfere with this home activity.

In this connection could be cited the seemingly endless anachronisms of that screwball era of prohibition, but one seems particularly pertinent. You could, if you chose to do so, write to your congressman and get from the Government Printing Office a thick book of testimony adduced from witnesses by an obliging senator who hated prohibition. The questions and answers were such that they added up to a great compilation of recipes for making alcoholic drinks in the home.

So, the manufacture and sale of hopped malt syrup was strictly legal, profitable and highly competitive. In traditional fashion, Anheuser-Busch was determined to make the best malt syrup and succeeded so well that soon it was spending hundreds of thousands of dollars each year to advertise its brand.

When, in 1933, a majority of the American people decided that prohibition had accomplished its absolute worst, the relegalization of beer caused Anheuser-Busch to have its third "founding." Much new equipment was needed, but the most important factor of all—brewing skill—had never departed from the plant. The then president, August A. Busch, and his sons, Adolphus Busch III and August A. Busch, Jr., were schooled in the art of brewing. Moreover, they were fortunate in having still their brewmaster of many years of service, the late Dr. Rudolph Gull, a scientist of the highest order, well known to his colleagues in the best breweries of his native Switzerland and of England, Germany, Denmark and Czecho-Slovakia.

Dr. Gull soon had Budweiser beer in production on a huge scale and he was training other brewmasters in his technique, including the man who was to succeed him so notably, Frank H. Schwaiger.

Meanwhile, the company decided to abandon malt syrup for the now extinct home-brewer but continue with the varied enterprises that had helped it to weather the prohibition tempest. While young "Gussie" managed the brewery division, his elder brother, Adolphus Busch III, continued to have charge of all other activities. Both sons had been schooled in the art of brewing. Adolphus always had had a warm spot in his heart for the company's bakers' yeast, which had entered a field that was virtually a monopoly and yet was able to emerge as an aggressive competitor. Indeed, that business grew to such stature that it was necessary to construct a second big yeast plant at Old Bridge, New Jersey.

After beer's return, it seemed for months that the demand for Budweiser beer never would be met. Then, suddenly, there was a noticeable slowing up. While business with other brewers, whose products were not premium-priced, was booming great guns, Anheuser-Busch found the task of recapturing pre-prohibition markets an arduous one.

Consumers, accustomed during the dry era either to sweet soft drinks or sweet carbonated beverages for masking the taste of bootleg liquors, had forgotten for the most part the slightly tart taste of fine beer generously flavored with costly imported and domestic hops. Criticism of Budweiser beer's taste and character began trickling in from sales forces in different parts of the country. The trickle became a tide and the protest was always the same—"You've got to change the brewing process; people say that Budweiser beer is too bitter."

Matters came to a climax at the company's sales convention in January, 1934, when all its branch and district managers were in St. Louis. August A. Busch, Jr., presiding, told the convention of the criticism and asked for a raising of hands to show who favored a change in the taste of Budweiser. The hands plainly showed that a majority was in favor.

Thereupon, August A. Busch, Sr., took the speaker's stand. He was in failing health, but a combination of anger and conviction lent to his voice a robustness that was not to be forgotten. He was answering that question, "What would Grandfather have done?"

"In the first place," he said, "to the sophisticated palate, Budweiser is not bitter. You might say it has a dash of tartness. It is not, therefore, the product which is on trial, but the consumer. The consumer, during prohibition, mixed his bootleg concoctions with ginger ale, soda and similar sweet mixers to disguise the liquor's raw taste. At the moment, he may favor the sweet beers, but that can't last.

"My father and Dr. Gull knew more about brewing skill and beer quality than you younger men who are just beginning to sell it. They created the distinctive taste of Budweiser—by, among other things, spending millions of dollars for imported Saazer hops to be blended with our best American blossoms. That distinctive taste is what made Budweiser outsell all other beers, year after year.

"To the uninitiated, a sweet beer may seem desirable for a time, but eventually it begins to cloy. Our competitors' sweet beers will re-educate the public to appreciate the taste of Budweiser—and it won't be long. Nobody will tinker with the Budweiser process or the Budweiser taste as long as I am president of Anheuser-Busch.

"And, another thing; when the public does become educated and the demand for Budweiser is greater than the supply, somebody is going to suggest that we can sell more Budweiser and make more profit if we produce it faster. That we won't do, either.

"Budweiser is America's finest lager beer. Only by kraüsening and long aging can you produce Budweiser—and we're going to produce Budweiser, not a second-rate beer masquerading as Budweiser."

Soon thereafter, Anheuser-Busch began inviting the public to make "The Five-Day Test." The test was the brain-child of Eberhard Anheuser, the grandson. The consumer was urged to drink Budweiser for five days and, on the sixth day, to try a sweet beer. "You will want the Budweiser flavor thereafter," the invitation concluded.

How sound was the thinking of August A., Sr., was shown by a trend back to Budweiser as sudden as had been the trend away from it. It was the competitors who changed *their* formulae and tried with no success to duplicate the Budweiser beer taste.

Thus, August answered the question, "What would Grandfather have done?"

The demand for Budweiser beer began soaring to embarrassing proportions. Each year, despite constantly expanding facilities, the product had to be rationed to dealers because of the constantly soaring demand. Since 1935, there never has been a year when demand did not exceed supply—an unprecedented tribute to a product.

When the annual output of Budweiser beer reached three million barrels (U. S. standard of 31 gallons) in 1941 the Sales Department felt that the impossible had happened. The newspapers, always reluctant to give any commercial product a free ride, published photographs of the three-millionth barrel and attendant ceremonies and printed fine tributes to Anheuser-Busch and its Budweiser beer.

Then, in 1950, the annual productive capacity of the St. Louis brewery reached six million barrels. Its counterpart in Newark in the following year had a productive capacity of 1,250,000 barrels, with expanded facilities there already planned for.

And the other-than-brewing activities of Anheuser-Busch increased at a corresponding rate.

What once was only a brewery now finds itself not only the world's largest brewery still, but an institution of multilateral businesses as well. It is a supplier of enormous quantities of ingredients to the pharmaceutical and food industries. Its nutrients go into baby foods and military rations. Its starches aid in the drilling of oil wells and the making of paper, textiles, adhesives, ammunition, batteries and many other necessities. It processes frozen eggs for bakers and supplies them with yeast, enrichment wafers for bread, malt syrup, corn syrup and jellies. Its syrups are widely used in the making of ice cream and candy. Anheuser-Busch products are employed in the making of such diverse things as rubber, aluminum and soap.

The material you have read thus far has been an attempt to give you a panorama-in-a-capsule of an institution that is unique. It is unique not just for its success and its magnitude. Those attributes are commonplace in this country, which has been blessed so abundantly.

It is unique because of the character of the institution and the characters that knit the corporate personality into a whole. You might rhapsodize for pages on this point, but it can be summed up best by saying that the story of Anheuser-Busch proves to anyone interested in happiness and success that there will be neither frustration nor failure where there is friendship . . . that the fruit of friendship is a bumper crop.

Now that you've had your panorama-in-a-capsule, you have in the chapters that follow a much more detailed chronology that seeks to explain why, what might have been hit-or-miss, became thus-and-so.

In the end it will all add up to, "MAKING FRIENDS IS OUR BUSINESS."

Chapter *I*

FAILURE—THEN A

MIDGET BECOMES A GIANT

NEITHER prosperity nor promise attended the origin of what was to become Anheuser-Busch, Inc. In 1852, a St. Louisan named Schneider—first name unknown—founded a small brewery on a site a few blocks from the Mississippi River and near the location of the present plant on the South Side of St. Louis. The little brewery had a productive capacity of 3,000 barrels a year.

One of the reasons for choosing the location was that there were caves close by. Such underground caverns were highly desirable for brewing operations in those days of no artificial refrigeration. Their temperature was cool and constant and provided good if not optimum conditions for ageing beer. Moreover, Schneider was able to cut blocks of ice from the frozen Mississippi River in winter and store the cakes in sawdust for use in the summer.

St. Louis, where the Ozark Mountains' northern slope begins, had several large caves. The largest and best known exists today under one of the city's busiest intersections, Jefferson Avenue and Washington Boulevard. At the turn of the century, the spot for many years had included a summer garden known as Uhrig's Cave. To this garden came traveling theatrical companies to entertain St. Louisans who enjoyed Uhrig's fine food and beer.

Mr. Schneider's cave, on the other hand, served a purely utilitarian purpose. It was more than ample for his dwindling trade, but destined to prove inadequate for the booming business of his successors in later years. In fact, man-made caves that served as annexes were dug out of the earth and chipped out of the rock in the later years. When mechanically created refrigeration came into its own, the caverns were abandoned and forgotten. Their presence became known again in the 1930's when deep excavations were made for new stock houses for Budweiser beer.

In one of the rediscovered caves was an ancient package crate that contained advertising novelties and a miscellany of records. The box apparently had been placed in the cave for temporary storage and then forgotten.

Three years after Schneider built his brewery, he found both his cave and his cash box empty. There is no record to indicate whether it was because he was a poor brewer, a poor salesman, or both. His business was taken over by a competitor, Urban & Hammer. The new owners renamed the property The Bavarian Brewery and launched an expansion program, largely with a $90,000 loan obtained from Eberhard Anheuser, a prosperous soap manufacturer of St. Louis.

The new operators managed to get production up to 8,000 barrels of beer a year, but The Bavarian Brewery failed in 1857, with Anheuser its major creditor. He chose to buy up the interests of the minority creditors and thus became sole owner of the brewery.

Eberhard knew that the rehabilitated and expanded property was a valuable one and that, rightly operated and exploited, could be made very profitable. He undertook the job of management himself while continuing to operate his soap business. After eight years of this, he came to two conclusions. The first was that trying to manage the two enterprises was too much for one man and that he would do badly to neglect the one which originally had brought him success and wealth. The second conclusion was that The Bavarian Brewery needed new blood and a younger man to give it all of his time.

Eberhard wanted a man who knew beer, who loved beer, and who could brew and sell beer.

He chose Adolphus Busch for three very sound reasons: Adolphus understood beer. Adolphus was one of Eberhard's warmest friends. Adolphus was the husband of Eberhard's daughter, Lilly.

Eberhard Anheuser knew nothing but good of his new general manager and son-in-law. He knew that Adolphus had been born on July 19, 1839, at Mainz, Germany, the youngest of the twenty-one children of Ulrich Busch, a prosperous wine merchant and dealer in brewing supplies. He knew that Adolphus had migrated to America in 1857 in the wake of those early German-born St. Louisans, who had sought freedom in their native land in the revolution of 1848 and then, failing, fled across the Rhine and then the Atlantic to the freedom that the United States gave for the asking.

Adolphus knew that one thing that America did not give for the asking was success. For that you worked. So, he worked at first as a clerk on a Mississippi River steamboat and got to know the people who inhabited the Midwest that was to help him become a world figure. Commerce was very much in the air in those steamboating days and it did not take the young immigrant long to decide that increasing commissions were more profitable than a steady salary. He became a salesman and began to get acquainted with prosperity through the medium of brewing supplies, just as his father had done.

When the War between the States began, there was strong sentiment for the South in St. Louis, but a majority favored the North. Adolphus decided that the Union which had offered him freedom and a future was worth defending. He enlisted in the United States Army, served in the Missouri campaigns and was honorably discharged as a corporal. Thereupon, he returned to his brewers' supplies business. His employer was the Charles Ehlermann Hops and Malt Company.

It was during the War between the States that brewers favoring the Union volunteered to pay a tax of $1.00 a barrel to help defray military costs. Anheuser was one of these volunteer taxpayers. The tax remained after cessation of hostilities. It was the beginning of federal excise taxes.

Beer-loving St. Louis with its breweries was a good market and Adolphus was a good salesman.

The changes that Eberhard wanted he got fast when Adolphus was put in charge. Just exactly what startling innovations the new general manager created is unknown, but one startling fact is history. In five years, Adolphus increased the brewery's capacity from 8,000 barrels of beer that was difficult to sell to 18,000 barrels of beer that was snapped up wherever offered. By 1873, production had jumped to 25,000 barrels and the need for further expansion of facilities became a certainty.

In that year of 1873, Adolphus became a full-fledged partner and the name of the concern was changed from The Bavarian Brewery to The E. Anheuser Co.'s Brewing Association. Six years later the name was changed again, this time to The Anheuser-Busch Brewing Association.

In the year of 1875, the business had been incorporated for the first time. Its capacity was 34,797 barrels of beer. The total investment was valued at $240,000. On this investment, 480 shares of stock were issued, each worth $500.00. The stockholders were Eberhard and his son-in-law and daughter, Adolphus and Lilly. This was the corporate structure that was to remain unchanged for fifty years.

From that time on, the Anheuser-Busch Brewery, as it came to be known first to St. Louis and then to all America, touched off a veritable chain reaction of accomplishment. Success followed success and innovations and improvements assumed fabulous proportions.

As noted in the Introduction, Adolphus Busch was the first to build

ADOLPHUS GROWS A TRADEMARK—The carefully-trimmed mustache and goatee was to become famous at home and abroad.

CARL CONRAD—He collaborated with Adolphus Busch in producing the most famous beer the world has ever known—Budweiser.

and operate a successful refrigerator car. He shrewdly decided that a great market was his for the taking in the southern states. The climate was conducive to thirst and unfavorable to proper fermentation in cool cellars. So, he built his trackside ice-houses and tackled Texas.

The success of the venture was so great that he next went into Louisiana and then into other states in the South. A similar spread into midwestern areas followed. Eventually he was to expand all over the United States.

Between 1875 and 1880, sales were nearly quadrupled, going from 34,797 barrels to 131,035. Another five years brought sales to 318,082 barrels. The record was more than doubled in still another five years—702,075 barrels. There was a leveling off period between 1890 and 1895, sales in the latter year touching 739,000 barrels. Then came another upward spurt and in 1900 the production reached 939,768 barrels.

From then on, a momentum that was to be stopped only by prohibition swept Anheuser-Busch sales into 1,600,000 barrels by 1913, with ten percent of the output being shipped to countries the world over.

In 1893, the newspaper, the St. Louis Star, published a book describing the industries of St. Louis. About Anheuser-Busch it said in part:

> Our design is to give some idea of the present extent and power of the business of the Anheuser-Busch Brewing Association, celebrated among the first brewing companies of the world. The frontage of this beer manufactory, when it first started, was twenty-five feet on a little by-street in South St. Louis. Today the plant takes in 100 acres of ground, covered thickly with the various buildings necessary to the business, and undermined with magnificent cellar vaults, ice houses and storage rooms, which it is a privilege to visit and inspect.
>
> The buildings are not only placed with due regard to the convenience of the manufacture, but they have been constructed with an eye to architectural beauty, and their spires and domes and towers and perfect proportions —massive and imposing here; light, graceful and sky-piercing there—give particular pleasure to the eye and excite wonder in the beholder. It is one of

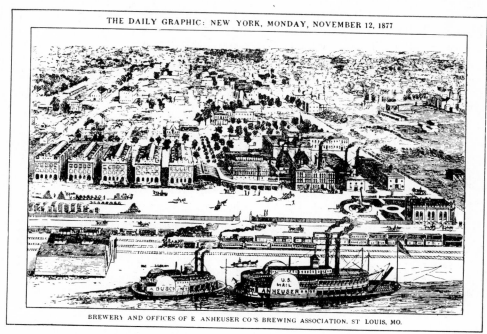

THE DAILY GRAPHIC: NEW YORK, MONDAY, NOVEMBER 12, 1877

BREWERY AND OFFICES OF E ANHEUSER CO'S BREWING ASSOCIATION. ST LOUIS, MO.

OUR FAVORITE BREWERY, 1883

THE ANHEUSER-BUSCH.

A BREWERY BECOMES NEWS—Expansion of the plant was so rapid and great that journalists visited it to describe it for their publications.

the sights of the grand city of St. Louis, which no visitor, who has the opportunity offered him, should fail to see.

The brewing capacity of this great concern is now equal to 1,800,000 barrels per year, or about 5,000 barrels per day. One remarkable feature of the progress of the Anheuser-Busch Association is the bottled beer trade. It was the first in this country to manufacture the bottled article with the Pasteurization process. The bottled beer trade had previously been monopolized by European brewers. Whole cargoes were imported from time to time to this country. In a few short years the trade was revolutionized. The imports were largely changed to exports, and today the bottled beer of the Anheuser-Busch Association, of St. Louis, is well and favorably known, not only in Europe, but all round the world. It has proved itself so decidedly superior to all the German and English brands, that it has virtually driven them out of the American market and is making a bid for the trade in Mexico, Central and South America, Australia and the islands of the Pacific that will soon put all competition aside.

The bottling department of the brewery is the largest in the world, and its capacity is 100,000,000 bottles per annum. The brands are the "Anheuser-Busch Standard," the "Original Budweiser," the "Pale Lager," the "Pilsener or Exquisite," the "Old Burgundy," and "Faust Beer," and include all varieties of beer from very pale and light brewings to dark and heavy beer, to suit the taste and demand for cold and hot climates.

We have in another article given some attention to the life and career of Mr. Busch, president of the Anheuser-Busch Association. There are other men in the association who deserve special mention: George Krumsick is the first vice president; August A. Busch, the second vice president and general superintendent; E. Muhlemann, the secretary and treasurer, and Adolphus Busch, Jr., the assistant secretary.

This concern has a daily consumption of 12,000 bushels of malt and 7,500 pounds of hops. With these figures in mind, one cannot be astonished when told that only last year Mr. Busch was offered by an English syndicate $8,000,000 for the Anheuser-Busch plant.

Mr. Busch stands in the front rank of the business men of St. Louis. His great wealth and income have enabled him to become interested in many of the important enterprises of St. Louis. He is a large owner of bank, insurance and trust stocks; has put much of his means in manufactories of various kinds, and is the owner of a great many valuable city and country lots and acres. With all his success and high-standing he has suffered no detriment at all in his character as a kind-hearted, easy-mannered, pleasant gentleman, his purse always wide open to private and public charity, his greeting to his old friends always cheery and cordial, his devotion to his family always loyal and most affectionate.

This is an excerpt from an article appearing in "St. Louis Up To Date," published by Consolidated Illustrating Company, in 1895:

ANHEUSER-BUSCH BREWING ASSOCIATION

Their beer is noted for its rich color, purity, bouquet, delicious flavor and nourishing tonic properties. It has been subjected to exhaustive tests by skillful analytical chemists, whose reports have established its purity and healthfulness; it has been awarded the highest premium wherever exhibited, even in competition with the renowned products of the old world, and it is shipped through agencies and branches to all parts of the United States, and exported to Mexico, Central America, the West Indies, Brazil, Australia, the Sandwich Islands, China, Europe and, we may state, all parts of the civilized world. The leading brands are: "Standard," "Budweiser," "Pilsener," "Pale Lager," "Burgundy," "Liebotschauer," "Erlanger" and "Faust," each of which is absolutely unexcelled, in its particular sphere, by any beer that is made.

The lager beer which is bottled here undergoes a process known as "Pasteurizing," enabling it to successfully resist the effects of changes of climate, and to be opened as fresh and sparkling in the Torrid as in the Temperate zone. This firm will go down in history as the originators of the present system of bottling beer for shipment to all parts of the world, the year 1873 marking the inception of this new departure, upon a scale of considerable magnitude. This mammoth establishment consumes no less than one-thirteenth of the total amount of water supplied to the people of St. Louis, while 15,000 carloads of coal is the annual allowance. The Association owns and operates 1,250 refrigerator cars for the shipment of beer, which is delivered to all the chief centers of the country, in the same splendid condition in which it leaves the storehouse.

An army of 2,200 skilled hands are employed in various capacities, and it would be difficult to estimate the value and beneficial influence of this concern, with its large pay roll and diversified operation, upon the general trade and the steady development of St. Louis.

The plant is a city in itself. Its elevator storage capacity is 1,400,000 bushels of grain. In the bottling houses the enormous number of 100,000,000 bottles can be put up each year. Boiler houses with eight batteries of two boilers each have a combined horse power of 6,000. The plant has coopers' shops, blacksmith shops and stables where the 150 splendid horses in service find excellent accommodation. The ice and refrigerator houses contain great De La Vergne machines, one of which, having a capacity of 500 tons, is the largest in the world.

Mention must however be made of the immense malt house, in which barley is malted by a pneumatic process, the annual capacity being upwards of 2,000,000 bushels. The manufacture of bottles was formerly conducted by the Association at two places in the state of Illinois, Belleville and Streator, but works have recently been acquired in this city for this purpose, in which a complete modern outfit has been installed, including patent self-feeding furnaces, and appliances which are the most improved embodiment of correct mechanical principles, in the manufacture of glass bottles.

Unlike other aspirants for supremacy in this line in the world, this brewery has the great advantage of facilities for transportation by water as well as by land, the ice houses, in fact, being located directly on the west bank of the Mississippi River. As regards the future, one thing appears certain, and that is, that the same skill and enterprise, which have been the chief factors in placing the Anheuser-Busch Brewing Association in its present position, as the undoubted leader in every respect of the brewing concerns of the world, will soon cause it to become as pre-eminent over the largest European manufacturers in quality of products.

The brewery of 1866 had one 25-horsepower engine, but the Home of Budweiser had the power of a giant by 1919. Total boiler horsepower was 12,665, engine horsepower 11,725 and electricity output 3,740 kilowatts. It owned the largest ice manufacturing machine in the world. Refrigeration facilities produced the equivalent of 4,250 tons of ice a day.

The value of the property, which in 1913 covered 142 acres containing 110 individual buildings, was estimated at $40,000,000.

Certainly, Adolphus knew a trend when he saw it. He guessed right when he guessed that beer was destined to become one of America's most consumed beverages. Twenty-three million Americans were consuming the output of 431 breweries in 1850, but ten years later 1,269 breweries were supplying a population of 31,500,000 persons.

The term "genius" was applied to Adolphus over and over again in his lifetime. It would seem from the record that the first to discover the genius was father-in-law Eberhard. He seemed quite content to play the role of pater-familias and let his general manager with the big ideas and big, booming, friendly voice take the wheel.

Given a free rein, Adolphus made each day a demonstration of boldness in both imagination and the means to implement it. He was positive that in order to make money you had to spend money—and he spent it lavishly, but always with discretion.

According to a book by James Buel and J. A. Dacus entitled "A Tour of St. Louis," published in 1878, The E. Anheuser Co.'s Brewing Association had just completed an expansion program involving a new fermenting and lagering cellar. The book describes the new cellar as follows:

> The beer vault is constructed after a new design and is an illustration of the originality of the proprietors. It is built of solid masonry and brick, the walls being thirty inches in thickness. It is two stories in height, each story being twenty feet in the clear. The first floor is laid with heavy granite flagstones and contains the fermenting tubs and two tiers of lager beer casks, one of sixty and the other of forty casks, each cask having the capacity of sixty barrels. The second floor is of iron on which an immense quantity of ice is packed from which drafts of air constantly descend through conduits in the wall to the first floor by which the contents of the huge casks are kept at a uniformly very low temperature.

Chapter II

THE WORLD'S MOST

FAMOUS BEER IS BORN

Anheuser-Busch was producing sixteen brands of beer in 1876, when Budweiser beer made its first appearance. It is pure presumption, but seemingly a reasonable one, to conclude that this variety of brands was dictated by marketing conditions and consumer preferences.

Anheuser-Busch records indicate that the co-founders of the company saw to it that the "A & Eagle" trademark was displayed on the label of each brand of beer so that the consumer would recognize it as a product of a house whose fame for highest quality was spreading.

Adolphus, once he realized what he had in Budweiser beer, was shrewd enough to sense that sixteen brands were in competition with one another and incapable of enjoying the benefits of advertising and marketing effort that could be concentrated behind fewer brands. Gradually, he reduced the number.

Again he was far ahead of his time in visualizing what he could do with bottled beer. True, his pioneering of the refrigerator car for shipping perishable draught beer was a technical and financial success. His trackside refrigeration plants not only re-iced the refrigerator cars, but they sold ice to their communities at a profit. Successful as it was, this operation never could be as profitable as shipping an unrefrigerated product anywhere in the world.

How far ahead was Adolphus in his thinking is shown by industry records which display in Anheuser-Busch's hundredth year a steady trend toward the bottle and away from draught beer.

Moreover, the retailing of draught beer in itself was a costly and cumbersome operation. The brewer, rather than be at the mercy of a saloonkeeper's whims, usually found it expedient to be the mortgagor of the retailer's property and thus have a voice in how it was to be operated. And, in addition, in each large market, horses, wagons and stables had to be maintained for regular deliveries.

Bottled beer, on the other hand, could be delivered anywhere and at any time. Too, it opened new outlets in homes, hotels, restaurants and out-of-the-way places.

Certainly, Adolphus Busch had not been standing still between the time that he took over management for Eberhard Anheuser and the time that Budweiser beer came into being. But, with his new product, he was destined to display speed of expansion and growth of prestige on a scale not often matched in American industry.

The origin of Budweiser beer was a thoroughly businesslike procedure, yet a fanciful legend about that origin persisted for many years. The story, with no basis whatever in fact, was so often told that not a few officials of Anheuser-Busch believed it through the years.

The tale was that Adolphus and a St. Louis friend, Carl Conrad, were traveling in that part of Czecho-Slovakia known in past years as Bohemia. They obtained lodging for a night in a monastery in a little town. There Adolphus was so impressed with the beer brewed by the monks that he forthwith made a deal with them to give him the recipe, the yeast and right to brew it in St. Louis. Adolphus was pictured as carrying the precious race of yeast across the Atlantic in an ice cream freezer.

A romantic story, but not a shred of truth in it!

Actually, Adolphus and Carl Conrad collaborated on the new beer, with the understanding that Carl's restaurant in downtown St. Louis was to be the guinea pig that would try the new brew on the public. Carl's restaurant had prestige—and the new beer was to have a prestige of its own.

The requirements for Budweiser beer were several. It was to be brewed from premium-priced ingredients. The barley was to be carefully graded and the smaller grains discarded because their ratio of husk to carbohydrate and protein was too great. Since American barley contains more protein in proportion to carbohydrates than European barleys, the supplemental carbohydrates would come from costly brewers' rice, not corn grits.

The choice of rice over corn was a fateful one. Rice contains much less oil than grits and that little oil is so bland as to make rancidity no problem. Moreover, brewers' rice contributes to the quality of the beer's foam, its brilliance and its stability. Through the years, brewers' rice has been considerably more costly than brewers' corn grits. Competitors tried unsuccessfully to turn the asset of rice into a liability. The taste and quality of Budweiser beer defeated their aims.

Another "must" for the new beer was a very generous portion of expensive Saazer hops to be blended with costliest American hops. Finally, the beer was to be a true lager beer—kräusened and left to go through a leisurely secondary fermentation that would bring it to mellow maturity enlivened with natural carbonation.

From his earliest days as general manager of the brewery, Adolphus demonstrated an interest in exploration that was to keep him far ahead of his competitors. He visited Europe repeatedly and studied the advancements of its brewers. In so doing, he learned of Louis Pasteur.

The French scientist had been called into service by his government, because a large segment of the Republic's population was showing an increasing interest in beer imported from Germany, with a consequent loss of revenue to the French vintners, brewers and government. Beer brewed in France was so inferior to that imported from Germany that it went begging.

Pasteur found that it was primarily a lack of cleanliness that made France's beer bad. He knew that for many decades German brewers were given to cleaning their equipment with boiling water. It was a practice started by German monks in the breweries that were part of nearly every monastery. The monks didn't know why boiling water helped as a cleansing agent; they just knew from experience that it did.

Thus it was that Pasteur discovered the presence of micro-organisms in the atmosphere. The discovery resulted in pasteurization—the killing of micro-organisms in beverages and foodstuffs with heat—and laid the groundwork for antisepsis, without which even the simplest surgery was a gamble.

Adolphus ordered his technical staff to perfect a method for pasteurizing bottled beer—and it was accomplished in 1873 after many heartbreaking reverses.

In a book called "Commercial and Architectural Structure" published in 1888 by Jones and Orear, this statement was made on page 275:

> The city's (St. Louis) export trade in bottled beer dates from the introduction by Anheuser-Busch of the pasteurizing process for the preservation of bottled beer. Previously, this trade had been monopolized by European breweries but, today, there is hardly a country in the world where the superior excellence of the Anheuser-Busch bottled beer is not known and appreciated.

> Though properly dating only from the accession of President Busch in 1865, this establishment has outstripped the largest breweries of the old world. Its output, in 1886, being 379,237 barrels against 363,017 barrels for the Spaten Brewery of Munich, 348,600 barrels for the Dreher Brewery of Vienna and 235,950 for the Pschorr, Munich. In like manner, all the

great breweries of Milwaukee, New York and Philadelphia have been left behind. For the year ending on January 1, 1888, its product was 456,511 barrels and its sales now are at the rate of 500,000 barrels a year. Its bottling is the largest in the world and the output exceeds 25,000,000 bottles a year.

The Anheuser-Busch Brewing Association employs 1,200 men, consumes 1,100,000 bushels of barley and over 700,000 pounds of hops, uses over 400,000 barrels and boxes, consumes 500,000 bushels of coal, and the meter shows 250,000,000 gallons of water used in beer making, cooling machines, washing, etc.

While pasteurization was a great step forward for Anheuser-Busch, as well as other brewers who copied the new technique, bottling troubles were not ended for any of them. Consumers, ignorant of the reason why, looked with suspicion on a sort of milkiness that clouded beer in the bottle to the extent that it had a marbled appearance. Actually, it was quite harmless, but uninviting to the eye. It was caused by oxidation of some of the beer's constituents. The problem was how to get rid of the oxygen that remained in the bottleneck after the cork was inserted.

The solution came from Dr. Rudolph Gull, brewmaster whom Adolphus had brought to St. Louis from Switzerland. Adolphus firmly believed that Gull was a brewing perfectionist, an opinion which the venerable doctor shared in a naïve and most inoffensive way.

Dr. Gull's solution was simple: A jet was made a part of the bottling equipment. The bottle was filled in the customary way and then, just before it was corked, the jet sent a sudden squirt of beer into the liquid already in the container. The agitation thus caused stirred up the beer's CO_2 just enough to form a gaseous "piston" that expelled the bottleneck oxygen on its own way out. The result was beer of brilliant clarity.

Adolphus's determination to perfect pasteurization of bottled beer was one of his most farsighted decisions. It equipped him to exploit the beer that was to make him and his company world-renowned—Budweiser.

Chapter III

A SON'S "TINKERING"

BECOMES A TRIUMPH

PUBLIC ENTHUSIASM for the new beer called Budweiser was instant. Sales grew at an enormous rate and there was never to be a time until national prohibition that the supply exceeded the demand. In 1878, the trademark was registered with the United States Patent Office.

Adolphus couldn't get bottles fast enough in the open market, so he established the Adolphus Busch Glass Manufacturing Company and made his own bottles.

Two years after its introduction, Budweiser beer was being exported. Buel and Dacus, authors of the book, "A Tour of St. Louis," previously referred to, said that Budweiser beer was popular in Cape Town, Hong Kong, Shanghai, Calcutta, Singapore, Nagasaki, Tokyo, the Sandwich Islands, Hawaii, England, Melbourne, Sydney, Valparaiso, Rio de Janeiro and all coastal cities of Central and South America.

Such popularity is easier to understand when one remembers that within the year that it was introduced, Budweiser beer took the highest award for any beer from anywhere at the Philadelphia Centennial Exposition in 1876. Subsequently, it took highest awards at expositions in Paris, 1878; Amsterdam, 1883; New Orleans, 1884; Chicago, 1893; Vienna, 1898, and St. Louis, 1904.

This story appeared in the St. Louis Republican, on May 10, 1879:

ANHEUSER BREWING CO. WINS GRAND PRIZE

AT PARIS EXPOSITION

ANHEUSER BREWING COMPANY TRIUMPHANT

They Have the Gold Medal
The Highest Premium Awarded
at the Paris Exposition of 1878

Yesterday we had the pleasure of seeing the gold medal awarded to this firm over all others, for the best beer on exhibition, also of reading the original letter accompanying it, a copy of which is appended:

UNIVERSAL EXPOSITION OF 1878
OFFICE OF THE U. S. COMMISSIONER GEN'L.
DEPARTMENT OF STATE

Washington, May 6, 1879

To the Anheuser Brewing Association
St. Louis, Missouri

I have today sent you, by Adams' express, the gold medal awarded to you by the International Jury, for your exhibit at the Universal Exposition of 1878, held at Paris.

Very respectfully
W. C. McCormick
Commissioner General

As it will be seen, St. Louis carries off the prize. We congratulate the company and its enterprising manager, Adolphus Busch.

A great triumph came in Bohemia in 1903. Competing with world-famous Bohemian beers, Budweiser was voted the world's finest bottled beer by the State Brewing Station.

1878
PARIS

1893
CHICAGO

1884
NEW ORLEANS

1904
ST. LOUIS

1908
BERLIN

1883
AMSTERDAM

1898
VIENNA

1876
PHILADELPHIA

SOME OF THE AWARDS PRESENTED TO ANHEUSER-BUSCH

Adolphus told the world about his product when he had printed on the label, "America . . . Europe . . . Africa . . . Asia . . . Australia." That was now his market—the entire civilized world. Also, he boldly printed on the label a guarantee that Budweiser would keep in any climate.

A dramatic illustration of the soundness of his claim was to come in August, 1919, when a bottle of Bud that was 22 years old was opened and tested. The bottle had been parachuted from a balloon as a stunt for a street fair in Alton, Illinois. A resident of the community recovered the bottle and presented it as a souvenir to John Elble, the manager of the Anheuser-Busch branch in Alton. Twenty-two years later Elble became curious about the contents and had the bottle opened and the Budweiser sampled publicly. It was declared "pure, palatable and delicious."

Adolphus decided that he, personally, was going to sell Budweiser in style and he saw to it that his package had style. In those days, before the invention of the metal crown cap, Budweiser was made to appear like a fine vintage wine. It had unquestionably the most eye-appealing beer label on earth. Each cork was branded with the name of Anheuser-Busch and, after insertion, was wired down and the bottle neck wrapped with metal foil.

The president of Anheuser-Busch liked to travel and Budweiser beer gave him a good reason for doing so. Up and down and across the country he went, perfecting his sales organization, seeing to it that the best hotels and restaurants appreciated what they had to offer their patrons in the St. Louis beer.

Few men have had a better understanding of word-of-mouth advertising than Adolphus. On his journeys, he always gave gold coins to the train crew. He gave ornate pocketknives containing a peephole portrait of himself in one end to those who made a pleasant impression on him. He was a gracious and even lavish host.

As the popularity of Budweiser soared and as Adolphus covered the country on goodwill missions, he demonstrated his acumen again. There were to be no franchises. All business was to be transacted on an order-to-order basis.

In the remote Island of Ceylon in the Indian Ocean the name, Anheuser-Busch, was a household word. This was our agency at Colombo

This was the Anheuser-Busch agency at Manila, where our dependents learned that one of civilization's finest products came from St. Louis

Here at Port Arthur Anheuser-Busch products were distributed to parts of Russia, China and Japan

In Batavia, Java, the South Sea Islanders preferred Anheuser-Busch's famous beverages to their own matchless color.

In Hong Kong the Chinese translated the A and Eagle trade-mark into their word sign for quality

The Oriental knows a good thing when he sees it, so we had to establish this agency at Tientsin, China

THE BREWERY GROWS AND SO DO THE WRITE-UPS.—Adolphus was an elegant host and editors and writers rewarded his hospitality.

Thus, he kept the door always open to a more aggressive wholesaler if the incumbent proved phlegmatic. If sales were not up to par, there was no apathetic franchise owner to keep them in the rut.

The policy proved itself. An ambitious wholesaler realized that he could make a fortune from the privilege of selling a beer whose popularity, year in and year out, climbed steadily. The result was that the turnover of wholesalers through the years was astonishingly small.

In the year of 1952, the order-to-order basis of business still stood.

One of the big reasons for Adolphus's confidence in his product and its future sprang from the conviction that not only was his brewing process sound but it was attended by everything that science and sanitation could give it. He told friends often that he could turn his entire plant and his brewing ingredients over to the most sagacious competitor and that competitor could not brew beer up to Anheuser-Busch standards because the man just would not have the proper understanding of cleanliness.

On one occasion, a competitor published some large-space newspaper advertisements in which he pictured his brewery as a paragon of cleanliness. The inference was that no other brewer went quite so far in the matter of sanitation. Adolphus squelched that with his own advertisement, whose headline said in effect, "A good brewer would no more brag of his cleanliness than a gentleman would boast of washing his face."

An Anheuser-Busch house organ, called The Tatler, said: "Anheuser-Busch made its own 'pure food laws' long before the Congress of the United States or the Legislatures of the several States ever thought of enacting statutes on the subject. It would be impossible to write pure food laws so stringent that their application could add one iota to the purity of Anheuser-Busch products."

How well that creed was followed by the descendants of Adolphus was demonstrated several years before Anheuser-Busch reached its hundredth birthday. The grandson-president, August A. Busch, Jr., plagued by a demand for Budweiser that constantly and embarrassingly exceeded the supply each year from 1935 on, entered into preliminary negotiations with a brewer whose property had been described as adaptable to the Budweiser process with a minimum of new construction.

August and his brewmaster inspected the brewery minutely and voted against buying the plant. "One thing that turned me against it," the president told his brewmaster, "was the pile of debris—broken bottle cases, beat-up barrels and just plain junk—that I saw piled against a wall outside the plant. That's no way to run a brewery. If it's spic and span it ought to *look* spic and span, inside and outside."

Even the wagons which delivered Adolphus's Budweiser beer to dealers reflected the immaculate interior of the brewery. They sparkled with polished brass and varnish. Horses were the best of their breed and their saddle-soaped harness glistened with brass trim.

Adolphus tried to think of everything that would make America more aware of Budweiser and Anheuser-Busch.

One of his ideas was to give wide circulation to a picture entitled "Custer's Last Fight," depicting the slaughter by the Indians of the General and his cavalrymen in the battle of the Little Big Horn in the frontier days.

The Custer picture has been belabored and belittled by artists as pure "corn." If this seems a reflection upon Adolphus, remember that his taste in art-work for his personal surroundings was on the highest of planes. He simply saw in the Custer picture a dramatic value that the motion pictures were to exploit in their "Westerns" many years later. It was the sort of thing to stop passersby in their tracks, make them gasp, make them talk about Anheuser-Busch.

Best estimates are that "Custer's Last Fight" ran into well over a million prints—and in the hundredth year of the company requests still came in at a tremendous rate.

Both the picture and the Berninghaus works are depicted and described in more detail in a later chapter having to do with Anheuser-Busch advertising ideas, which were always unique, always productive.

Yes, Adolphus had America and much of the rest of the world very conscious of Budweiser and Anheuser-Busch. His travels became more frequent, taking him away from but never out of touch with his brewery. He longed to spend more time in Europe, where he was to form close friendships with Edward VII of England, the German Emperor and Prince Henry of Prussia.

Adolphus decided that it was high time, now that his son, August A. Busch, was nineteen, to get the young man in harness so that he would be fitted to take over in more mature years. Then and there, young Gussie figuratively set off a firecracker under the old gentleman's chair. He had what modern day parents know as the Hopalong Cassidy complex. He wanted to be a cowboy.

That this came as more than somewhat of a blow to Adolphus is no exaggeration. He marshalled his best explosive capacities and brought the whole matter into final focus with the single question, "What kind of a situation is this where you build up a marvelous business for a boy and then the boy wants to be a cow-poke?"

Gussie was adamant. Adolphus, being no fool about either his business or his family, was yielding. After all, hadn't he wanted to blow off steam in Mainz, Germany? And hadn't Father Ulrich given his consent to his son's exploration of that faraway wilderness called America?

Adolphus saw to it that young Gussie was properly outfitted, including a six-gun, and sent him on his way. That did something for the young heir-apparent—in six months. It convinced him that brewing and Budweiser offered a much more inviting career. Chagrined and chastened, August came home to St. Louis and, having learned a great lesson by his own admission, voiced no protest when told he was being bundled off to Europe to learn the science of brewing.

How diligently he applied himself, how well fitted he became to succeed his father is described in a later chapter devoted to the personality, the power and the humility that made August A. Busch a truly great man.

In this chapter, we can skip those years of apprenticeship and picture

NEW PACKAGE FOR AN OLD FRIEND—At the turn of the century the Budweiser bottle appeared with its newfangled metal crown cap, the wired-down cork covered with foil continued to be seen for several years.

August seated at his desk at the turn of the century. He and his associates are quite happy about an experiment that promises to turn into a bonanza. It is the newfangled metal crown cap. They have put it on Budweiser beer bottles and it looks good. It's a big time saver, too. No more plugging-in and wiring-down of expensive, branded corks from Spain. No more metal foil neck wrappers. A disc of cork, a disc of tin, a crimp and there's your bottle of Bud.

While August at his desk in St. Louis is enjoying near-ecstasy, Adolphus on vacation in Germany is having near-apoplexy. He has heard about the new closure over the trans-Atlantic cable. Gussie has been holding this out on him. He remembers his proud boast on the label—"Guaranteed to keep in any climate." And now this meddling. It could ruin reputations—of Budweiser, of Anheuser-Busch, of Adolphus Busch.

His rage becomes uproarious. He is taking the next boat for America.

Well, Budweiser hadn't missed the boat, either. It had sailed, with its newfangled closure, from chilly New York past the equator and down to South America—and then back again. Climate changes gave Budweiser the worst they had to offer and Budweiser came back to give its best from a perfectly sealed bottle.

August, knowing that his father's boldness rested on a secure foundation of caution, had insisted that the new package get the extremes in the way of a treatment before going on the market.

Confidently, he awaited the irate homecoming.

Back in St. Louis, Adolphus's wrath rose mightily and, quite as abruptly, subsided behind a broad smile. Piles of reports from the laboratory, from branches, from wholesalers and from retailers gave ample evidence that August's "meddling" was the kind that deserved a medal.

From then on, Adolphus knew that in the years left to him he could indulge his love of travel with never a fear about whether or not his beloved brewery was in safe hands. He knew that his job was finished. It had been a titanic job and he had proved himself a titan. He had amassed a fortune—and given away fortunes. He had worked hard, yet he had found time to enjoy the elegance and opulence that was so dear to his nature.

He had taken Eberhard Anheuser's brewery so far uphill that in 1901 Anheuser-Busch sales passed the million-barrel mark for the year, far exceeding the output of any other brewery anywhere on earth. His Adolphus Busch Glass Manufacturing Company had become one of the country's biggest manufacturers of bottles, with plants in St. Louis and over in Illinois in the cities of LaSalle, Belleville and Streator. He had become president of the South Side Bank, the Manufacturer's Railway Company and the Busch-Sulzer Bros. Diesel Engine Company. He was a generous donor to and a director in the Louisiana Purchase Exposition Company that was to bring to St. Louis in 1904 one of the most colorful and successful world's fairs in all history.

The name Adolphus Busch now was the name of a truly great man—the same name that half a century earlier had identified a truly humble if ambitious immigrant clerking on a Mississippi River steamboat.

Let us, in the next chapter, go back to those steamboating days and, with less emphasis on business, live a bit of daily life with Adolphus and study his personality and habits. We'll find that he let not one day slip by as either uninteresting or unproductive.

Chapter IV

OPULENCE, ELEGANCE

AND SALESMANSHIP

WHEN ADOLPHUS BUSCH settled in St. Louis in 1857, the city was beginning to establish itself as the gateway to the great Southwest. Each year saw its trade with trappers increase, pointing to the day when it would become the world's greatest fur market. Its hardware business was booming, because the frontiersmen who came to sell their wares bought heavily of traps, knives, guns, pots, pans, stoves, nails and knick-knacks.

River trade, too, was booming. Steamboats stood in the middle of the stream, awaiting their turn to get to the levee, discharge cargoes and take on new freight. Their forest of tall stacks sent up great clouds of smoke that hung like a black mushroom over the city.

In such a mercantile community, why would a man destined to become one of America's greatest salesmen take to clerking on a packet? Well, for one thing, the youngest of twenty-one children had to have a job and a wage—a job he understood, not one that he had to learn from scratch.

"First Citizen of St. Louis"—The title was bestowed upon Adolphus Busch by a forum of civic leaders including clergymen.

Young Adolphus felt at home on the river. He had spent his earlier years on the Rhine and Main rivers in Germany, guiding rafts of lumber, a commodity in which his father had a financial interest. He was to astonish friends while on vacation in Germany in 1895 by demonstrating that his feet had lost none of their nimbleness on rafts. On this occasion, Adolphus and his guests were riding in a carriage on the banks of the river Main when they came to a spot where a log jam had river traffic tied up in knots and confusion. Adolphus jumped from his carriage, leaped from raft to raft until he reached and freed the jammed lumber, then leaped from raft to raft back to the shore.

In a city so promising as St. Louis, the steamboat clerkship could mean only a temporary job to Adolphus. He was frugal and, when his purse had been fattened, he sought to see if he could make a success of selling brewers' supplies.

What he sought he found. That was the first of a string of successes that were to show the touch of Midas.

There are no records, save production and sales figures, to show just what it was that Adolphus did to get the slow-moving Bavarian Brewery up on its feet and give it wings. But, whatever were the methods he used, they must have had a goodly splash of the grand manner that was to characterize all his later operations.

Biographers have no choice but to agree that Adolphus Busch could have become a great figure on the stage had he not chosen brewing. In his simplest activities, he gave a great performance. He couldn't give a ham performance, because he was playing the role he loved, merchant prince. He played merchant and he played prince with such conviction that a group of clergymen, never frantically enthusiastic about alcoholic beverages, voted him St. Louis' "First Citizen" and President William Howard Taft called him "Prince Busch."

Adolphus was not particularly tall, but he was certainly commanding. He walked with the ramrod stiffness of a Prussian sergeant-major, relaxed with the loose-jointedness of an adagio dancer. He was stern in the hour of decision, jovial in the time for hospitality.

Young Busch was a handsome man, but middle-aged and ageing Busch was a far more handsome man. His hair, goatee and mustachios were impressive in younger days, magnificent when they became touched with gray.

Contemporary biographers agreed that most striking of his physical characteristics were his eyes and their elongated lids, a characteristic quickly discernible in his children and even in his great grandchildren. From his barrel of a chest came a voice that boomed, thundering disapproval or cannonading acclaim. One of those contemporary writers declared that Adolphus never greeted anyone, whether important or unimportant, with anything less than a jolly explosion and a half-Nelson handshake.

He was an elegant dresser. And, after he had dressed himself to his very best, he dressed up his surroundings—with furniture, carpets, carvings, ceramics, chandeliers, stained glass, teak, rosewood, mahogany, marble. Then, when prosperity permitted, he dressed up his favorite landscapes with architecture, gardens, birds, animals.

In the 1870's, when Adolphus had his brewing operations in high gear, business offices and counting rooms in downtown St. Louis followed pretty much of a pattern. The wooden floors were unadorned so that they could be scrubbed and sanded back into clean plainness. Desks and chairs were utilitarian and uncomfortable. Wooden boxes filled with sawdust stood about for the convenient unjuicing of those who chewed tobacco—and there were many.

There was none of that for Adolphus. Buel and Dacus, in their book, "A Tour of St. Louis," published in 1878, described the brewery's headquarters as follows:

> The office is one of the finest and most tastefully used of any in the city and bears the characteristics of the President's office of a large bank. It's Gothic in the exterior with small Doric skylights and modern windows and antique decorations. The floor is of tessallated marble and the furniture is of the most exquisite workmanship and elegantly veneered.

The private office of Mr. Adolphus Busch, secretary and manager of the association is simply sumptuous with its beautifully designed and immaculate marble mantle, Axminster carpets, ornamented French Plate Glass, luxurious chairs, elegant paintings, etc. In addition to its handsome appointment, the office is provided with every possible convenience and with an arrangement for expediting business unsurpassed.

With growing affluence, Adolphus made each day somewhat of a pageant. Each morning's arrival at the brewery brought enthusiastic greetings from employees of every station and the greeting was boomed back with a wave of the hand. In his elegant office, he seated himself at an ornate desk over which hung an elaborate pendant of a chandelier.

In the rim of the desk were push buttons that summoned secretaries, key officials and even a telegraph operator, since Adolphus had a private wire over which to transact his spreading business.

Alvina Berg was secretary to Adolphus and took dictation in both English and German. She was a very competent woman, in whom he had great faith and confidence and she served him with untiring devotion. Her work was her life. Miss Berg traveled extensively with Adolphus and Lilly in this country and abroad.

Close by the brewery he built a small company-owned hotel, where out-of-town people with whom he transacted business were his guests. Horses and carriages were on hand for their convenience.

Conferences and business occupied the forenoon. Soon after twelve o'clock it was time for luncheon—and that was no small matter. On two or three days a week, Adolphus entered his fine carriage and, with the horses rhythmically clop-clopping on Broadway's cobblestones, the journey to downtown St. Louis began. Greetings flew thick and fast between carriage and curbstone as friends and acquaintances were recognized. Occasionally, the horses came to an impressive halt to permit a special greeting to some special friend and then they were off to an equally impressive start.

The destination was the luxury restaurant of Tony Faust, close to the famous Southern Hotel and not very far from the equally famous Planters' House. The cuisine of each of these hostelries was nothing to be sneered at, yet the guests considered a stay in St. Louis incomplete without sampling the savory splendors that brought national fame to Tony.

There was a long table reserved for Adolphus and at its head he sat with bountiful dignity. The menu was a gourmet's delight. To what you might expect in a fine restaurant were added such now legendary things as bear steaks, venison and a great choice of wildfowl. The prices were nearly as attractive as the dishes themselves. And, to pay homage to the food and impart its own delicious touch, there was good Anheuser-Busch beer aplenty.

These were the days of a more leisurely pace in America and luncheon was a leisurely affair that seldom consumed less time than two hours. After food, drink and fellowship, the coffee and cigars brought a business note into the proceedings. Whatever deals he made, Adolphus made them quickly. They were concluded with a nod or a word, for he was proud all his life that he signed contracts only when legal considerations made it imperative. Adolphus wanted the world to know that the word of Anheuser-Busch was sufficient without written whereases and whomsoevers.

The banking business in the early days of St. Louis was largely in the hands of French-speaking men. With them, Adolphus got along famously, since he spoke their tongue as fluently as he spoke English and German. He was able to converse within limitations in Spanish and Italian, also. He had studied languages diligently in the Gymnasium of Mainz, the Academy of Darmstadt and the Collegiate Institute of Brussels in Belgium.

The bankers trusted deeply in his business acumen and were in later years to see their judgment vindicated when the man who had borrowed from banks found himself able to lend to banks.

The journey back to the brewery differed from the trip downtown. Now, instead of the cheery halloos and handwaving, there was dozing in the carriage.

In those days, remember, the business man's post-luncheon nap was as firmly entrenched as if it were guaranteed by the Constitution.

Arriving refreshed at the brewery, Adolphus made the afternoon a busy one. There were conferences with department heads, correspondence to be reviewed and signed, the daily talk with the chief brewmaster, visits to the malt house, the brew house, the lagering cellars.

Then, when the long shadows of the brewery chimneys sun-dialed the ending the day, he strolled over to his home and his family at No. 1 Busch Place, just a stone's throw from the brewery that was always growing bigger.

On days when he did not go downtown for luncheon, Adolphus invited business friends with whom he was currently dealing to join him in the spacious dining room of his home. It was not uncommon for him to bring as many as twenty men home with him for the midday repast, which rivaled the best that Tony Faust had to offer.

Number 1 Busch Place was a big home—a great, big, fine house. It reflected the good fortune, the opulence, the great ideas and the grand manner of its owner. No question about it, the place was lavish in its proportions, its architecture and its appointment. It had had for a forerunner very modest quarters, indeed, at Second and Hickory streets, just two blocks from the Mississippi shore.

It had been to Second and Hickory that young Adolphus had taken his bride, Lilly Anheuser Busch, after a colorful wedding in 1861. It had been a double wedding, with Eberhard Anheuser giving away Lilly to Adolphus and her sister, Anna, to Adolphus's brother, Ulrich. Pretty, seventeen-year-old, blonde Lilly was known as "the curly head." Anna was tall, dark and distinguished for her dashing manner.

The marriage ceremony had been solemnized before a large gathering by the Rev. Dr. Hugo Krebs, pastor of the Evangelical Lutheran Church of the Holy Ghost in the fashionable residential section at Eighth and Walnut streets, later to become the Chinatown of St. Louis. Dr. Krebs, a colleague of

Carl Schurz, had swum the Rhine to escape Germany in the 1848 revolution and, like Adolphus, emigrated to America and St. Louis.

The bearded and imposing clergyman, who was to serve as a chaplain in the Union Army, had acted as toastmaster for the many speeches and toasts which followed the wedding. His wife, Mrs. Mathilde van den Bergh Krebs, had opened the evening's dancing by leading a polonaise with the father of the brides.

Happy evening—and a happy little home at Second and Hickory, where you had the steamboat whistle if not the nightingale. Adolphus longed for more pretentious surroundings and Lilly caught his spirit, as she was always to do as they worked and frolicked through life together.

The next home of Mr. and Mrs. Adolphus Busch was on Third Street near Plum, a nicer home, a smarter neighborhood. On quiet nights—all night long—you could hear the splash of paddles as the packets churned commerce up and down Old Man River. Nine blocks westward, the bells and whistle blasts in the railway terminal ballyhooed the booming that was making St. Louis go places—and its products, too.

The future that was to be fantastic already looked fine to Adolphus. He wanted a fireside that matched his future. The answer was No. 1 Busch Place —and it answered everything that he wanted.

Would you like to visit it?

The door is in the next chapter.

Chapter V

AT HOME WITH LILLY

AND ADOLPHUS

YOU ARE GOING to be introduced to No. 1 Busch Place, not by seeing it go up brick by brick, but by hearing a swan song that preceded the razing of the residence in 1929. A reporter for the St. Louis Post-Dispatch visited the mansion. It made such a deep impression upon him that he should be pardoned for going on a rhetorical rampage. He began his story in a rather matter-of-fact manner, writing:

> No. 1 Busch Place, deserted mansion of Adolphus Busch on the brewery grounds, for many years a spot of brilliant and lavish entertainment, is soon to be razed.
>
> August A. Busch, Senior, President of Anheuser-Busch said the land-scaped plot containing the twenty-room brick mansion and another twelve-room home nearby, formerly occupied by other members of the family, will become the site of a switching yard and perhaps a factory, the latter producing one of the many lines taken up by the company since prohibition wrecked the brewing trade.

The reporter said that the house had been virtually deserted since Adolphus died in 1913—that his widow divided her time between Pasadena and Europe with occasional stops at the old mansion. After her death in 1928, it had been unused.

The son and daughters divided the furnishings and art objects which covered every available inch of space—rugs, paintings, statuary, tables, chairs and tapestries, the reporter added.

The home was described as one of great richness. Inlaid floors creaked underfoot where the small inlays had warped. Some light filtered through many stained-glass windows. Chandeliers, incredibly massive and ornate, hung overhead.

The reporter then pulled out all the stops and went on to say:

In the huge salon, plump women in filmy red garments float across the ceiling. Under it, full-breasted contraltos once brought forth ponderous Wagnerian arias to the delight of their host. Here Sarah Bernhardt smiled at the flatteries of the enraptured merchant prince. Here Caruso, flushed with wine, gave full play to the voice that has never been duplicated.

In another room, Roosevelt sat and discussed commerce and business with Busch, Taft tarried for a taste of Busch hospitality, Carl Schurz found welcome. General Franz Sigel quaffed a goblet and resumed his trip. Melba, Nordica, the de Reszkes, Lotte Lehmann, Leslie Carter, Sothern and Marlowe, Nat Goodwin, Maxine Elliott, Billy Crane, Joseph Jefferson —all those touched by beauty, cleverness or distinction, guests for a time of the city, became guests of Busch. One imagines they will sigh and turn away when this Valhalla is destroyed.

Thus stands the deserted castle of the baron, its guests fled, its garlands dead, the glory of its era departed. Where carriages drawn by four horses once moved up the gravel drive and handsome women stepped out beside the mulberry trees at the entrance, pudgy switch engines will soon be chugging and stolid factory buildings rear their bleak walls skyward in incongruous monuments to a faded age of life and gaiety.

In all of this word-embroidery you sense a way of living that was unique.

HOST TO PRESIDENTS AND PRINCES—Many were the distinguished visitors entertained royally at No. 1 Busch Place.

You would have sensed it also in the magnificent stables and carriage house.

Loving all horses, Adolphus was not one to let the animals that brought guests to his home shiver outside under a blanket. Horses and carriage, after discharging their passengers, were driven into a large rotunda in the carriage house. Thus were beast and cushions kept warm against the late home-going. There was a recreation room, where the coachmen could play cards, read or chat. And plenty of good food and Budweiser were at hand.

The Globe-Democrat, on October 11, 1913, carried a story under the headline, "Busch Stable One of Finest." The newspaper said:

Among the attractions at the Anheuser-Busch brewery is one of the finest stables in America and the finest collection of pleasure vehicles owned by any American. The vehicles include nearly everything on wheels —tallyho coaches, barouches, landaus, broughams, depot wagons, shooting traps, carts, stanhopes and phaetons. In the roomy box stalls, before the event of the automobile, Busch kept about thirty fine traveling horses of the various types, and in glass cases around the wall were beautiful sets of harness mounted with silver and gold.

He encouraged his son, August A., to go in for fine horses of the carriage and saddle type, but had no inclination to own race horses.

Number 1 Busch Place had been built by Eberhard Anheuser and occupied by him and his immediate family for a number of years. With the marriages of the girls, he found the house more than ample for his needs and, by mutual agreement, Adolphus and Lilly took it over. Adolphus immediately began enlarging the home to suit his entertainment needs.

The family residence was one of Victorian splendor. The spacious rooms were designated by their color scheme—the Rose Room, the Green Room, the Blue Room. The floors were covered with Aubusson rugs and on the walls hung the works of artists of note.

The Post-Dispatch of October 12, 1913, quoted a St. Louis art dealer, who was unnamed, but described as caretaker for the preceding ten years of the brewer's gallery of pictures in his home. The dealer said that Adolphus once remarked, "I am through with buying pictures by foreign artists. Hereafter, I shall buy only pictures by American artists." The dealer considered this a patriotic stand to take in that Adolphus was the owner of such wonderful paintings as Lenbach's "Bismarck," Kulbach's portraits of his wife and children and Zorn's portrait of Adolphus himself, which was one of the three greatest paintings of that artist. It is now in the St. Louis Art Museum. The dealer said Adolphus was one of the first connoisseurs to recognize the talent of William Keith, one of America's great landscape artists. He said that after the Louisiana Purchase Exposition, Adolphus bought a mammoth scenic painting of the entrance of American troops into Manila.

The art treasures of the United States were destined to be greatly enriched as a result of the marriage of Adolphus Busch's daughter, Edmee, to Hugo

Reisinger, an officer of the Siemens Glass Works of Dresden, Germany. After two visits to the United States, Reisinger came to America permanently to represent his firm here.

Adolphus and his son-in-law found themselves kindred cultural spirits. When Adolphus gave Harvard University $100,000 toward founding a Germanic Museum, Hugo promptly donated an additional $50,000. (In 1950, Hugo's widow made a grant of $300,000 more and the name of the institution was changed to The Busch-Reisinger Museum of Germanic Culture and, in that same year, Hugo's son, Curt, holder of a Bachelor of Arts degree, class of 1912, made a grant to found the Samuel Hazzard Cross Professorship for Slavic Languages.)

Hugo Reisinger was an enthusiastic art connoisseur. His private art collection of modern paintings was one of the finest in the United States. His American canvases included those of Browne, Bellows, Childe Nassam, Chase, Dougherty, Dewing Dearth, Hitchcock, Lawson, Metcalf, Melchers, Murphy, Redfield, Schofield, Sargent, Winslow Homer, Weir and McNeill Whistler. German art was represented by Boecklin, Habermann, Hofmann, Kampf, Liebl, Lenbach, Liebermann, Menzel, Putz, Schuch, Slevogt, Thaulow, Thome, Truebner, Uhde, Zuegal Schoenleber and Schram-Zittau; and among his French examples were those of Boudin, Blanche, Besnard, Cazin, Courbet, Corot, Dupré, Degas, Mauve, Manet, Monet, Menard, Pissarro, Renoir, Raffaellie, Fautin-Latour, Harpignies, Isabey, l'Hermitte, Lepine, La Touche and Maria; other artists represented are Israëls, Jongkind, Mesdag, Mastenbrook, Van Essen, Sorolla Zoro Liljefors and Lund.

President Theodore Roosevelt and Nicholas Murray Butler, then president of Columbia University, in 1908 inaugurated a plan for the interchange of modern American and German art. Hugo Reisinger was one of those chosen to bring the plan to its successful fruition. As a result of his work in bringing an exhibition of German art to the Metropolitan Museum in that year, he was named an honorary fellow of the museum for life.

In 1910, Hugo exhibited two hundred American paintings in the Royal Academy in Berlin under the official auspices of the Prussian government. His object was to prove to the European schools that contemporary American art was the equal of any other in the world. Most of the pictures were from his own collection, but some from the Metropolitan and from the Pennsylvania Art Society were included.

After the exhibition at the Metropolitan, Hugo was instrumental in arranging for similar displays for the Copely Society in Boston and the Art Institute in Chicago. He also helped to arrange an itinerary for a committee representing the Munich Museum, which studied American museums to arrange for improvement of the Munich institution.

Although most of the Hugo Reisinger collection of pictures was sold in 1916, his widow and sons retained some. Curt, in 1948, presented a Whistler and a Sargent to the National Gallery of Art in Washington. They are reproduced on the next page.

Hugo died little more than a year after his father-in-law. He died in the same place—Langenschwalbach near Wiesbaden in Germany.

One son, Walter Reisinger, was for many years until his death in 1948 a member of the Board of Directors of Anheuser-Busch. His brother, Curt, succeeded to the directorship.

Mrs. Webster Tilton, formerly Alice Busch, granddaughter of Adolphus, said of No. 1 Busch Place in memoirs which she wrote for the members of her family:

> Then came the dining room, a huge, narrow, long affair with a bay window at the end. It had to be long to seat the House of Busch. Off this room came my favorite spot, because there I could find my dearest friends and the sweetest people I ever knew: Wenzel, the butler, who ushered me in and always made me feel that I was a Princess out of my favorite Grimm's fairy tale; Babette, my grandmother's maid, who never failed to tell me that I was getting to be quite a young lady—music to my ears; little Barbara, the parlor maid; Big Barbara, the waitress, whom I

Head of a Girl—
by James Abbott McNeill Whistler

Repose—by John Singer Sargent

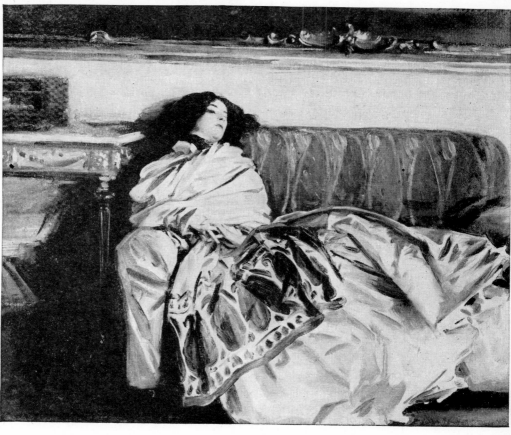

loved; and Struzie, the cook, who made the most delicious cinnamon waffles in all the world with huge waffle irons with birds printed on them.

Anna Schuman, remembered in the will of Adolphus, was housekeeper at No. 1 Busch Place for many, many years and was affectionately known by all the family as "Annschen."

As Busch Place was never closed during the absences of Adolphus and Lilly, Anna Schuman was the custodian and looked upon as the "mother" in charge.

There was a large park around the residence and the brewery. There, in the first week of each December, one of the watchmen impersonated St. Nicholas and went about ringing bells. Next morning, the children found their stockings filled with a rarity of that era, oranges, as well as candy, gingerbread Santa Clauses and sweetmeats.

On Christmas Eve, there was a huge tree on a revolving stand. At its top was a large waxen angel. In those days of candlelighted trees, a guardian always stood by with a huge bucket and mop when the tree was illuminated.

On one Easter, Adolphus decided to have an Easter egg hunt for his and the neighbors' children. It proved to be such a success that each year the number of "neighbors'" children increased to the point where hiding the great quantities of colored eggs among the shrubs and flower beds of the garden became a problem. The huge crowd of children prompted Adolphus on one year to buy so many eggs that the whole ceremony was moved to Forest Park.

On less festive occasions, life at No. 1 Busch Place still was impressive. Adolphus made it so from the moment he arose in the morning. A barber-servant awaited him in a bathroom so large that it contained not only a barber's chair, but a magnificent mahogany table in the center. After having his hair trimmed, Adolphus sat patiently while the barber meticulously arranged the flowing goatee and twirling mustachios. These had become such a well-known identification of Adolphus Busch that he had another barber's chair in a room close to his brewery office.

Yes, life rocked on gently and pleasantly in Busch Place. Son August became so skillful at handling the business reins that Adolphus was letting him have his head more and more. A large comfortable home known as No. 2 Busch Place was built for August.

Adolphus could really indulge his taste for travel now. He had a railroad spur run from the trackage at the brewery over to the park so that his private railroad car, The Adolphus, could be backed up virtually to the back door.

The private railroad car was a gift from Anheuser-Busch stockholders. The newspapers reported that it had been built at a cost of $50,000.

In 1905 Adolphus lent his private railroad car to a Dr. Stewart who was one of the organizers of the Tuberculosis Society in Missouri. Dr. Stewart was the first public school doctor retained by the Board of Education. The railroad car traveled for several months over the Frisco and Rock Island Railroads throughout Missouri with Dr. Stewart and his group organizing the Society.

Periodically, Adolphus went to New York, where he was as well known as he was in St. Louis. A writer, Gerald Holland, wrote in The American Mercury magazine in 1929 that his studies had convinced him that Adolphus Busch was the greatest salesman America ever had produced and added that when Adolphus registered at The Holland House in New York that simple formality consumed half an hour, so busy was he with shaking hands and greeting friends.

The American Mercury writer used these phrases to describe the emissary from No. 1 Busch Place:

> He scoured the nation and eventually the world, preaching the gospel of Budweiser. His work was done magnificently. His name was revered at home and abroad he was received with the deference due a merchant prince. He had outguessed all his rivals; he was king of the brewers. He was essentially great and grand; the commonplace stifled him. He liked the role of benevolent monarch and he played it well. But, he never took himself too seriously.

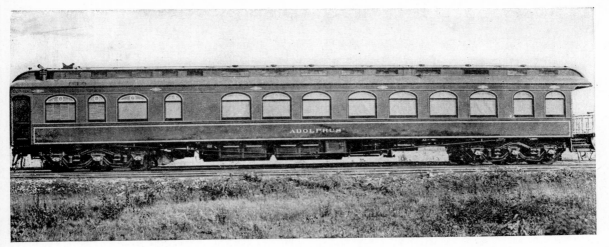

A Private Car for the Traveler—With it, Adolphus could indulge his love of travel and his liking for visiting with distant friends.

Interior of The Adolphus—Here friends in distant cities were wined and dined sumptuously.

The late George Rector, according to Cosmopolitan magazine's M. I. Pitkin, pictured Adolphus as one of New York's bon vivants in what the writer called the "golden nineties." Rector told of being summarily yanked out of his third year's studies in Cornell's law school to go to Paris to obtain a recipe, because "Diamond Jim" Brady, just returned from Europe, had told Rector's restaurant-owning father of the wonders of Filet of Sole Marguery.

What enraptured Brady was the sauce served only in the Cafe Marguery in Paris. Young Rector worked fifteen hours a day for months in the Parisian cafe, learning the knack of making the sauce. When a jury of seven chefs voted his sauce perfect, he cabled his father that he was taking the first boat home.

Charles Rector and Diamond Jim met him at the dock and hustled him to Rector's restaurant uptown. Then Brady invited Victor Herbert, Sam Shubert, Klaw, Erlanger, other notables—and the graduate gourmet of Tony Faust's, Adolphus Busch.

The company sat down to dinner at eight and finished at midnight—and why the dinner didn't finish Diamond Jim is a mystery. He told Rector, "I had nine helpings of Filet of Sole Marguery—and right now I could eat a Turkish towel drenched with that wonderful sauce."

Then back to Busch Place and the family for Adolphus . . . and being host himself . . . and being sure that nothing that could make life good and worthwhile was overlooked. There was a day close at hand when the fine horses and elegant carriages of No. 1 Busch Place, while keeping their importance in their owner's heart, were to yield a bit to a new and faster means of individual transportation. The jesting days of the "horseless carriage" were over just as surely as were the days when the one-cylinder "buggies" made thirty-mile "endurance runs."

A magnificent Pope-Toledo automobile became a factor in the Busch household—not just a run-of-the-mine touring car, but a vehicle with a specially-built body of wicker-and-yellow with brass trunk fittings on its top. For a long time, this motor car was one of the few seen on the streets of St. Louis.

MRS. LILLY BUSCH—Portrait painted by Anders L. Zorn. Wherever in the world that Adolphus chose to go, his wife went with him.

ADOLPHUS BUSCH—Portrait painted by Anders L. Zorn. Now hanging in the St. Louis Art Museum.

Having been many times to California, Adolphus decided that anyone who could afford it should live there part of the time. He could afford it. He chose Pasadena. There he bought a house that rivaled the one in St. Louis. He and Lilly named it Ivy Wall. They bought another close by for "the family."

There was neither smoke from brewery chimneys nor the bite of severe winters in Pasadena to take their toll of flowers and so Adolphus decided that here he was going to have a garden that really was a garden. What he came up with kept fifty gardeners permanently busy—and kept tourists streaming in and out of the place. What it looked like and how it eventually brought a fortune to the cause of war wounded veterans will be told in another chapter.

And, lest the impression be created that money was to Adolphus something for only self-indulgence, another chapter will show how he gave away fortune after fortune to charity.

To get on with the way of life of Adolphus Busch: his next longing was for a home on the river Rhine in Germany—the river on which he once worked as a humble raft guide, leaping from log to log. Having made the decision, he enlarged upon it and built two houses at Langenschwalbach. The first, which he named the Villa Lilly after his wife, was for themselves and their guests. The second was for his children and grandchildren, because "the family" must always be in the picture.

Just a glance at a photograph of Villa Lilly is enough to prove that it was an elaborate establishment—and to disprove that it was a "castle on the Rhine," as imaginative newspaper correspondents always called it. Such extravagant description is understandable when you remember that one to enjoy the hospitality of Villa Lilly was Edward VII, King of the United Kingdom of Great Britain and Ireland, Emperor of India and the Dominions Beyond the Seas, Defender of the Faith, etc., etc. A personage like that just isn't supposed to be at home any place except in a castle or a palace.

Deer roamed on the estate and Adolphus, proud of his shooting eye, saw to it that they were harvested seasonably. Even when the illness that was to

IVY WALL—Adolphus Busch's winter home in Pasadena, California.

THE BLOSSOMS—Also in Pasadena, where Adolphus entertained his family and friends.

VILLA LILLY—Summer home in Langenschwalbach, Germany.

end his life was upon him, he would have himself taken out into the forest preserve in a wagon and from it shoot a buck or two.

While Adolphus was enjoying his lush years at Villa Lilly, he still had a mind for business. Hops merchants from Bohemia were regular callers and their blossoms were rubbed between palms, sniffed expertly and bought or rejected. Budweiser had to have the finest. And the cable tolls! Often the exchange of messages between the Villa and the brewery amounted to $100 a day—and in those days with their tolls you could say a great deal for $100.

Pleasure-loving, business-respecting Adolphus also kept up with his correspondence. For the very important matters concerning Budweiser beer, sixteen-page letters in his own hand to son Gussie or faithful General Superintendent Menzenwerth were not uncommon.

Buying hops from Bohemia on his trips to Europe gave Adolphus an excuse to acquire another house—this one at Cooperstown in New York State's hops growing district. He, who insisted that every one of his employees become an American citizen as soon as possible, wanted to be American in the matter of hops and use them as well as the distinctive Saaz variety.

Adolphus's son, August, was an ardent baseball fan and was right at home in Cooperstown. It was there in 1839 that Colonel Abner Doubleday, later an Army general, invented the national game of baseball. The National Baseball Museum was established in the town. Each year its display of uniforms and paraphernalia of famous players and other relics of the sport attract thousands of visitors.

Because his business was so dependent upon farming, Adolphus read books on the subject avidly. He had the same reading ability that Theodore Roosevelt had—the knack of digesting whole paragraphs at a glance. In time, he became something of an expert on agriculture and he was one of the creators of the Crop Improvement Bureau with headquarters in Chicago. He was fond of riding through the beautiful countryside about Cooperstown and chatting with farmers. At his Pasadena home, he kept a large flock of finely bred chickens and used them to stimulate interest among farmers and breeders.

Adolphus Busch so loved his home life that he wished all of his children to own houses of which they could be proud. So, on his and Lilly's golden wedding anniversary in 1911, he presented each child with a home.

Mr. and Mrs. August A. Busch, Senior, received a mansion built in the French chateau manner on a farm near St. Louis once owned by General U. S. Grant. Mr. and Mrs. Edward A. Faust built their home at No. 1 Portland Place in the city. The newspapers, given to extravagant phrases whenever reporting news about the Busch family, described the Faust residence as one of the handsomest and costliest in America with "one room furnished entirely with gold fixtures and hardware and special rooms decorated with materials imported from France and Germany."

Mrs. Hugo Reisinger was given a mansion at 993 Fifth Avenue in New York City. Mrs. Paul von Gontard received a mansion in Berlin, Mrs. J. W. Loeb a fine home near Lincoln Park in Chicago and Mrs. Edward A. Scharrer one in Stuttgart, Germany.

The golden wedding anniversary which occasioned these gifts caused a celebration in St. Louis unlike anything ever before or since seen in America It was all the more remarkable, because Adolphus and Lilly in Pasadena were not present to witness it. Adolphus was seriously ill.

The scene was the old Coliseum in St. Louis, a huge arena-like building that attracted big conventions and the fashionable Veiled Prophet's ball. While a fifty-piece band played, the 6,000 employees of the brewery, singing and waving flags, marched in and out of the building. Lights played on a fountain in the center of the arena. It threw a thirty-foot jet of water and was banked with golden orchids. Altogether, 13,000 employees and friends attended the affair. Dancing continued far into the night. Forty thousand bottles of Budweiser were consumed with a hundred thousand sandwiches. If ever a good time was had by all, this was it.

The brewery personnel sent a telegram of congratulations etched in a solid gold replica of a Western Union telegram. Other gifts were gold loving cups from Theodore Roosevelt and Kaiser Wilhelm of Germany; a new $20 gold piece designed by St. Gaudens in an ivory case from President Taft; and from the children solid gold dinner plates and a gold basket on which a goldsmith had worked for five years.

The newspapers reported that Adolphus had presented Lilly with a gold crown and they solemnly reported its value at $200,000.

All the joy and merry-making was soon to be succeeded by intense sorrow. The illness that beset Adolphus Busch in Pasadena was growing worse. His end was growing nearer.

Chapter VI

FINIS FOR "THE FIRST
CITIZEN OF ST. LOUIS"

ADOLPHUS, 76 YEARS old and now unable to walk unaided, was with his wife at Villa Lilly in October, 1913. He had hoped that the brisk German autumn would prove a tonic and help to restore him to health.

Late in the afternoon of October 10, he dictated some letters. After dinner, he enjoyed some music while he puffed on a cigar. Later he asked to be assisted to his desk and, while seated at it, he collapsed from a heart attack. He remained conscious and seemingly only uncomfortable until 8:30 p.m., when he died, suddenly and peacefully.

At his side were his faithful Lilly and faithful son, August.

Present, too, were two daughters, Mrs. von Gontard and Mrs. Scharrer.

The death came as a thunderbolt to the family in St. Louis and to the city as a whole. None had suspected that the end was so close at hand. August had arrived at Villa Lilly just a few days before, believing that his father was in no grave danger and preparing to accompany him home in a few weeks.

69

His Last Portrait—Always a commanding figure, Adolphus became actually imposing as age added greater dignity to his presence.

Weeping with the family in the villa was Carl Conrad, who had collaborated with Adolphus in producing and perfecting Budweiser beer and who had been his traveling companion for years.

On the morning of October 11, 1913, the St. Louis Globe-Democrat carried the news of Adolphus's death under a four-column headline on page 1 with the story flanking a three-column portrait. The headlines said:

ADOLPHUS BUSCH IS DEAD

IN HIS CASTLE ON THE RHINE

GRANDSON GETS CABLE TELLING END OF BREWER

AND CAPITALIST—NEWS UNEXPECTED

TO BRING BODY HOME

ELDEST SON UNAWARE OF ILLNESS WHEN HE SAILED

FROM NEW YORK TO ACCOMPANY FATHER BACK

WEALTH WAS $60,000,000

GERMAN NATIVE AMASSED RICHES IN ST. LOUIS AND

WAS LEADER IN BUSINESS AND PHILANTHROPY

The news story, in part, was as follows:

Adolphus Busch, St. Louis' best-known citizen and philanthropist, died last night in his castle on the Rhine in Germany. Mr. Busch was preparing for his return to St. Louis where he loved to spend autumn and early winter months. While in uncertain health the last few years, his family knew of no special crisis in his condition. He often commented upon the fact that he had outlived two of his physicians who predicted his death.

The news of Mr. Busch's death came in a cablegram from his son, August A. Busch, to his grandson, Adolphus Busch, III.

The Globe-Democrat carried additional sidelight stories on page 2. There was a two-column portrait of Lilly under the caption:

WIDOW OF ST. LOUIS' BEST-KNOWN CITIZEN

WHO WAS BY HIS SIDE AT DEATH ABROAD

The newspaper said that in addition to his many donations to charities, Adolphus gave substantial financial help to many of his friends and that, indeed, quite a few St. Louisans could trace their success to help given by him in the beginning of their careers.

The newspaper also quoted a number of prominent citizens who eulogized Adolphus in lavish terms.

On page 3, the Globe-Democrat pictured the so-called castle where Adolphus died.

A separate story on another page carried the headline:

EMPLOYEES WILL BE SINCERE

MOURNERS AT THE FUNERAL

The story follows in part:

The Busch and Anheuser families owned a large lot in Bellefontaine Cemetery where the bodies of Adolphus, Jr., Peter and several other children of Adolphus Busch are buried. This is where the body of the head of the family will be buried, but as yet the relatives in St. Louis have no information as to when or other details.

Among the mourners at the funeral, they will not feel the loss more keenly than the old employees of the brewery who had the highest regard for Adolphus Busch. It is said he never neglected the family of an old employee and when a man died in his employ, the widow and children were cared for, in many cases drawing the salary of the dead father until the children were able to care for themselves and the widow.

Nat Klein, who has been in the employ of Adolphus Busch as city representative of the brewery nineteen years and whose daily association with the 6,000 employees of the Anheuser-Busch Brewing Association enables him to speak for them, said: "Mr. Busch was dearly beloved by everyone in his employ. They all respected and loved him because they knew their interests were uppermost with him at all times. It was his practice on visiting the brewery to go about among the employees and greet them personally, calling the older employees familiarly by their first names and asking about their condition. There are many men in his employ who had been working for him for thirty to thirty-five years and they all had a kind word for him.

"Men who worked for him regarded their places as lifetime jobs and, as a rule, they stayed with him as long as they were able to work. I can say for myself he was the grandest man I ever knew to work for. I have always felt he took a personal interest in me and I am sure he always had the interests of his employees at heart, and everyone in his employ always had a good word for him. The news of his death was a great shock, as we all looked forward to his return the latter part of the month as one of the most pleasant events of the year."

The Globe-Democrat of Sunday morning, October 12, 1913, published these headlines and story:

TO SAIL OCTOBER 21 WITH BUSCH'S BODY

Son Cables Effort Will be Made to
Get Earlier Steamer if Possible

Heart Disease Fatal

Smoked Cigars, Dictated Letters,
Collapsed and Died in an Hour

August A. Busch and other relatives will sail from Germany, Tuesday, October 21, or sooner, accompanying the body of Adolphus Busch, foremost citizen of St. Louis, philanthropist, patron of art, successful businessman and shrewd manager of a fortune estimated at $60,000,000, who died Friday night at his summer home in his native land.

The newspaper then reviewed details previously published.

The death of Adolphus and the preparations for his funeral continued to be page 1 news for days. The Globe-Democrat of Thursday morning, October 28, 1913, printed these headlines:

BUSCH'S BODY HOME; THRONG BRAVES RAIN

Several Hundred Wait Hours Until Arrival of Train—Some Near Collapse

CASKET IS DRAPED

The funeral train, which brought the body from New York the newspaper said, arrived by Pennsylvania Railroad and the Manufacturers Railway and stopped on the brewery property adjacent to the family home at No. 1 Busch Place. A crowd of several hundred persons stood for several hours in a pouring rain awaiting the arrival of the train.

The Globe said that a special marble casket awaited the body at Bellefontaine Cemetery, where a concrete vault was ready. The marble casket was made of stone imported from Italy.

The German Emperor directed an attache of the Germany Embassy in Washington to attend the funeral and place a wreath on the grave and the following message was received:

> By command of his Majesty, the Emperor, I have the honor to express to you and the other members of the family his Majesty's condolence at the great loss sustained by the death of your highly esteemed father. His Majesty has commanded that a member of the Germany Embassy attend the funeral and place a wreath upon the casket.

It was signed by von Haniel, Imperial Charge d'Affaires.

The funeral was conducted on October 25, 1913, the day being a Saturday. The Globe-Democrat of the day before described arrangements for the funeral from No. 1 Busch Place.

The funeral services were to be private. The 6,000 brewery employees appointed a committee to ask the family if they could take charge of the casket just before the funeral procession got under way. The committee pointed out that it had been Adolphus's daily custom to visit several, if not all, of the departments of the brewery where he would fraternize with the workers, many of whom he had known for many years. The employees wanted to have the casket taken through each department of the brewery, just as Adolphus had visited those departments while living. The request was granted.

The same newspaper account said that for two days so many orders for floral tributes had accumulated among St. Louis florists that their stocks were depleted. They sent to other cities within a range of 300 miles for more flowers.

The Post-Dispatch published a four-column photograph on page 1 of scenes of the funeral, and under a two-column heading, "Twenty-five truck loads of flowers sent to Busch funeral," was a story about the ceremonies. The newspaper estimated that 20,000 persons filed through the home at No. 1 Busch Place to view Adolphus's body and that simultaneously with the services in St. Louis services were held in thirty-five cities and towns in which Anheuser-Busch had branches.

The service in the home was conducted by the Reverend John W. Day of the Unitarian Church of the Messiah with Charles Nagel delivering the eulogy. At the grave was an address by Congressman Richard Bartholdt.

At the house, a portion of the St. Louis Symphony Orchestra played Rubinstein's Kammenoi-Ostrow, Tschaikovsky's Andante Cantabile and Ase's Death from the Peer Gynt Suite by Grieg.

According to the Globe-Democrat of Saturday, October 25, 1913, the number of persons who viewed the body in the family residence was 30,000 as contrasted with the Post-Dispatch's estimate of 20,000.

Mayor Henry W. Kiel, at the direction of the City Council, predecessor to the Board of Aldermen, asked business firms of St. Louis to suspend business for five minutes at the time that the services were to begin.

The Post-Dispatch of October 26, 1913, said the funeral procession moved from Busch Place west on Pestalozzi Street to Grand Boulevard and then through Tower Grove Park to Kingshighway and then north on Kingshighway to Bellefontaine Cemetery. The newspaper said that there was an unbroken throng of people from the starting point to the cemetery, a distance of nearly twenty miles.

The street railway system stopped all of its trolley cars for five minutes at the moment that the funeral service began.

By the time services at the grave were over, it was growing dark.

According to the Globe-Democrat of October 26, the Planters and Jefferson Hotels extinguished all their lights for five minutes at the time of the funeral services.

The Globe quoted Congressman Bartholdt as describing Adolphus as a "high priest of the square deal."

Rabbi Samuel Sale addressed the congregation of 2,000 in Temple Shaare Emeth and paid Adolphus high tribute.

The St. Louis Symphony Orchestra dedicated the first number on its November 7 program to the memory of Adolphus.

Charles Nagel, formerly Secretary of Commerce and Labor in the Cabinet of President Taft, delivered this eulogy at the home services:

> The life of a great man like a great composition of music appeals to and is understood by all the people. Adolphus Busch was a giant among men. Like a descendant of one of the great vigorous and ancient gods, he rested among us and, with his optimism, his far-seeing vision, his undaunted courage and his energy, he shaped the affairs of men.
>
> He was acquainted with the great book of life as few men are. Instinctively, his mind travelled the true course, received and welcomed the good message, accepted the wise counsel and threw his tremendous influence invariably to the right side of every human conflict. Never a visionary, he was always an optimist, who could smile away the errors of a day in the triumph and the success of a lifetime. He believed in the ultimate progress of the world, he believed in the ultimate good of men and he based all his activity and all of his conduct upon that belief.
>
> He dared to appeal for all he stood for and for all which is good in human nature and that was the meaning of his success. He believed that the people ultimately wanted that which is right and that they were ultimately entitled to that which is right. This was the secret of his success and this was the meaning of his relation to all his men and to all his associates. His relations with the men in his employ was unlike anything we knew; it was a personal relation and if his advice and his counsel had been heeded and generally accepted, our Statute Books would not be burdened down with the humiliating confession of man's inhumanity to man.

Although embarking in new plans up to the last moment, he left his successor with great responsibility.

As to his gifts, he was his own executor. He did what he wanted to do. He enjoyed giving. He loved success and he loved to share it with others. He has given what he loves to those who succeed him with the privilege and the opportunity to enjoy as he did. Confiding still with the confidence which had once been rigid, he entrusted to them the protection of his fortune and his fair name.

The following editorial was published in the Post-Dispatch, October 11, 1913:

What purpose can an obituary serve in the case of a man whose career and life are known to everybody? There was no citizen of St. Louis better known in more than one sense than Adolphus Busch. The press cannot tell the public, either of St. Louis or the country at large, much about the world's leading brewer that it has not heard many a time.

The very human qualities of the man drew the public to him in an unusual intimacy. He was as well liked as he was widely known. There was no mock philanthropy about Mr. Busch. He did not patronize the public with overwhelming benefactions. He did not consider that he owed the public an apology for his great wealth and he did not sue with huge bribes for forgiveness, forgetfulness or favor. He erected no monuments to vanity.

He legitimately went about his own business with an independence which forced admiration from free American citizens, and his generosity, his kindliness were real, prompted by the heart. Measured by the deeds that sprang from it, it was the heart of a big man.

Of what use is it to recount the mere money gifts of a man of vast wealth? How little of the true character of the donor can be told in a column of figures?

Too often they are set forth for want of something better; too often they conceal, they mislead, they lie. The real generosity and genuine quality of a man are more likely to be expressed in a charity of his right hand of which his left hand neither receives nor gives a sign. Many there are whose tears of grief alone tell of the secret kindness of Mr. Busch. Yet no public appeal, no worthy cause ever sought of him in vain.

In his death, the world has lost a singular example of successful enterprise coupled with high integrity. St. Louis has lost a big private citizen actively identified with a half century of its growth and thousands of men and women and children have lost a good friend.

The corporation of Washington University adopted this resolution:

The community's loss in the death of Adolphus Busch is so universally and profoundly felt, that we are but one of many institutions to record our last tribute.

The real expression of sorrow will come from the multitude of people who felt for him as he felt for them and who saw in him a natural leader with a place which they had created in their own hearts and of their own will.

Coming to our country as a young man, he never surrendered a keen interest in the welfare and success of his native land, but in the rarest manner did he know how to harmonize that interest with absolute loyalty and devotion for his adopted government.

He was a citizen of the United States who sought to bring to our aid the experience and all the advantages of an older civilization. He was a master in the affairs of men. In business of the widest scope, he displayed the rarest imagination, boldness, experience and judgment.

The distribution of a large part of his fortune showed the greatest generosity and discernment. He loved success, but no success was so welcome as that which was shared by friendly colleagues or which enabled him to register some new triumph for a public cause dear to his heart.

Liberal, open minded and tolerant, he discriminated in neither conduct nor gift against belief or intellectual convictions. Whatever the form in which the charity appealed, it always found warmest welcome from him.

For the growth of common tolerance and intellectual freedom, he trusted to education, giving freely of his means to aid where distress had overtaken the less favored. His larger influence and support went to the development and upbuilding of those institutions whose charge it is to spread enlightenment and to prepare for the battle of life.

From the day when he entered this board, every plan for the development of Washington University placed before him received his thoughtful consideration and his substantial support. His name is engraved upon our structure. His strong sympathy for our work will outlive him to urge us on to the accomplishment of greater and better things. This was the inspiration which prompted him in his activity among us and its taking away registers our loss.

The general faculty of the Department of Arts and Science of Washington University on October 21, 1914, adopted a resolution which said in part:

> In him, the University loses one of its most benevolent friends and one of its most generous contributors.
>
> Mr. Busch's magnificent donations have been among the chief factors in the progress and extension of our activities. The wholehearted belief in the dissemination of knowledge by which Mr. Busch's gifts were prompted and his proven confidence and civic pride in Washington University have served by their example to widen and to deepen the public interest in the welfare of this institution of learning. By the admirable spirit in which Mr. Busch's benevolences were bestowed, nor less than by their imposing amounts, he has the earned and the lasting gratitude of the entire corps of instructors.

The St. Louis Merchants Exchange adopted this resolution:

> It is seldom that any community sustains such a loss as the city of St. Louis now mourns in the death of Adolphus Busch, one of its foremost citizens, noted equally for his public spirit, his brilliant business talents, his untiring energy and progressiveness and his open hearted charity. Probably no man ever did more for the advancement and development, not only of his own city, but also of the country at large, than did Adolphus Busch, his activities and charities being world-wide; and certainly none were ever more loyal to the interest of his city or nation. In this regard, the career of Adolphus Busch is one which commands universal respect and admiration and should prove an inspiration to all of his fellow citizens as an example worthy of the most earnest emulation.

Resolutions of sympathy and praise were adopted by the St. Louis City Council, Chamber of Commerce of Dallas, Texas, of which he was an honorary member, and the San Francisco Chamber of Commerce.

In connection with the death of Adolphus Busch, the St. Louis Post-Dispatch of October 12, 1913, published a number of anecdotes, which are paraphrased below:

Henry Menzenwerth, general superintendent of the company for thirty-two years, said that Mr. Busch was always concerned about the poor on the South Side and that, in very cold weather, it was his custom to order several railroad cars of coal put at the disposal of the poor. He would inform the police that the coal was waiting and ask the police to send worthy and needy people to get it.

———

James Campbell, multimillionaire president of the North American Company and a director and stockholder in thirty other public service corporations, began life as a brakeman for the "Katy" (Missouri-Kansas-Texas) Railroad. He dabbled in stocks and began acquiring means. He also made the acquaintance of Adolphus. On one occasion, he found himself in a financial jam and asked Adolphus for help. When Adolphus asked how much he needed, he said he thought $100,000 would be sufficient. "That's easy," said Adolphus and instantly wrote him a check.

———

For years Adolphus was called by the press "First Citizen of St. Louis." In 1911, a number of the city's religious leaders began a campaign called the Men and Religion Forward Movement. As a preliminary, a sort of civic census had to be taken by a number of clergymen. They voted overwhelmingly in favor of Adolphus as "First Citizen."

———

Adolphus on one occasion was invited by President McKinley to expound his beliefs on alcohol and regulation. The interview was described in the memoirs of a congressman who introduced the brewer to the President. Among the data which supplied the information for this history was a page torn from the legislator's book—a page yellowed and brittle from age and bearing marginal notes describing the author as a member of the House of Representatives, but failing to give his name.

Of the meeting, the congressman wrote:

> They had never met before. Encouraged by the President to give his views on the temperance question, the brewer king proceeded, in his candid and inimitable way, to express his convictions on this vital subject. He first explained that he was taking pride in furnishing only the best and most wholesome beverage, that the production of good beer had converted us from a nation of hard drinkers into a sober and temperate people and how, consequently, the brewers had really accomplished more for the cause of true temperance than all the paid apostles of prohibition combined.
>
> "All the brewers I know," he said, "are reputable citizens and honorable men. There is no case on record of any one of them ever having even attempted to cheat the Government, and they have always paid their taxes loyally and ungrudgingly, enough every year to maintain the whole American Navy."
>
> The President seemed very much interested, and so my friend continued by asking whether catering to a legitimate public demand was not an entirely respectable business, especially when the demand came from eighty-five to ninety per cent of the adult population.
>
> "Mr. President," he said, raising his voice, "the demand I speak of is prompted by human nature itself, and, believe me, if fanatics should ever succeed in preventing its being satisfied legitimately, the people will resort to narcotics or stimulants so injurious as eventually to undermine the health of the nation."
>
> For nearly half an hour he went on, logically advancing one argument after the other and winding up finally with a strong plea for the unrestricted maintenance of our personal freedom and the right to self-control of the individual citizen.
>
> The President was visibly impressed by these candid representations, and

next day, when a matter of business again called me to the White House, he said to me: "Your friend Busch is a most remarkable man. His personality no less than his arguments challenge my admiration."

It will be remembered that under the McKinley administration our social quacks made no headway whatever with their nostrum, and the same is true, by the way, of the administrations of his predecessors and his two successors, Roosevelt and Taft.

———

One of the works of Adolphus's later years was establishment of a "Happiness Fund" of $75,000 a year for the benefit of brewery employees. The fund was divided into departments. There was a pension fund for all employees, a fund for widows and orphans of workmen, a sick benefit endowment administered by the Relief Association, a fund for bravery medals and awards for workmen only, an entertainment fund for workmen, the annual picnic fund for all employees and the Christmas presents fund for office workers only. Administration was in the hands of seven men—the president and three selected by the workmen and three by management.

———

In the spring of 1913, two robbers jumped onto the observation platform of Adolphus's private car as it was traveling between St. Louis and Kansas City. Before they could accomplish their holdup, they were thrown off and arrested. This happened in the jurisdiction of Kansas City. When Mr. Busch found out that they were only twenty years old, he pleaded with the Kansas City prosecutor to drop the charges and give them another chance, which was done.

———

On one occasion, Adolphus wanted to buy a certain tract of land and found that it was on the site of an Episcopal Church of modest proportions. He built the congregation an entirely new and better church and thereupon acquired the land that he was anxious to have.

Edward Faust, a son-in-law, said that he had been associated with Adolphus for fifteen years, having charge of his private investments and holding his power of attorney during the absence of Adolphus and his son, August. He continued: "It has been a great pleasure to be associated with him. He was one of the greatest commercial geniuses of the country and would have made a great success in any business."

It now is quite apparent that Adolphus exhibited great sagacity in his choice of business associates and counselors. One, because of the quality of his guidance, the ethical imprint that he left upon the business and his love and loyalty for "the family," deserves special mention. He was Charles Nagel.

Businessmen by and large were neither excited nor impressed when young Nagel began to practice law in St. Louis in the late seventies. They discerned then none of the attainments that were to make this man a beloved national figure in the years to come.

Adolphus, on the other hand, won the confidence of the over-modest young attorney and thus learned of his impeccable character, ability to reason rightly and unflinching refusal to compromise with expediency. The new friend virtually underwrote Nagel's professional beginning, presumably positive that some day he would be chief of counsel for Anheuser-Busch and personal advisor to son and grandsons, but he did not know that this young attorney was destined to be a member of the cabinet of a President of the United States.

The childhood and youth of Charles Nagel were as colorful as those of Adolphus. Charles's father was a physician, who, after his marriage in 1846, migrated in the following year to the United States. He was one of the thousands of Germans who preferred the liberty of America to the abuses that were to plunge Germany into revolution in 1848.

CHARLES NAGEL—Life-long friend and advisor to Adolphus Busch and a member of the cabinet of President Taft.

Dr. Nagel's choice of Texas for his residence was purely a matter of chance. The North German Lloyd ship which sailed from Bremen was bound for New Orleans. It had taken many an emigrant there before and a sort of colony of Germans-turned-Americans had grown up in San Bernardo, sixty miles from Houston. There Charles was born in 1849. Soon thereafter, the family moved to the nearby village of Millheim, a peaceful, liberty-loving community of a hundred and seven families.

When war threatened, Millheim voted 99 to 8 against secession in the state election of February, 1861. Although this had been a free expression by ballot, the village's neighbors never forgave the Millheim folk once hostilities began. Dr. Nagel found life now so unlovely that he fled into Mexico with Charles, went northward by sea and settled eventually in St. Louis, where he soon was reunited with the other members of his family.

Again under happier auspices, Charles was able to proceed with an education that was to be greatly enriched, year after year. He went for a while to a boarding school in South St. Louis, then attended the old Central High School, from which he was graduated in 1868 as valedictorian of his class.

With a classmate, Washington Fischel—who was destined for a brilliant medical career—Charles visited Europe. The journey proved to be a great cultural awakening for Charles. He delighted in the art museums of Dresden and Munich; in the opera, the theatre and the concerts; in the industry and tidiness of Switzerland; in the beauty of the Harz Mountains; in the gaiety and splendor of cruising down the Rhine. In boyhood he had hoped to become an actor or a painter, but his visit abroad convinced him that many years of preparation would be necessary if mediocrity were to be escaped.

It was his reading of William Thackeray's "Vanity Fair" that was to chart his lifetime course. The classic gave him a new conception of the scope and sparkle and great strength of the English language and made him an avid reader of poetry, novels, essays and history. After studying the speeches of Pitt, Burke, Macaulay and others, Charles was determined to make the law his career.

In 1870, Charles Nagel entered the St. Louis Law School. Completing its course in 1872, he enrolled in the University of Berlin, where he studied Roman law, constitutional history, political economy and medical jurisprudence.

Upon his return to St. Louis, Nagel was employed by a law firm at fifty dollars a month. After a bit of puttering about here, he and a friend formed a partnership that soon was dissolved for lack of business. One of the reasons for Nagel's slowness to catch on was his innate modesty that all his life bordered on self-effacement. A second partnership brought four more years of near-penury.

Then, in about 1881, began his friendship with Adolphus Busch and more and important clients were attracted. With maturity, experience and a taste of success had come a fine presence, dignity mingled with humility and a powerful adherence to convictions. Adolphus was convinced that in Charles Nagel he could have complete confidence for the guardianship of Anheuser-Busch's integrity in all of its legal dealings. Moreover, in matters of policy, Adolphus leaned heavily upon the advice of Nagel.

In 1894 the firm of Nagel & Kirby was formed. Subsequently, it became Finkelnburg, Nagel & Kirby and so remained until Judge Finkelnburg was appointed to the federal bench. As the two-partner firm found its activities expanding, new partners were acquired and the firm became Nagel, Kirby, Orrick & Shepley. (In the hundredth year of Anheuser-Busch, its legal advisor was the firm that grew out of the original Nagel & Kirby—Shepley, Kroeger, Fisse & Ingamells.)

Nagel never sought public office, but public office sought him. His service would have been one of reluctance had it not been for his exalted sense of duty. He was a member of the Missouri House of Representatives from 1881 to 1883; president of the City Council from 1893 to 1897; Republican National Committeeman from Missouri from 1908 until 1912 and Secretary of Commerce and Labor in the cabinet of President Taft.

As a cabinet officer, Nagel was instrumental in the enactment of more humane immigration laws, in the establishment of a code for court-dissolved combinations in restraint of trade and in a great improvement of the nation's lighthouse service.

With all of his multiple activities, Nagel found time to give regular lectures in the School of Law of Washington University for more than twenty-five years and to serve as president of the school's board of trustees.

Anyone who confused Nagel's inherent modesty with timidity was sure of a jolting awakening, whether before the bar or in personal dealings. To his great satisfaction, he was greatly responsible for the defeat of more than a few demagogues seeking public office and, when anarchy threatened to overwhelm St. Louis during a street car strike, he formed a sheriff's posse that patrolled the streets with guns that kept order.

It is not often that a man of ninety finds his counsel still sought, but to Adolphus Busch III and August A. Busch, Jr., Nagel's guidance was as welcome as it had been to their father and grandfather. Death brought a good life to its conclusion in 1940.

In the following year, at a meeting of the Missouri Historical Society in the Jefferson Memorial in St. Louis, Adolphus III and August, Jr., presented the organization of which Nagel had been president, with a bronze likeness of Charles Nagel done by Carl Mose.

Addressing the society on behalf of his brother and himself, August said:

> My brother, Adolphus Busch, and I have wished that by some power we might enable those who in the days to come will here look upon the sculptured features of Mr. Charles Nagel to see not only the dignity and fineness of those features, but also the gentleness, courtesy, understanding, tolerance and helpfulness which we always saw there.
>
> Those who knew him need no reminder of how he looked. Those who in future days may know of him only by his enduring works, we hope may supplement their appreciation by viewing here the gift which it is our great privilege to make.

The Globe-Democrat of October 11, 1913, interviewed someone whom it described as one of Adolphus's associates and quoted that associate as saying about the Busch fortune, "I think the amount will be $60,000,000, and there is no estimating what it would have been if he had showed a grasping disposition. He gave away more money than many millionaires have. In addition to the immense sums he gave outright, his business policy was open and liberal instead of close and grasping. He paid top prices for everything and stood a loss cheerfully rather than have an argument.

"It was a hard matter to get Adolphus Busch into court. He abhorred litigation and would take all the worst of it before he would appear on either side of a case. I don't recall his ever being a party to any lawsuit. He hired good lawyers to keep him out of court, not to get him into litigation."

After Prince Henry of Prussia visited St. Louis as Germany's representative to the World's Fair, Kaiser Wilhelm conferred the Order of the Red Eagle on Mr. Busch in recognition of courtesies shown his brother. When Mr. Busch celebrated his seventy-second birthday in Carlsbad in 1909, the Order of Commercial Councillor was conferred on him by the Duke of Hesse. Later, the Emperor conferred the Order of Philip the Good on the distinguished St. Louisan.

According to the Post-Dispatch, October 12, 1913, Adolphus in his lifetime made the following gifts:

Harvard University	$350,000
The Louisiana Purchase Exposition	100,000
Busch Hall, Washington University	120,000
Sisters of the Good Shepherd	100,000
San Francisco Fire Relief	100,000
Dayton, Ohio, Flood Sufferers	50,000

| Washington University, Chair of German | $ 30,000 |
| University of Missouri Hospital | 10,000 |

The Post-Dispatch of October 12, 1913, quoted Edward Faust, a son-in-law, as saying that Adolphus had been to some extent an invalid for nearly seven years before his death. The decline from his former robustness dated from Christmas Eve, 1906. At that time, his daughter, Mrs. Scharrer, was returning to St. Louis from abroad and Busch was determined to greet his "little girl" as he called her. The night was cold and raw, the train was long delayed and Adolphus, pacing the station midway impatiently, caught a cold which soon developed into pneumonia.

The attack was severe and the inflammation of the lungs passing slowly brought on dropsy. From that time, it was necessary for the patient to be in close touch with his physicians and to avoid fatigue.

The disposition of Adolphus Busch's estate naturally was a subject of much concern to the newspapers.

The St. Louis Post-Dispatch of October 30, 1913, carried a three-column headline on the filing of the will. The paper said in one headline, "Busch Heirs' Income $1,000 a Day." In a second headline, the paper said "$50,000,000 Estate Left to Family." The third headline said, "Son, With Double Share Has Wide Power."

The figures were supplied, the paper said, by Daniel N. Kirby, the family lawyer. The Post-Dispatch said that an income of approximately $2,000 a day fell to August A. Busch and an income of $1,000 a day to his mother, Mrs. Adolphus Busch, under the terms of the will. The will created a trusteeship and divided the $50,000,000 estate, with the exception of $210,000 for charity and $20,000 for two women employees. The heirs, besides August A. and the widow, were the daughters, Mrs. Jacob Loeb, Mrs. Hugo Reisinger, Mrs. Edward A. Faust, Mrs. Paul von Gontard and Mrs. Eduard Scharrer. The paper said the widow and each daughter got one-eighth each. August received, in addition to his own eighth, the equal share which his invalid brother, Carl Busch, would have received but for his helpless condition. August was required to care for Carl, spending on him whatever was needed, up to $12,000 a year.

The newspaper quoted Kirby as saying that the estate represented $3,000,000 a year or a six percent return on a $50,000,000 valuation. It continued that, divided by eight, this would make the income of each share equal to $375,000 a year. The paper continued, saying that an income of $375,000 a year meant more than $7,000 a week, but that the expenses of administration would reduce this somewhat.

The Post-Dispatch said the will gave August A. complete power over the Anheuser-Busch Brewing Association, the Manufacturers Railway, the Busch-Sulzer Bros. Diesel Engine Company and the American Bottle Company. It said that the engine company and the railway had been built up by August without too much help from his father.

In a box on page 1, the Post-Dispatch said: "Six Busch Heirs to Pay $15,000 Income Tax; August A. Busch, $30,000." The paper stated that this was an approximate figure and added that for each share an income tax of $15,810 would have to be paid each year.

Adolphus, by his will, entrusted to his son, August, the job of carrying on as follows:

It is my desire and purpose that August A. Busch be President of the Anheuser-Busch Brewing Association, because I believe that his management will promote the interests of the Association and, therefore, will serve to secure the several interests in the Association which I bequeath by the terms of this, my will.

My trustees and their survivors and successors are, therefore, hereby requested and instructed and it is made part of their duty as such trustees to vote all the shares in said Anheuser-Busch Brewing Association which they may receive or hold as such trustees by the terms of my will for such officers and directors as that may, from time to time, be requested or directed to do by said August A. Busch and in such manner and for such measure as may serve to secure the continuance of August A. Busch as President of the Anheuser-Busch Brewing Association. If August A. Busch, for any reason, cannot serve, then I recommend trustees elect Edward A. Faust, President.

Faust, a son-in-law, had managed the personal business of Adolphus for many years.

Under August's management, the business of Anheuser-Busch began to roll smoothly again, but the vast brewery was a much different place now. Contrasted with his father's booming heartiness, August's charming personality was one of reserve nearly to the point of shyness. August, too, was deeply sentimental. For six years, he kept his father's desk just as its owner had left it when he sailed for the last time to Europe.

Then he moved the desk into his own office and to the spot where it stands today. When that desk was moved, it was as though the change symbolized the death of an era—a peaceful and ever more prosperous era.

Trouble had come—and was to keep on coming, blow after blow after blow.

AUGUST ANHEUSER BUSCH, SENIOR—His mission was to face adversity—and fight back.

Chapter VII

PROBLEMS COME IN A
TREMENDOUS TIDE

THE ROLE OF Adolphus Busch had been magnificent and now the role of August
A. Busch was to be just as magnificent, but on a vastly different stage.

The life of Adolphus had been a sort of light opera, in which Fortune
smiled upon him endlessly.

The life of August was all drama—at times nearly melodrama—in which
his part was to smile back bravely each time that misfortune or failure struck.

The new president of Anheuser-Busch had been in office less than a year
when World War I began and immediately and inexorably changed the American economy. And above the barrages of war could be heard the steady rumble
of one of America's most unspeakable "war babies"—prohibition.

When hostilities began, his mother was visiting her villa in Germany.
August cabled, urging her to return to St. Louis. She demurred, thinking as
many others did that the war would be short lived. Instead, the fighting spread
and she found herself bottled up in Germany.

Since she was in her seventies and not too strong, August worried greatly about his mother and tried repeatedly through different channels to have her returned.

Finally, in 1917, August sent Harry B. Hawes, his friend, an attorney, and former United States Senator, to fetch her home. Hawes expected to accomplish this in a matter of weeks but instead it took him seven and one-half months. In Switzerland, he was able to meet Mrs. Busch with a nurse and a companion. Mrs. Busch was ill with fever. Hawes obtained a hospital car from the French government, and got the three women aboard. At the Spanish border they were turned back and sent to Paris. Hawes wandered from bureau to bureau for two weeks, trying to get out of France. When at last they arrived in Spain, they stepped into a revolution.

Late in June, 1918, the party reached Key West. The three women were subjected there to indignities by a male physician in the Custom Service, who had a spy phobia. He stripped all three of their clothes and searched them for concealed messages from the enemy. On Mrs. Busch's person the doctor found a prescription given her by a Spanish doctor, a newspaper clipping of a patriotic poem, a receipt for $100,000 which she had given to the American Red Cross and a snapshot of her husband's grave.

Hawes, in a newspaper interview, branded the incident as "unexcelled in brutality." After a lengthy investigation, the Attorney General of the United States apologized to the Busch family.

Thereafter, Mrs. Busch lived peacefully at No. 1 Busch Place and in Pasadena, until at the age of 84, she died of a heart attack.

Lala (Clara) Conrades, who was left a nice bequest in the will of Lilly Busch, was a faithful friend and traveling companion to Mrs. Busch long before and after the death of Adolphus. She was Mrs. Theodore Conrades. Her husband was a traveling salesman for the company.

To August's great sorrow, as the trend grew steadily toward United States participation in the conflict, his mother's enforced three-year residence in Ger-

AUGUST A. AND LIFE-LONG FRIENDS, JIM HARVEY AND HARRY B. HAWES

AUGUST A. BUSCH AND FAMOUS SONNENSCHEIN HOP MERCHANTS OF BOHEMIA

many provoked gossip that the family was pro-German. These rumors were spread despite the fact that the family had contributed heavily to the American Red Cross and to funds for war orphans on both sides in Europe.

Vindication was complete, once America got into the fight. August turned over to the government the entire facilities of the Busch-Sulzer Bros. Diesel Engine Company—and the Navy was able to obtain quickly the huge diesels needed to power its submarines. The Army asked for and got tremendous storage space in one of the largest buildings of the brewery and when the rental was paid August turned the money back to the Treasury.

The family bought heavily of each Liberty Loan, buying well over $1,000,000 worth of bonds in addition to the very large purchases made by the company.

While Americans fought overseas for liberty, other Americans fought at home—for prohibition. To their contention that alcohol in any form was the ruination of mankind, they added an argument that many found plausible. It was that it was wrong to turn corn into whiskey and barley into beer when those grains would feed the populations of our own country and our allies. The fact that the Caucasian race always has consumed relatively little barley as food did not enter into it.

August A. Busch had seen the handwriting on the wall. One year, he devoted all of his Budweiser newspaper advertising to wonderfully expressed messages regarding the part that the struggle for personal liberty had played in history. The messages won many over to his side, but not enough.

August still hoped that the nation would not embark upon an experiment that he was convinced would fail, but he resolved to be prepared for the worst. He directed his technical staff to try to produce a nonalcoholic beverage that would taste like beer. What resulted was Bevo, made from barley malt, rice, hops, yeast and water. The name was derived from the Bohemian word, "pivo," meaning beer.

The new beverage had a negligible alcoholic content. It was produced by

THE BEVO PLANT—Bevo runs with the ball. The nonalcoholic beverage Bevo, with a beer taste, became a spectacular success—and a sudden failure.

ANHEUSER-BUSCH'S ST. LOUIS PLANT TODAY—It covers seventy city blocks and produces Budweiser and Michelob beers, yeast, bakery products, malt, corn products, and refrigerated cabinets.

hastened fermentation, which required considerably more yeast than was needed for brewing beer. While beer brewing still was legal, plenty of residual yeast was available for the Bevo process.

Bevo hit the jackpot overnight. Soon it was known and sold all over America. In the remainder of that year, 1916, when it was introduced, 2,250,000 cases were sold. Its popularity grew at such a heart-warming rate that August happily OK'd the expenditure of $10,000,000 for what is still the largest single bottling plant in the world.

The plant was equipped with eighteen bottling lines and so designed that eighteen more could be installed at any time. The building also housed a laboratory and space for the offices of the personnel concerned with producing and marketing the new product. The building was unique in design for bottling operations particularly in that the bottling equipment was on the top floor. It was when Bevo was going strong that a railroad depot was built in the basement.

Five million cases, which brought Anheuser-Busch $6,000,000 were sold in 1918. In the next year, the beverage was being sold in Cuba, Jamaica, Canada, India, Japan, China, Liberia, South Africa, England, France, Italy, Holland, New Zealand, Portugal, Spain, Russia, Java, Ceylon, the Philippines, Mexico and Central and South America.

August A. Busch had good reason to feel happy about his foresight in bringing into being his popular soft drink, because in 1918 came "wartime prohibition." All brewing operations came to a halt in the world's largest brewery in October of that year, but with Bevo booming it appeared that Anheuser-Busch would ride out the storm.

August was a temperate man, enjoying good beer and wine, but having no liking whatever for hard liquor. He was sickened and sad by what became the new American scene.

Soon hoarded liquor bought at exorbitant prices disappeared. The bootlegger appeared. So did the sawed-off shotgun, the corrupt public official, muscling in, high-jacking, organization, gangs and gang warfare.

Rum Runners In Gang War; 5 Die In Mysterious Sinking Of Speed Boat

GRAND JURY INDICTS THREE U. S. DRY AGENTS

Slayer of Woman Hates Prohibition

Dry Raider Who Shot Woman Held For Manslaughter

DRYS SEND 50 SHOTS INTO TWO FISHING BOATS

MILLIONAIRE BOOTLEGGER

INSIDE STORY OF AMAZING CAREER OF . . .

Dry Agent on Trial for Slaying Farmer In Home Brew Raid

JURY INDICTS BOOZE SNOOPER FOR MURDER

GUN BATTLE BETWEEN OFFICERS AND SMUGGLERS AT FALMOUTH

LIST 200 SLAIN BY DRY SPIES

Head of Biggest Whiskey Conspiracy, Involving Several Thousand Men, Tells How He Operated to Defy the Government

Youth, 22, Sentenced to Life Imprisonment As Habitual Criminal

Boy 17, in Rum Car Slain by Dry Agent

1 Killed, 5 Wounded In Raid On Liquor Depot

VILLAGE FILES PROTEST ON DRY TERROR REIGN

Bullets Intended for Tires, Virginia Officer Says; Auto Yields 3 Gallons

190 DEATHS IN RAIDS UNDER PROHIBITION; SEARCH CURB ISSUED

WOMAN ACCUSED OF BOOTLEGGING LOSES CHILDREN

Attempt to Buy Nationwide Protection by Paying Over $250,000 to Friend of U. S. Attorney General

$40,000,000.00 SPENT FOR DISTILLERIES, LIQUOR AND PROTECTION IN TWO YEARS

5 UNIVERSITY OF MICH. FRATERNITY HOUSES RAIDED, 84 ARRESTED

The American people took to drinking on a scale never before known or believed possible. The hip flask became as common as the match book. The reason? Probably the age-old American spirit of mutiny against shackles imposed by a minority. Besides, a spirit of fun entered into it. Any time that you visited a speak-easy or a night club illegally selling liquor, you might be treated to the sight of enforcement officers bursting in on a raid.

You could count on juicy headlines in the daily newspaper (see p. 99) with supporting stories of automobiles filled with gangsters racing through the streets, killing one another off in a spectacular fashion. These homicides came to be looked upon as a good thing for the community, like shooting crows. Motion pictures, scenting good box office, whetted the public interest by picturing the gangsters in action with machine guns.

Yes, people were having a lot of fun playing the popular new game of breaking an unpopular law—sometimes at the price of blindness from drinking "liquor" made with wood alcohol. In fact, bootleg liquor was so universally raw in taste and bite that few undertook to drink it straight. So ginger ale became the most popular mixer and people became accustomed to expecting a sweetish taste in their highballs and gin rickeys.

Bevo, with its slightly tart taste of beer, could not fight that trend. Moreover, prohibition regulations caused the unique quality and character of the drink to be impaired. To produce Bevo called for those large amounts of brewers' yeast, although the beverage's alcoholic content was limited to less than half of one percent. When it no longer was legal to brew beer, the essential residual yeast was lacking, a lack which forced modification of the manufacturing process to its distinct disadvantage. It just wasn't—nor could be—the same Bevo that millions of persons had taken to their hearts. Sales began dropping off as rapidly as they had sky-rocketed. They fell to virtually nothing by 1923, yet the product was manufactured until 1929 in the vague hope that it might make a sudden come-back. More than $15,000,000 had been invested in Bevo, of which $4,000,000 was lost forever.

Moreover, August A. Busch provided the funds to erect in an outlying part of St. Louis a restaurant called the Bevo Mill. Its management was a separate entity, but under his watchful eye. Its purpose, aimed at oncoming prohibition, was to prove that a high type of restaurant could be operated without a bar—suggestive of the saloon—if good food and drink were served at the table in the European custom.

The Bevo Mill, which actually simulated a huge Dutch windmill for its main entrance and was resplendent in Old World atmosphere, quickly became one of the smart showplaces of St. Louis, despite its location far from the concentrated residential section of the city.

August's restaurant failed in its endeavor to stem the dry tide, but, because of the excellence of its cuisine, in 1952 it remained one of the most popular and packed dining spots in St. Louis.

The blow of Bevo's sudden collapse after its great success barely had subsided when a new reverse began shaping up in the guise of a godsend.

Congress, seeing the growing sickness of national prohibition, sought a palliative in "near-beer"—real beer made in the real way and then dealcoholized.

As mentioned earlier, "wartime prohibition" made its appearance in 1918, coming to a focal point when the war ended November 11. However, for technical reasons, a "state of war" continued to exist into the 1920's. Legislation forbidding the manufacture and sale of beer, wine and hard liquor, except for export and medicinal purposes, was enacted into law by the Congress.

President Wilson, who opposed prohibition publicly, signed the bill on November 21, 1918. Why, when his views were well known, he made the resolution into law is anybody's guess. Perhaps, girding for his historic and fatal battle for his League of Nations, he feared the loss of strength and prestige which would result from an overriding of a veto. In any event, he signed and the law became effective July 1, 1919. Anheuser-Busch ceased brewing operations in October, 1918.

Followed the ratification of the Eighteenth Amendment to the Constitution

THE FAMOUS BEVO MILL—It was built just before prohibition by August A., Sr., and is still one of the great eating places of the Midwest.

and the enabling Volstead Act. On January 1, 1920, the country was bone dry—on the books and on the books only.

As prohibition became more farcical, liquor prices became more fancy. Price-cutters in the bootleg liquor business were "rubbed out" with gunfire or dropped into rivers in barrels of cement or, in other ways, brought either to their senses or a sad ending.

The man of soft purse couldn't afford to pay hard liquor prices. He didn't suffer too long, because in those days there was always some genius to see to it that the thirsty were ministered to. "Home-brew" was the answer—a concoction of malt syrup, hopped water, sugar and yeast fermented in a basement crock until "dead," then revivified with extra sugar for carbonation and bottled.

To call home-brew beer is to torment generations of honest brewmasters into turning over in their graves at a whirling pace. It could best be described, charitably and idiomatically, as swell swill. It resembled beer in a cloudy way, tasted like beer in a far-fetched fashion, but it did have a kick.

The new law-buster caught on so rapidly that soon every neighborhood shopping center had its store for home-brewing supplies and the owner was an overnight master brewer who cheerfully schooled his customers in the new cellar science for free.

Thereupon, the prohibition legislators decided that if the public liked beer that well it better have beer—except that it would be "near-beer" containing less than one-half of one percent of alcohol by volume. The brewing of real beer to be humiliated into becoming near-beer was made legal.

August A. Busch and his staff were heartened by this turn of events. To keep alive the love of good, temperate beer was their goal. They began, with the best facilities at their disposal, to make Budweiser—not Budweiser Lager Beer of great repute, mind you, but just plain Budweiser near-beer. If this malt beverage caught on at all, it would keep the famous name before the people and replace the waning Bevo.

The Budweiser beverage caught on fast, when it appeared on January 1, 1920. It was crystal clear and had a fine flavor, although the flavor could not compare with that of the lager beer whose esters held in suspension in alcohol brought such delight to the palate. What made it quickly popular was the bad and unstable taste of home-brew.

Once more, August grinned back at misfortune and approved the installation of costly equipment to complete the dealcoholization process. In the first year, five million cases of the new Budweiser beverage were sold. Things began to look good again—but briefly.

The thirsty public was used to getting a "kick" out of its drinks. Budweiser beverage had no kick. Besides, the techniques of the home-brewers were improving with practice and with felt strainers, screened siphons and other devices invented by American know-how.

Budweiser sales accordingly soared and sank, although they did remain at a low-profit level throughout the remaining years of prohibition. The beverage continued to be popular with many people who liked it for itself and with others who, unappreciative of the plight of the pancreas, poured a small jigger of grain alcohol into their bottle of near-beer because they wanted the "kick."

Now that the brewery was making real beer first to make near-beer afterward, not a few people in St. Louis began to envy the Anheusers and the Busches on the assumption that they managed to smuggle their lager beer into their households. That's what not a few people thought—but the many who knew August A. knew better. He told a Globe-Democrat reporter in an interview that he had forbidden everyone in his family and in the brewery to taste the real beer. The newspaper quoted him as saying:

> If I should go over there and take a glass of beer, my two boys would want to do likewise and then the other officials and pretty soon the workers. It is up to me to set the good example.

Since he had seventy city blocks of equipment, August decided to try to perfect a soft drink to succeed the nearly dead Bevo.

Anheuser-Busch produced several carbonated soft drinks. One, with a chocolate flavor, was called Carcho. Another, coffee-flavored, was named Kaffo. Buschtee, flavored with the costliest of imported tea leaves, Grape Bouquet and root beer were others. All of these drinks were supported by generous advertising and merchandising efforts, but they fizzled. The public had all the soft drinks it required and was having too much fun with prohibition.

Busch Extra Dry Ginger Ale, made with pure fruit juices instead of extracts, was successful for a number of years, but eventually succumbed when the demand for cheap mixers for bootleg liquor prompted soft drink bottlers in virtually every community to enter the ginger ale business with products of lesser quality as well as a lower price.

Some other forms of activity and other non-beverage products were needed.

August A. sensed that soon and acted quickly.

Here again is a good place to reflect and compare. To repeat, "What would Grandfather have done?" Who knows?

It is surely a fact that the son of an illustrious father suffers one nearly insurmountable difficulty. If he does something well, folks say, "He should; look at the father he had." If he fails, they shrug and say, "He certainly isn't the man his father was."

Adolphus Busch was a great man in great times.

His son, August A., was a great man—and a sorely tried man—in bad times.

Adolphus conquered, August never quit.

The father had a magnificent brewery and a brewery only.

The son had a brewery—and suddenly only a mass of bricks . . . and 6,000 workers dependent upon him for a livelihood. The bricks and the people had to start all over again.

Chapter VIII

A NEW SKIPPER SALVAGES

THE SINKING SHIP

AUGUST A. BUSCH was determined that the vast plant which his father had built would continue to operate in some capacity and that its activities would be guided by Anheuser-Busch and Anheuser-Busch only.

In 1916, when every sign indicated that prohibition was no longer just a threat but an eventual certainty, the company took stock of itself and its situation. The company's net worth was $30,800,000, invested in plant, barrels, bottles, bonds and other properties. Best estimates were that, if the investment were liquidated, only a fifth of its value could be realized.

Anheuser-Busch never had taken such a beating and August was resolved that the company wouldn't take it now. Department heads were told to put on their thinking caps and plan for eventual conversion.

In this thinking cap business, August A. relied heavily upon Eberhard Anheuser, who more than lived up to the expectations. Tireless and resourceful, "Ebie" contributed more than hard work to each day. His cheerfulness simply

106

wouldn't take "no" for an answer from adversity. His attitude was that the long haul wasn't helped by a long face and that get-up-and-go began with a grin. August never ceased to heap praise upon Eberhard for the latter's zeal in those zero hours.

When the prohibition that August A. had feared in 1916 became a horrible reality in 1919, the president could be grateful that the thoughts of his staff and himself had focused on what was to be done to avoid a crash. Assets and potentials had been thoroughly catalogued. And there were the human assets, too.

Adolphus III long ago had proved his fitness for the responsibilities that the future had in store. Brother Gussie, busy with his brewing studies, was demonstrating his fitness for the multilateral activities that were to be his lot.

Leicester Busch Faust, son of the astute Eddie Faust, had inherited his father's flair for business and management.

A fourth grandson of Adolphus Busch, père, had not grown up under the very eye of paterfamilias August A., and, when he joined the company in 1923, he had to be very much on his toes to prove his mettle. That grandson was Adalbert (Adie) von Gontard, the son of Baron and Baroness von Gontard, who was recently arrived and armed with a Master's Degree in Engineering awarded in Germany.

For a few years, Adie was assistant to the Technical Director, Dr. Gull, who, as has been noted, was somewhat of a taskmaster with very firm ideas. That there would be flare-ups between the young upstart and the old master was inevitable. In these early days of Adie's career, Uncle August, as well as Dr. Gull, entertained some skepticism about the young engineer. Skepticism to the contrary, the young man continued to exhibit the energy and drive that were to carry him to a high place in management.

Adie contended, for example, that the per-kilowatt cost of power could be reduced by two-thirds, proved it and did it. Then he came up with some revolutionary ideas on boiler installations . . . so radical that outside consultants

EBERHARD ANHEUSER—Chairman of the Board in the centennial year, the right-hand man of Anheuser-Busch through many years.

were called in to check on the novel procedure. The consultants voted the new departure not only good but perfect.

One day August A. demanded his nephew's presence. Adie went to the president's office prepared for some stiff questioning if not a reprimand. The older man scowled at the younger, then grinned broadly and said, "I sent for you to tell you that some day not too far away you will be our Chief Engineer."

As the twenties rolled on and what had been the world's largest brewery became a beehive of many other activities, reconstruction of plant and facilities became constant and gave Adie the opportunity of proving his ability beyond question. It was excellent training for a man who was, in the thirties, to have to rebuild the vast plant back into a brewery—and a very modern brewery that would encompass the many changes that had been brought about by brewing science abroad during the thirteen years of prohibition at home.

Now that we have reviewed who of the family was on the active list in management in 1916-19 and who was to join that active list, let us return for the moment to the time that August A., Sr., decided that Anheuser-Busch would stay in business.

No new-product plans were being made a few blocks away by one of the company's biggest competitors of long standing, the William J. Lemp Brewing Company. It gave up in 1920, selling its huge buildings for factory and warehouse use for reportedly ten cents on the dollar.

All over America, breweries folded up for keeps—and, remember, that their number was only slightly lower than the peak year of 1910, when the country had 1,568 plants producing an even greater number of brands of beer.

For many decades, Anheuser-Busch had maintained extensive shops for wood work and metal crafts. These were essential to keep delivery wagons and trucks spic and span. It was only natural that when prohibition did come, these shops were put to work building truck bodies and refrigeration cabinets —and, because Anheuser-Busch, as usual, took no short cuts on quality, it was natural that this department became a profitable department.

Then there were the adventures with soft drinks already related.

But, as early as 1916, with an eye toward the blackening skies of the future, August began entertaining a bright idea—although it didn't seem at the time to be too bright to some of his counselors.

He reasoned thus: Since fermentology always has been an important factor in our brewing science, why shouldn't we plan to enter the bakers' yeast business?

If this conclusion caused near-swooning among some of his advisors, they can be pardoned for it. Here was a big corporation having plenty of trouble, facing double doses of more trouble and yet its president was asking for still more. The discussion went on for years.

In tribute to August A. Busch's courageous heart and excellent sense, it must be said that he knew he was asking for trouble, but he was ready to fight it.

To understand fully the boldness of such a plan, one must remember that the bakers' yeast business was conducted by one large company and a few small competitors for many years.

Dr. G. S. Bratton and Arthur E. Weber had been in the employ of one of the small competitor companies which went out of business, the former in technical work, the latter in the Sales Department. They met with Mr. Busch in St. Louis, planned ahead and joined Anheuser-Busch on January 21, 1926. Conversion of the brewery's idle Stockhouse No. 3 into a yeast-producing plant was begun immediately.

One of the many problems of the new yeast business was the threat of patent litigation, but all such obstacles were successfully overcome.

August A. decided that the time had come for his eldest son, Adolphus Busch III, to try his wings and, accordingly, he gave him active management. The Third, as he was affectionately known to family and associates, appointed the late Homer F. Ziegler as head of the Yeast Sales Department.

Toward the end of 1926 yeast production got under way. While The

Third was in complete charge, August A. still was head of the dynasty. So, not too confidently, Adolphus brought his father the first samples of yeast—and the big question, "What would Grandfather have done?"

The father promptly decided that the yeast had neither the odor nor quality standards that his own father always had insisted upon. No yeast was marketed in what remained of 1926. It was a year of costly discouragement, but August insisted that the battle go on. In March of 1927, such progress had been made that samples of Anheuser-Busch yeast and the big competitor's yeast were sent to commercial laboratories in unidentified but coded packages. The laboratories found the new product up to baking standards in every detail.

On Monday morning, March 28, sales operations began. It proved to be not just a blue Monday, but one of deep indigo.

When the day was ended, 506 pounds of yeast had been sold for cash and 10 pounds for credit. Samples amounting to 323 pounds had been given away.

Tuesday was Monday all over again, but dyed a deeper blue. Thirty-one pounds were sold for cash and 13 for credit. On the next day, 62 pounds brought cash and 87 pounds went out on credit.

The new business began to grow, but at a slow and discouraging rate. Also rumors and stories began to grow. Bakers—and Anheuser-Busch— heard that the new yeast business was about to be sold. They heard, too, that because Anheuser-Busch had one plant instead of several, a mechanical failure, fire or similar calamity would leave in the lurch bakers relying on St. Louis for yeast.

The usually mild-mannered August A. became hornet-mad when this sort of gossip was over-worked and he decided to work it over. In every publication and into every channel of information that could reach members of the baking industry he sounded this challenge:

We are in the yeast business to stay.

We will continue as leader in yeast quality.

We will expand, in size and in service, to meet the industry's needs.

ADOLPHUS BUSCH III—This kindly man was tough enough to help his father make a great success of the yeast business after many business people had predicted rank failure.

We are now, and will remain, firmly on the side of the baker.

This statement not only made a hit, it made a dent. Orders began to tumble in and more and more Anheuser-Busch yeast began to pour out to bakers in most of America. August's boldness was beginning to pay off, was beginning to build a giant new industry for his heritage. He and Adolphus III began arising long before daylight to make personal calls upon bakers in their oven rooms and receive renewed assurance that their product was what the bakers wanted.

In June of 1927, August A. issued a statement under the caption, "Wholesome Competition Is the Spice of Life" in which he outlined his policies for the Yeast Department, which was destined to become such a success. Excerpts from the statement follow:

> It is a well-recognized fact that yeast is the foundation of all fermented beverages. It is, therefore, perfectly natural to assume that in the production of Budweiser it has always been necessary for us to have a yeast of the highest and most uniform quality in order to produce a product as delicate and palatable as Budweiser, which has been the leading brand of its kind on the market for a period of more than sixty-five years. During this long stretch of time we learned how to treat and make yeast, which explains why we are now able to supply a yeast product that is second to none in any respect.
>
> One of the most important factors in the distribution of yeast is the keeping of this product at a uniform temperature. We have developed Busch refrigerated automobile truck bodies equipped with automatic brine circulating systems. In this connection, I believe it is appropriate to mention the fact that we have been wagon builders for upwards of fifty years. With the progress of time and the advent of the automobile, the business of our Vehicle Department naturally developed into the building of automobile truck bodies for ourselves and other business concerns. Consequently, we are today equipped and qualified to make our own automobile truck bodies, and it goes without saying that the best equipment money and experience can provide is represented in our yeast delivery system.

Two other vitally important factors which enter into our yeast delivery system are the railroad refrigerator cars in our service and the ice and cold storage plants located throughout the country which we own or in which we have controlling interests. These ice and cold storage plants are manned by splendid organizations and supervised by capable managers recognized as leading citizens in their respective communities.

Such facilities are exceptional and they will be utilized to insure a prompt delivery of, and uniformity in, the quality of Anheuser-Busch Yeast.

When prohibition descended upon the country our problem was not merely one of numerous unoccupied buildings. We also had a valued clientele and a vast organization to consider. The personnel of the Anheuser-Busch manufacturing and distributing organizations would do credit to any institution in the world.

It is my earnest desire to hold these two organizations together and at the same time perpetuate the name and continue the activities of the House of Anheuser-Busch. In these organizations were men who had spent the greater part of their lives in our service; who had given us the best they had to give, and for whom my good father and I had a warm personal attachment. Their interests and welfare were always ours. I therefore wanted to keep these two great bodies intact. For I realize that no institution can have a greater asset than we knew we had in the thousands of friendly patrons handling and distributing Anheuser-Busch products throughout the country.

My hope was to continue a relationship which was founded on something deeper and stronger than a mere business connection. In not a single instance has it ever been necessary for us to enter into a contract with any of our distributors or representatives. Between these men and the House of Anheuser-Busch is a bond of confidence born of long association that rendered unnecessary anything more binding than the word of either party. It certainly would have been hard indeed to sacrifice friends like these.

I could have advocated liquidation, the proceeds of which would have netted a very comfortable sum to our stockholders. Personally, I could have retired to the historic and beautiful Grant's Farm which it is my good fortune to own. The pride in our organization, knowledge of the loyalty of our patrons and a firm conviction that we deserved and would have the confidence of the public in our new undertakings inspired me to go on and seek out the new fields into which we have ventured.

Then there were my own two sons, who had ambitions to realize and for whom I, too, had ambitions. It was my hope that they would follow in the footsteps of their illustrious grandfather and in my own, as long before and since my good father's death I have been active in the interests of Anheuser-Busch. It is my belief that a career alive with interest and activity is the only proper and natural one for any man.

I wanted to see my sons carrying on the business established by their forefathers more than seventy years ago. I have had this satisfaction and the great gratification of being able to continue business relations with our countless friends throughout the country and have been able to keep intact our splendid organization—not a man among the many having ever been found wavering in his loyalty to Anheuser-Busch. But I want to emphasize that all of this would not have been possible had we not branched out into the new undertakings that have become such an important part of our present business.

In conclusion I want to say that I will not at any time countenance or permit our people to take any unfair advantage of, or make any attempt to belittle the products of those with whom we come into competition. I want each and every one of our men to understand that we are out for business based on the merits of our products alone. I believe "wholesome competition is the spice of life."

I am a respecter of the rights of the other man and any business that comes to us must come on a clean basis and on a representation of the facts. Our products must sell, as they always have, on their merits. I feel that everything we are producing is as good as can be made, which should entitle us to the consideration of the buying public.

It is my conviction that "only a thoroughbred can win" and I want our people to always bear in mind that the articles they are representing live up to this designation in the fullest sense of the word.

In 1928, August A. made this statement to the baking industry:

Your business and our business are both founded on service. Our efforts are being concentrated to give you a finer yeast and finer service than you have ever known before—for we know that unless our yeast is a better yeast, we cannot live. Unless our yeast is uniformly fresh and strong, we cannot live. Unless we deliver our yeast to your shop without interruption or delay, we cannot live. And we propose to live and prosper and grow.

In the next four years, the yeast business grew to the point where it accounted for more than one-third of Anheuser-Busch sales. It was then that a $2,000,000 yeast plant in Old Bridge, New Jersey, was built. The company widely published an advertisement saying:

> Our promise four years ago of a better product for the baking industry has been fulfilled. Our pledge that we are in the yeast business to stay finds emphatic expression of proof in the building of a new, modern yeast plant on our own propery of 19 acres, located at Old Bridge in East Brunswick Township, New Jersey, just 40 miles from New York City. This extensive expansion and investment is not alone due to the inherent qualities of Anheuser-Busch Yeast, but has been made possible by the bakers' recognition of a quality that has resulted in better bakery products at lower cost and in less time.
>
> This new factory will produce Anheuser-Busch Yeast exclusively in conjunction with one of the largest plants of its kind in the world at St. Louis. It is the seal of our pledge of permanency in manufacture and service to the thousands of bakers who have placed confidence in our product with their patronage. The production of kindred products for which Anheuser-Busch have long been famed will in no way alter the relationship so firmly established with bakers of the country nor retard our expansion to better serve the baking industry. We are in the yeast business to stay.

In April of 1927, a branch was opened in Milwaukee and in May branches were opened in Chicago, Marion and Quincy, Illinois. At the close of the year, twenty branches were operating, including such markets as Kansas City, St. Paul, Detroit, New Orleans and others.

Before the end of 1927, the following cities had branches for the distribution of Anheuser-Busch yeast: St. Louis, Milwaukee, Chicago, Marion, Quincy, Chicago Heights, Kansas City, Grand Rapids, Louisville, Racine, St. Paul,

Detroit, Indianapolis, Dallas, New Orleans, Breman, Ind., Fort Worth, San Antonio, South Bend, and Waco.

Sales by months during 1927 were as follows in pounds:

April	19,649
May	44,151
June	69,409
July	79,695
August	118,513
September	151,985
October	186,287
November	207,448
December	216,789
TOTAL	1,093,929

Perhaps the most outstanding and happiest account of all in the beginning was the Ward Baking Company of New York City. Beginning June 4, 1927, Anheuser-Busch shipped 400 pounds of yeast per day—and that was the biggest thrill of all to the sales department.

August A. was never again to have to worry about his harebrained idea of 1916 that scored such a hair-raising and happy success. It was really big business that was to become even bigger business and call for more expansion, more personnel and more baking industry products.

In this one venture more than in any other, August A. had fulfilled his wish of creating a new kind of business that would hold his plant and his people prosperously together against the day he was certain was coming—the day of repeal.

When 1947 marked the twentieth anniversary of the company's advent into yeast production, August A. Busch, Jr., published this statement in every publication that would reach the baking industry:

My dad said it 20 years ago—and on our twentieth anniversary, I say it again—"We are in the yeast business to stay"—but not to stay still.

On March 28, 1927, Anheuser-Busch courageously embarked on a great new adventure.

On that same day, twenty-three equally courageous bakers in St. Louis did likewise—for on faith alone, they purchased a new and heretofore unknown product—Anheuser-Busch yeast.

A humble beginning this! And especially so when viewed in terms of national marketing objectives. But to those hardy founders of the House of Anheuser-Busch, here was simply history repeating itself as it had so often during the illustrious years preceding.

For Budweiser did not overnight become the world's most popular beer. Nor was the world's largest brewery built in a single day. Both came slowly, surely, as the inevitable reward of the uncompromising quality standards, integrity, sincerity of purposes, highest ideals of service and a very human understanding of customer relationship.

Surrounding this new bakers' yeast with these same time-proved ingredients for success, my father August A. Busch, early in 1927, confidently made public this simple forthright promise to the baking industry:

"We are in the yeast business to stay."

Today as we celebrate our twentieth successful year in the yeast business, we wish to convey our deep appreciation to those bakers who embarked with us that first day on our great adventure—and to the thousands of bakers who, in the days which followed, have become our valued friends.

Yes! I can assure you again, Anheuser-Busch is in the yeast business to stay. But not to stay still! Ahead are tremendous sales opportunities for the baking industry and for us. By working and planning together, we can turn these opportunities into new sources of volume and profit. Here at Anheuser-Busch, we are busy on many new and interesting projects. They should prove of great mutual value in making 1947 the biggest year in our respective history.

It was in 1946 that the head of the Yeast, Malt & Corn Products Department, Adolphus III, died. When the matter of choosing a successor came up, Adalbert von Gontard, vice-president and chief engineer, said that he would like to try his hand at selling. To some, this came as a surprising request, since Adie had so distinguished himself in keeping the Engineering Department abreast of the increasing demands that increasing production was forever making upon it. The request was granted and results proved the decision to have been a most happy one.

Adie demonstrated quickly that he had inherited his grandfather's gift of personalized selling. He subscribed heartily to the idea that "Making Friends Is Our Business." Granted that you have products of superior quality, how can you sell them in volume unless you make friendships of such solidarity that your story is listened to in its entirety and believed wholeheartedly?

Maintaining the fine momentum generated by The Third and increasing it to keep up with increasing production facilities called for more contacts in more places. Adie decided that, like his grandfather, he would become one of Anheuser-Busch's most traveled representatives. At first he kept tab on the mileage he covered as an amusing pastime, but, as cipher after cipher was added to the imposing total he gave it up, feeling, "What's another ten thousand miles in this job?"

All of Adie's salesmanship was on a family level. When he was the guest of a prospect or the prospect and his wife enjoyed Adie's hospitality, the little touch of flowers for the lady afterward was never overlooked.

Making salesmanship a family affair paid off not only in fast friendships, but in new accounts. Some of the largest and hardest-to-crack accounts in the baking, confection and other industries came into the Anheuser-Busch fold to stay. So impressive was Adie's success that in April, 1951, he was made director of sales and advertising of all Anheuser-Busch departments everywhere.

With the entire Anheuser-Busch sales organization, Adie enjoyed an enviable reputation for the unique messages he delivered each year at the company's sales convention. His talks were, in every instance, a medley of wit, satire and down-to-earth information and advice.

A brief biography of Adalbert von Gontard appears in Chapter XIX.

The following is a memorandum to management from Arthur E. Weber, dated July 5, 1938, which said in part:

> The recognition accorded us by bakers in the eleven years that we have been in the yeast business has proved a sound and beneficial policy for their industry. It has brought results that it is impossible to measure in monetary value alone, but which nevertheless have had an important influence upon the continued advancement of the baking industry. In this consideration, the following factors stand out prominently:
>
> *Vastly improved quality.*
> *Greatly lowered prices.*
> *The elimination of dependency upon one source of supply.*
> *Focusing the limelight of publicity on the destructive policy of encouraging home baking at the expense of the commercial baker.*
> *The encouraging and active support of every worthwhile movement calculated to benefit the baker.*
> *An extensive and ever-growing research program that has developed valuable facts on many important subjects of interest and concern to the baker.*
>
> The saving to the baking industry from our program of increased quality at lowered price schedule reaches tremendous proportions. For instance, in 1926, the yeast quotations by the then leading yeast company ranged from 30 cents per pound down. Today, they start at 20 cents per pound with the same ratio of decrease applying all the way through. Another important development in connection with yeast prices is the narrowing of the spread between the basis for the small bakeries and the large national accounts.

Syrup was another factor in the rehabilitation of the brewery property. Since the company had considerable grain elevator storage space and buildings adaptable to processing of grains, it was decided to enter the wet corn milling operational field. This industry had always been closely held. There were only eight other wet corn millers besides Anheuser-Busch.

Plant installation began in 1922 and on August 15, 1923, the production of corn syrup (glucose) and crude corn sugar was a reality. The first grind for the first year's operation in 1924 was 1,722,080 bushels.

YEAST PLANT AT OLD BRIDGE, NEW JERSEY—It was built when St. Louis facilities no longer were able to cope with the growing demand for Anheuser-Busch bakers' yeast.

During this period, crude corn sugar was much sought after by bootleggers, who used it to make whiskey. Anheuser-Busch, of course, had no business with them, selling the sugar through legitimate channels.

Production through the years showed steady progress until 1934, the year after repeal, when the manufacture of corn sugar was discontinued.

Simultaneously with the production of corn syrup, Anheuser-Busch began the manufacture of malt syrup. Because of its excellent quality, it found ready acceptance from commercial bakers. Moreover, it helped to pave the way for distribution of Anheuser-Busch bakers' yeast. The new syrup soon found profitable markets among the manufacturers or processors of pharmaceuticals, cereals, special foods, textiles, dairy products, flavoring agents, confections and vinegar.

Within the next year or two after the inception of the malt syrup business of Anheuser-Busch, home-brewing, previously noted, began to take on serious proportions. August A. and his people, having great respect for fine beer, quite naturally looked with scorn upon such a makeshift substitute and ignored it until 1925, when there came a sudden change in thinking.

It had by now become obvious that a large segment of the American people were determined to have anything that resembled beer. The federal law enforcement agencies reached the same conclusion and, having their hands full with the hard liquor problem, made virtually no effort to discourage the home-brewer as long as he did not sell his product.

August A., convinced that there some day would be repeal, reasoned that the home-brewer was building up sentiment for the return of beer. He reasoned further that the home-brewer would brew better beer with better ingredients. Furthermore, the manufacture and sale of canned malt syrup was a legal and reputable operation. Finally, it was a promising source of badly needed profit.

Anheuser-Busch stepped up its production of canned malt syrup by leaps and bounds and did likewise with advertising and sales promotion. Having got into this business a bit late, the company found competitors well established, but before too long it got its share of the business through—again—sheer quality.

In 1921, when malt syrup was still pretty much of a baking ingredient, the company spent $1,411 on advertising in trade papers. In the next year, this was increased to $8,724. When the decision to expand the operation was made in 1925, $61,395 was devoted to advertising and 2,444,400 pounds of the product were sold. However, in the first nine months of the next year, 1926, sales jumped to 6,616,008 pounds and from then on until repeal sales remained well above the 6,000,000-pound level. In those same nine months of 1926, the advertising appropriation was increased to $234,444.

The advertising of malt syrup by all manufacturers of it was a curious thing. You could not even intimate that your product made better home-brew, but you could keep your name before the public in newspapers, magazines and on posters by speaking of the quality of your syrup's ingredients and solemnly insisting that it made better cookies and other home-baked goods.

Hence it was not at all uncommon for one home-brewer to tell another that his "last batch of cookies" had turned out beautifully.

This sort of nonsense was contrary to all Anheuser-Busch advertising policies of the past, but nonsense was the sign of the times. Anheuser-Busch violated no law, but it did advertise its malt syrup as a superior ingredient for cookie baking. For the sake of the record, that was a fact. If you used Budweiser Malt Syrup, you did get a better cookie if you baked—and you did get a better beer if you brewed.

As the Roaring Twenties began to approach the Terrible Thirties—in which the nation would count upon repeal to help it get back on its financial feet in the worst depression in history—August A. Busch could well be satisfied and proud. He had kept the corporate nose clean and the corporate body breathing—breathing deep, healthful breaths.

In all the years that he fought for survival, August A. often found himself very tired, but never too tired to fight prohibition every day of his life. His

PROHIBITION MADE THIS ANOTHER BIG BUSINESS— Anheuser-Busch was comparatively late entering the malt syrup field but the superiority of the product soon made it a great favorite among consumers.

thinking was clear and he was articulate enough, but he was much, much too busy to crusade constantly and singlehandedly. He needed help—and got it in generous measure.

George W. Eads was a political writer for the St. Louis Post-Dispatch. His sagacity and writing ability so impressed Mr. Busch that in 1918 he persuaded Eads to obtain a leave of absence from his newspaper to assist him in combating some proposed prohibition legislation in the Missouri legislature. Thus began a friendship and confidence that was to endure as long as August A. lived. Eads became so fascinated with his new venture and its possibilities of righting a national wrong that his leave of absence became permanent and he became a regular member of the Anheuser-Busch family.

Mr. Eads became such an authority on prohibition and temperance, the correction of the former and the furtherance of the latter, that his views and often his testimony were welcomed on both sides of the great controversy.

The following five chapters present excerpts from his records and they appear here with gratitude for his fine work and fine cooperation.

Chapter IX

THE BLUE-NOSE
PUTS A NATION TO SHAME

Liquor Prohibition Amendment

Article XVIII

1. After one year from the ratification of this article, the manufacture,
    sale, or transportation of intoxicating liquors within, the importation
    thereof into, or the exportation thereof from the United States and all
    territory subject to the jurisdiction thereof for beverage purposes is
    hereby prohibited.
2. The Congress and the several States shall have concurrent power to
    enforce this article by appropriate legislation.
3. This article shall be inoperative unless it shall have been ratified as an
    amendment to the Constitution by the Legislatures of the several States,
    as provided in the Constitution, within seven years from the date of the
    submission hereof to the States by the Congress.

This is the story of what prohibition promised. And what it gave us. It is
the story of small groups of men and women who believed that, once the
manufacture, sale, transportation or importation of intoxicating liquors was

banned . . . and they were determined that it would be . . . America would enter into a period of unparalleled moral, social and economic well-being.

Never were sincere men so wrong. In their zeal, they overlooked the fact that their action was the attempt of a minority to impose its standard of conduct upon all the American people.

Theirs was a well deserved defeat. But it was more. They lived to know the bitter disillusionment that they had been "used." For the shame of prohibition was that it succeeded in having propaganda made into laws. Actually, it was the culmination of twenty years of work by a band of zealots. Leading that band was Wayne B. Wheeler.

Opposed to him, was August A. Busch. The vigor and unfailing resourcefulness of August A. Busch were impressive. He was intensely aware of and responsive to every new development in the economic and social field that might affect his interests. He was abreast of most things that happened, and ahead of many.

Every generation has its own interests, and often total unawareness of what it owes to the leaders of the preceding generation. So it is very doubtful whether anyone who does not know the inside story of prohibition will realize all that its defeat owes to August A. Busch. To him, the coming of prohibition was more than a threat to his own personal interests. He saw it for what it really was . . . *a curtailment of the liberty of all Americans.* He trusted the people, and today, with the benefit of hindsight, we can see that his achievements were not only those of a singularly gifted and productive individual, but of the spirit and ways of America.

The Eighteenth Amendment had ruined Busch's prosperous pre-prohibition beer business. He found himself losing large sums of money by observing the law. Others were making fortunes by violating it. Convinced that when public opinion is aroused against an evil, the voting public, without political pressure, will put an end to it, he labored—at times almost singlehanded—to give the people the facts.

But before repeal came . . . the thirteen years and one month during which
the Eighteenth Amendment was embedded in the Constitution . . . America,
politically speaking, was to go through one of the blackest periods in its history.
Midway through that period, Gifford Pinchot, then Governor of Pennsylvania
and himself "bone dry," made this serious appraisal of the evil effects of
prohibition:

> We are living in an era of disrespect for law. We are, by the showing of
> cold figures, one of, if not the most, lawless nation on Earth. That is one
> reason why law enforcement today is an issue that no citizen who loves his
> country can afford to disregard.
>
> There is a wave of lawlessness all over America. Murder, banditry and
> violence in our great cities are the despair of citizens and the shame of the
> police . . . Why? The reason is not far to seek.
>
> It is common knowledge that when the Eighteenth Amendment was first
> passed, our people, law-abiding and law-defying alike, assumed that it
> would be enforced. It was expected that the Government of the United
> States would stand behind and enforce the law regulating the manufacture
> of alcohol in every form.
>
> Today what do we find? Among all the cities in America, Washington
> has become the conspicuous leader in disrespect for the law and the Consti-
> tution. Cabinet officers, judges, Senators, Representatives of Congress,
> leaders of official life in Washington publicly, notoriously break the funda-
> mental law of their country. Is it any wonder when these men set the
> example the criminal classes and all men everywhere should follow them.
> We have sowed the wind, and the nation is reaping the whirlwind. . .

How had the nation come to such a pass?

Apparently formed in 1899, the Anti-Saloon League held its fifteenth
annual convention in 1913. There it adopted the following resolution:

> We . . . declare for . . . an amendment to the Federal Constitution which
> shall forever prohibit throughout the Territory of the United States *the
> manufacture, and sale, and importation, exportation and transportation of
> intoxicating liquors, to be used as a beverage.*

Within seven years this resolution of the Anti-Saloon League was, almost word for word, written into the Constitution of the United States as Section One of the Eighteenth Amendment. Here is that Section:

ARTICLE XVIII

Liquor Prohibition Amendment

1. After one year from the ratification of this article, the manufacture, sale, or transportation of intoxicating liquors within, the importation thereof into, or the exportation thereof from the United States and all territory subject to the jurisdiction thereof for beverage purposes is hereby prohibited.

In those days, we did not know as much about the Anti-Saloon League as we do now. It held itself out to the churches, in Wayne B. Wheeler's own words, as an educational, scientific, and charitable institution.

Senator Reed (Dem.) of Missouri said:

> The Anti-Saloon League, then, had not been forced to reveal how its funds were collected and expended. It did not tell the small contributor that his silver offering was split 50-50 between the exhorter and the League.
>
> It concealed the fact that the Hon. Richmond Hobson, of Alabama, who was then a member of Congress and who introduced the original Eighteenth Amendment in the House of Representatives on orders from the Anti-Saloon League, was in its pay. This fact was uncovered by a special investigating committee of the Senate, of which I was chairman. . .
>
> . . . Introduced from the pulpit as a statesman from Washington, fighting the good fight for national temperance . . . Hobson received a commission on every dollar that the Anti-Saloon League received . . . in eight years from 1914 to 1922, his split of the money was more than $170,000. In the years 1919 and 1920, when prohibition was being fastened on the nation as a legal fact, the Anti-Saloon League paid him more than $30,000 each year.

The National Prohibition Act, which became popularly known as the Volstead Act, set up a unit in the Internal Revenue Department to administer the law. Nominally, the Commissioner of Internal Revenue was the chief enforcement officer. Actually, enforcement was delegated to the prohibition commissioner.

Taking notice of widespread violations, Internal Revenue Commissioner Williams, in a press release, acknowledged that all large brewers were obeying the law. That, ironically, meant that the patriotism of these brewery owners in obeying the law was ruining them. He promised full law enforcement against all violators.

Mr. Busch read the press release with interest. He wrote a congratulatory letter to the Commissioner. He was amazed to have the Commissioner ask him, "Would you be willing to cooperate with the Internal Revenue Department to fully and fairly enforce the laws against all, especially for the protection of lawful business?"

Think what that meant. Mr. Busch was opposed to the prohibition law. In addition to dissipating the fortune of the Busch family and industries, he foresaw the great evils it would bring upon the nation. His assistance in the enforcement of the law—if successful—might have the effect of making the law permanent. That, of course, he did not want. He took the position that the law should either be enforced or repealed.

In the end he made his decision. It was this. With complete trust in the common sense and honesty of the American people, he determined to investigate the methods and practices of the Prohibition Enforcement Department and to tell the American people the plain truth about it.

On May 12, 1921, Oliver T. Remmers, attorney for Anheuser-Busch, Inc., appeared before the Judiciary Committee of Congress, Mr. Volstead presiding. Details of outrageous conditions were reported. A booklet, "The Penalty of Law Obedience," was placed in evidence and copies of it placed in the hands of every member of Congress, the President and his cabinet and other high government officials. Requests were made not only to Congress, but to President Harding for an official investigation of the conditions outlined in the booklet. The government ignored the request.

It was plain that the prohibition law was not being enforced; that it was not capable of being enforced. It was plain, also, that it was fostering crime and enriching criminals; that it was driving into homes the manufacture of liquor of all kinds to the demoralization of women and children—debasing the character of citizens everywhere.

The first big exposures made by Mr. Busch broke in newspapers throughout the nation on June 14, 1922 . . . the fifth month of the administration of President Harding.

This is how it happened.

Albert D. Lasker, then chairman of the United States Shipping Board, had been head of the large advertising agency which formerly had handled the account of Anheuser-Busch, Inc. Lasker and Charles E. Staudinger, then Anheuser-Busch advertising manager, were friends. Mr. Busch sent Staudinger to Washington to arrange for the sale of Bevo on United States ships.

Staudinger met Lasker, who replied he would be very glad to put the Busch nonalcoholic beverage on sale on the ships, but that there would be no demand for it because the ships served liquor.

> Mr. Lasker, related Staudinger, stated very frankly how it all happened. He (Lasker) said that soon after he became Chairman of the Shipping Board, he found losses in operation were enormous. He took a balance sheet to the President (Harding) and told him that, by the sale of liquor on the ships, the losses could be reduced by $100 million a year. The President replied, "Mr. Lasker, you are Chairman of the Shipping Board."

So United States ships advertised in foreign newspapers, in all ports they touched, that "choice wines and liquors" were served on board and a prospective passenger was assured that "it is possible to secure not only real beer on our steamers, but we also carry all other forms of liquid refreshments." On one line alone, the United States owned and operated five saloons. Its wine list included ten popular brands of champagne; nine of red and white Bordeaux

THE PALL BEARERS.

"Courtesy New York World-Telegram & Sun"

THE VOLSTEAD MARKET DAY
"Courtesy New York World"

"Courtesy New York World"

PROHIBITION CARTOONS—Mr. Rollin Kirby, noted for his symbolic prohibition figure, the man in the frock-coat wearing a high hat, was awarded the 1922, 1925 and 1929 Pulitzer Prizes for his prowess as a political cartoonist.

wines; nine of red and white Burgundy; seven of Rhine wines; five of Moselle wines; five of Vermouth, Port and Sherry; and twenty-seven varieties of spirits and liquors including "old American Rye Moonshine" at thirty cents a pony.

The facts revealed were sent in a letter to the President. Copies were sent to Lasker, all members of Congress and all Washington newspaper correspondents.

The charges created an official explosion in Washington. The President shunted the responsibility back to Lasker. Lasker claimed that United States ships had the right to sell liquor outside the territorial waters of the United States and accused Mr. Busch of wanting to scuttle the United States Merchant Marine.

Actually, it was the prize of one hundred million a year that the federal government was trying to win—to "get the money" and wink at the violation of the prohibition law at sea while enforcing the law against its citizens on land at home.

Attorney General Daugherty finally ruled that American boats must be dry. Moreover, foreign governments were advised that ships of their registry could not enter American ports with liquor aboard.

Of the Daugherty decision, the New York World said, editorially, "Ships chartered in the U. S., according to Mr. Daugherty, are subject to the laws of U. S., are, in fact, American territory, but ships chartered in foreign countries are not foreign territory. As soon as they enter American waters, all vessels subject themselves to American law, which means, of course, the Volstead Act. How this comes about is not clearly explained.

"It would naturally be supposed that if an American ship were American territory, a foreign ship would be foreign territory. Mr. Daugherty cannot have it both ways. On one point or another he must change his mind. Or have it changed for him."

For nearly a year after Mr. Busch's sensational exposure, the Shipping Board defended its practices. Then, in November, 1922, the United States

Supreme Court decided that these maritime operations violated both the Eighteenth Amendment and the National Prohibition Law. The Supreme Court also held that it was equally illegal for *any* ship (Daugherty's position) of *any* registry to transport liquor into, or to possess liquor within, the territorial waters of the United States.

Thus, the great passenger fleets of Great Britain, France, Germany and Italy could not enter the ports of the United States with any liquor for beverage use. They could sell liquor on their westbound trips legally until they reached the three mile limit. Then any surplus supply had to be dumped.

The United States proceeded then to enter into treaties with foreign governments granting the latter the right to transport and to possess intoxicating liquors while in the territorial waters of the United States. The first of these treaties was proposed by the Secretary of State, Charles Evans Hughes, ratified by the Senate and approved by President Coolidge.

According to their own admission, the professional prohibition organizations spent $50,000,000 to bring about the ratification of the Eighteenth Amendment and the passage of national and state enforcement acts.

Chapter X

MR. BUSCH REPORTS
TO CALVIN COOLIDGE

In his message to Congress, December 8, 1922, President Harding outlined, as well he might, the demoralizing results of prohibition.

On the following September 23, the Department of Justice said, in part, ". . . the Department has been called upon to prosecute a member of the judiciary, prominent members of the American bar, high officials of Federal and State governments. The sordid story of assassination, bribery and corruption has been found in the very sanctums where the law was presumed to be held sacred."

On the death of Harding, August 2, 1923, Calvin Coolidge became President. Here was another opportunity for Mr. Busch to be of service to America. Writing directly to Mr. Coolidge, he said:

My Dear Mr. President:

We are informed by the daily press that you have called a meeting of the Governors of the states in Washington, October 20, to consider, among other matters, the enforcement of prohibition laws. We are also informed

135

that you consented to give a hearing at the White House to certain advocates of prohibition, who assembled in Washington, October 13, 14, and 15.

Mr. President, we believe that it will be conceded by all who are in the least informed on the subject that the attempt to enforce the prohibition law has produced disastrous results in at least three important respects:

First, it has corrupted the Federal service to an extent never before known.

Second, it has so uprooted respect for all law that crimes of intense violence have swept the country from coast to coast to such an extent that no citizen knows today when he is secure in his life and his property.

Third, it has set back the cause of real temperance many years by driving the illicit manufacture of alcoholic beverages into the home; by flooding the country with all sorts of imported or smuggled beverages, and creating an army of manufacturers and purveyors of beverages of doubtful or harmful quality.

Your late predecessor in office said to the Congress in December, 1922: "In plain speaking, there are conditions relating to its enforcement which savor of nation-wide scandal. It is the most demoralizing factor in our public life."

If it is true—as President Harding said, and our own experiences confirm the truth of his statement—that prohibition enforcement is the most demoralizing factor in our national life, then is it not time that our public officials and our thinking people were giving serious consideration to fundamental causes instead of being swept away by emotionalism aroused by false representations or by considerations of political expediency? For more than three years we have been trying to make the Government at Washington see these fundamental facts and we have been pointing out to our leaders that if they continued to permit the Federal service to be prostituted by corruption and if they continued a policy that incubated disrespect for all law, sooner or later the country would reap a whirlwind of disorders of a most serious and dangerous character.

Many former large brewing corporations of the United States, within six months after the adoption of the Volstead enforcement act, found themselves in a peculiar and embarrassing situation where they had to appeal to the Government for the enforcement of the prohibition law for the protection of the lawful business they had undertaken to establish.

The Government had confiscated their former business and immediately after the adoption of the prohibition law embarked upon a policy of lax enforcement and favoritism, which made it practically impossible for law-abiding manufacturers to do business. Some of the brewing corporations spent much time, money and practical effort trying to get a fair and impartial enforcement of the law. We think we may say to you, in truth, that they spent more money, time and effort trying to get the law honestly administered than all the so-called dry organizations and churches combined.

Some former brewing corporations that made complaint, we are informed, were put out of business by the Government agents for their temerity in asking for the enforcement of the law. We say to you in all sincerity and candor that our efforts to get the law enforced failed not only because we could get no effective cooperation from the Government itself, but because the law in its very nature is non-enforceable.

In fact, at the very time that we were trying to get a fair enforcement of the law, the Government, through the United States Shipping Board, was setting an example of law violation unparalleled in history by buying and selling large quantities of alcoholic liquors for the use of passengers on ships owned and operated by the United States Government. The Shipping Board pursued the policy of violating the Federal prohibition laws for a period of more than eighteen months, while at the same time the Government was prosecuting and punishing some of its own citizens for violating on dry land the law which the Government had set aside at sea.

Certain representatives of the brewing industry were moved by two considerations to demand the enforcement of the prohibition law, although they did not believe in the law itself, and fought its adoption with all the legitimate resources at their command. These considerations were:

First, inability to market their lawful products in competition with the flood of unlawful products manufactured and sold practically everywhere with the knowledge of the Government.

Second, on account of their contact with unlawful business they were able to discover that this unlawful business existed primarily as the result of the corruption of the Federal service for political advantages and, therefore, as good citizens, interested in the preservation of the sanctity of their Government, they felt impelled to demand the enforcement of the law. It may come as a surprise to you to know that when some of these representatives visited Washington to demand the protection of their lawful business they were denied an audience with the chief of the Prohibition Enforcement Department!

We believe, Mr. President, there are certain fundamental reasons why the prohibition law cannot be enforced. The prohibition propagandists are continually asserting that there is only a small minority of the American people opposed to the law and that this minority is in conspiracy against the Constitution and the laws and is comprised of a vicious and law-defying element of our people. Let us examine the facts and see what they show.

You, of course, understand that the question of national prohibition was never submitted directly to the American people for their approval or rejection. It was adopted during the war on a wave of emotionalism and prejudice. The best barometer of the sentiment of the American people with respect to prohibition is found in the result of referendum elections held in several states in advance of the adoption of the Eighteenth Amendment. We believe the facts are worthy of your most earnest and serious consideration. These facts show:

First, that fifteen states before ratification of the Eighteenth Amendment, had never adopted statutory or constitutional prohibition. In some of these states the issue had been presented and rejected by the people. The population of these fifteen states, according to the Federal census of 1920, was 50,257,517.

Second, that the legislature of ten states, without having submitted the prohibition issue to the people, had adopted statutory prohibition. The people of these ten states had no opportunity to express their opinion on the subject at the polls. The population of these ten states was 22,014,531.

Third, that twenty-three states had adopted constitutional or statutory prohibition by a vote of the people. The population of these twenty-three states was 33,000,701.

Fourth, that the vote cast for prohibition in these twenty-three states was 2,666,408, and against prohibition, 2,104,906. The majority for prohibition in the twenty-three states in which the people were given an opportunity to vote upon it was 561,502.

Fifth, these facts show that only 4,771,314 voters had exercised an opportunity to express themselves on a state-wide prohibition proposition in advance of the adoption of national prohibition and that approximately 44 percent of the electors in these states objected to prohibition as a state policy.

Sixth, that the actual vote cast for prohibition in people's referendums in these twenty-three states was only 2,666,408.

Seventh, that actually less than 2½ percent of the American people had expressed themselves as favorable to prohibition as a state policy prior to the adoption of the Eighteenth Amendment.

Eighth, that in the states in which prohibition was adopted as a state policy by a vote of the people, the principal issue was against the saloon, and not against the manufacture and distribution of mild and practically non-intoxicating beverages.

These facts, we believe, make it clear, that the people of states having a population of 72,272,348 had never given their consent to prohibition at the polls.

We are attaching a memorandum setting forth these facts in detail. A little study will present convincing proof that prohibition did not represent the will of the majority of the people of the United States, but, so far as sentiment found expression at the polls, it represented the will of only 2,666,408 voters—or less than 2½ percent.

We believe you will find in these facts, Mr. President, the real reason why prohibition is not enforced in the United States today and why it cannot be enforced.

May we be permitted to make a demonstration to you to prove that the will of the people was openly and flagrantly disregarded in the ratification of the Eighteenth Amendment, at least in our own state, Missouri?

There was submitted to the people of Missouri, at the general election of 1918, a proposed prohibition amendment to the State Constitution. At least 150,000 young men of the state, a large majority of whom, we believe, are opposed to prohibition, were absent from the state in the service of their country. The amendment was rejected by a majority of 73,964, but the members of the Legislature, elected on the very day that this referendum was held, in defiance of the expressed will of the people on the subject of prohibition, ratified the Eighteenth Amendment. We think this is a full and complete demonstration that state legislatures, under the whip of highly organized and richly financed leaders of minorities, have deliberately mis-represented the will of the people in the adoption of Federal Prohibition.

In our own state, in the campaign of 1918, most cruel and vicious methods were adopted by the dry organizations. In many parts of the state, publishers of newspapers were threatened with boycott if they published anything—even paid advertisements—opposed to prohibition.

The brewing industry as a whole was viciously maligned, and charged with being dominated and controlled by the German Government. The truth is that there was not a dollar's worth of German money invested in any St. Louis brewing corporation, but eleven St. Louis breweries were owned and operated by British stockholders. The final result of all this prejudice and falsehood was that the Government of the United States, by the adoption of the Eighteenth Amendment, destroyed millions of dollars worth of property belonging to our allies right here in St. Louis, but not a single dollar's worth of such property belonging to the enemy.

We cite these facts as proof that the Federal law on this subject does not truly reflect the sentiment of the American people. In a broad sense, there-fore, it is no law and this we believe to be the general attitude of the people toward it.

Within six months after the effective date of the Volstead Act, violations of the law had become so extensive and general that as a matter of self-protection and self-respect we were compelled to appeal to the Government for uniform enforcement of the law. When we presented evidence of wide-spread violation of the law to the Enforcement Department at Washington we were frankly—and we believe truthfully—informed that the depart-ment had become so corrupt that it could not enforce the law. This informa-tion was given to our representative by a former Assistant Chief of the department in charge of active enforcement.

At the request of this Assistant Chief of the Prohibition Bureau at Washington, our representatives presented the facts relating to prohibition law violations to a regional director in charge of enforcement in four great states. This regional director was as frank as his superior in Washington and he, too, declared that his department was so corrupt that he could not enforce the law.

We shall be very glad at your request, Mr. President, to have our repre-

| There was an old man | He had so many inspectors |
| who lived in a shoe, | He didn't know what to do. |

"From the St. Louis Post-Dispatch of February 8, 1920"

FITZPATRICK GAVE THE DRYS FITS—This great artist's cartoons were republished in newspapers and magazines all through the country and helped to give the death blow to the Eighteenth Amendment.

sentatives who conducted the negotiations with the department appear
before you and the Governors of the States and present the facts in detail.
We will be glad to tell you who these men were who admitted that the
department was corrupt and to outline to you the complaints that we made
at the time and also give you such information as you may desire on the
facts which we shall present hereinafter.

From the very beginning, it appeared to be the policy of the Prohibition
Unit to exempt entire states and certain large cities from the provisions of
the Enforcement Act. We believed then, and we believe now, that the
exigencies of practical politics had something to do with these exemptions.
Our observations confirm us in the conviction that wherever there have
been general and open violations of the law there have been considerations
of a political nature.

We shall point out a few instances. The State of Pennsylvania offers
perhaps the most flagrant example. Time and again we have brought conditions in the State of Pennsylvania to the attention of the Prohibition Unit
in Washington, under the administration of both Mr. Kramer and Mr.
Haynes. When, in a last final effort to get the law enforced in that state,
we presented the facts to the present Prohibition Commissioner and insisted
on knowing why the law was not enforced, he replied that a certain United
States Senator had just been in his office and was well pleased with conditions in Pennsylvania!

What were the conditions? The law was openly violated in many parts
of the state. A prohibition agent attached to the staff of general agents in
Washington was called in and discharged because he had interfered with
some law violator in that state and he had to appeal to a Senator from his
state to get himself reinstated in the department.

Let us look at some of the results. The people of Pennsylvania were denied
the right of an expression at the polls of their opinion on the wisdom of
prohibition. Popular sentiment, we understand, is against it in that state.
But since the Government had adopted a policy of prohibition it was its
duty to enforce the law with uniformity and fairness.

If you will refer to the September Annals of the American Academy of
Political and Social Science (of which Secretary Hoover is a vice-president)
and turn to page 205, you will find the following statement by Mr. T.

Henry Walnut, former special Assistant United States Attorney General at Philadelphia:

"Coupled with the temptation of extraordinary sums of money there were political influences of importance. The value of the office of the state director of prohibition as a political asset was soon demonstrated. It could control numerous highly desirable appointments, could afford protection to favored persons and provide permits in payment of political debts, and, what was still more important, could collect unlimited sums of money for campaign purposes."

Control of the office was eagerly sought by political leaders. The Republican leaders were alive to these considerations and their original selections, both in New York and Philadelphia, were men of prominence in political life—Judge Harte and Senator McConnell. Neither one lasted more than a few months and both were indicted within a year from the date of their appointment for the fraudulent issue of permits and in both cases there was a persistent rumor that the money collected was intended in part at least to be applied to important political purposes, one of which in Pennsylvania was the accumulation of a fund of great size for the election of a Governor in the following year.

However true the specific rumors may have been as to the political reasons involved, it is undoubted that enormous quantities of liquor were withdrawn from distilleries upon fraudulent permits and that enormous sums of money were paid for these permits. The permits so issued by the Pennsylvania office in a period of sixty days called for seven-hundred-thousand gallons of whiskey and alcohol. The corruption fund arising from these papers must have run close to four-million dollars, which price was added to the cost of the liquor that was withdrawn and bootlegged.

Mr. President, the observation of the former special United States Assistant Attorney General at Philadelphia that the Prohibition Enforcement Department has been used as a collection agency of campaign and corruption funds is in line with our own observations. You will understand that when all the powers of the investigating departments of the Government were unable to discover specific evidence that such funds were collected and distributed it would be very much more difficult for individuals to get the evidence.

We are informed, however, that in the city of Pittsburgh evidence was obtained that at least $100,000 a month was being paid for protection by law violators. We were also informed during the progress of the campaign last year that certain violators of the law were operating in Ohio upon the payment of specific sums for political purposes. Our information indicated that the money collected from the violators of the prohibition law was being used to support candidates pledged to a dry program and also to create public sentiment against a proposition to legalize the manufacture of non-intoxicating malt beverages and light wines.

The consequent activity in Pennsylvania and Ohio seems to have caused a shortage of bottles. We have positive knowledge that a short time before the general election of 1922 more than 10,000,000 bottles were shipped into Pennsylvania and Ohio from Milwaukee. Our experience teaches us that no such demand for enormous quantities of bottles arose from an appetite for lawful beverages.

We have protested with all the power we possess against these wholesale violations, because we were convinced from all the evidence we could gather that they were rooted in corruption which was not only enmeshing large parts of the Federal service, but also involving political parties as well.

It seems to us that, if the Government is going to permit the Prohibition Unit to become the collector of campaign funds from violators of the prohibition law, it should frankly tell the American public what it purposes to do. It should tell the people from whom it is collecting the money, how much money is being collected and who are the beneficiaries of this corruption fund. If Mr. Walnut is right in his assumption that a corruption fund of at least $4,000,000 was collected in a lump sum for the issuance of fraudulent permits and that this money was used for political purposes, we think the American people should be told the truth about it.

At the very time that these things were being done we were spending our money and time trying to get the law enforced for the protection of lawful industry and for the prevention of the corruption of the Government. Could it have been that certain representatives of the Government were more interested in the collection of corrupt campaign funds for political purposes than in the enforcement of the law?

We do know that at the very time we were confronted with this impregnable wall of law violations, the Government itself was bootlegging at sea and, according to our best calculations, the Government sold at least $10,000,000 worth of liquors and earned an incidental profit thereby of approximately $100,000,000 by attracting passenger traffic, which otherwise would have gone to foreign ships.

The moral turpitude involved is exactly the same whether a law violator of great proportions is exempted from the operation of the prohibition law upon the payment of a huge bribe for political purposes or whether the farmer is excused from its operation as a bribe for his vote. We were somewhat astonished recently to read in the daily press what purported to be a copy of a letter from prohibition Commissioner Haynes to Congressman Hill of Maryland, in which it appears to be the fixed policy of the department to exempt the farmers from the operation of the prohibitory laws.

We quote the following paragraph from the letter:

"While it is, of course, both the duty and intention of this unit to prevent the use of the cider and fruit-juice privilege from being perverted to the manufacture of intoxicating liquors for beverage purposes, nevertheless the prevailing customs and practices in the manufacture of this simple domestic article are such that it is believed to attempt to fix a definite prohibited per centum of alcohol strength, which was apparently not the intention of Congress, would have the effect to confuse, hinder and delay the plain farmers of the country in the enjoyment of a long-enjoyed right, and one which it is believed Congress never intended should be denied them."

If this statement means anything, it means that the farmers of the United States are to be exempted from the provisions of the Volstead Act with respect to the manufacture of intoxicating beverages in their homes. The president of our corporation is also a farmer. Under the operation of the law, he would lay himself liable to prosecution for the violation of the prohibition act if, in his capacity as president of the corporation, he permitted it to manufacture beverages in excess of one-half of one percent of alcohol, but would not be liable to prosecution if he manufactured ciders and fruit juices containing more than one-half of one percent of alcohol on his farm.

The Volstead Act itself exempts the rich with well-stocked cellars from the law. If the prohibition unit is going to permit certain favored manufacturers to violate the law upon the payment of contributions to political campaigns and permit the farmers to violate the law in order to win their support at the polls to the dry cause or some other political cause, where is such a policy leading us? Inevitably into a saturnalia of corruption the like of which has never been known in America and into a state of class prejudice that may be even more disastrous to our Republic.

With entire states and many spots in other states being exempted from the operation of the prohibition law, apparently for political reasons and with the Enforcement Department asserting that it was not the intention of Congress to interfere with the long-enjoyed privileges of the plain farmers to manufacture cider and fruit juices in their homes—notwithstanding the fact that cider is one of the worst intoxicants in the entire family of intoxicating beverages—it is not surprising that we were not able to make any substantial headway in our program of law enforcement for the protection of lawful business and for the preservation of the sanctity of the Government and its laws. We were not satisfied to let the matter rest with merely putting the issues up to the Government. We even set aside our pride and appealed to that holy of holies, the Anti-Saloon League.

We called the attention of this organization to the fact that the laws of the country with respect to prohibition were being openly and notoriously violated. We asked the Anti-Saloon League whether it was interested in the enforcement of its own pet law.

Yes, the League was interested, but only upon the payment of a fee of $500 for each case. Having exhausted our resources to induce the Government to enforce the law, we at length determined to find out whether the law could be enforced by yielding to the Anti-Saloon League's importunities for fees to enforce it. We found that where fees were paid in the sum of $500 for each case, the law could be enforced, but where they were not paid the law was not enforced.

Mr. President, can you imagine anything more incongruous than a state superintendent of the Anti-Saloon League, which proclaims itself as the political agency of the Christian Churches of America—a superintendent of this so-called righteous organization with a halo around his head—bow-

A GREAT MORAL VICTORY.

"From the St. Louis Post-Dispatch of April 23, 1925"

ing down before a "wicked brewer"—one of these individuals who has been pictured to the country as having horns and eleven hooves and a forked tail—and saying: "Oh, please, Mr. Brewer, give me $500 of your money and I will get my own—my great, sacred moral law—enforced by the Enforcement Department of the United States, which I control"?

If you can visualize that picture, Mr. President—if you can picture this saintly Anti-Saloon League representative, a former minister of the Gospel of Jesus Christ, begging a law-observing opponent of the prohibition laws for money to enforce them—if you can picture this same super-righteous man grafting upon business firms for procuring permits and favors from the Prohibition Enforcement Department and finally picture him as the financial backer of a bootlegging and narcotics peddling joint in which his young son was actively associated—we think that you will get some idea of what prohibition is doing to human character in this country of ours.

If it breaks down the morality of political parties which are willing to share in the fruits of corruption funds; if it breaks down the morality of departments of the Federal service that are willing for a share of the corruption fund to overlook or protect the law violators; if it breaks down the morality of the very men who used the funds of the great trust magnates to override the will of the people and write prohibition into the Constitution and the statute books of the United States; if it breaks down the character of the citizen and makes him a hypocrite or a law violator or a vicious criminal—then there must be something fundamentally wrong with the law itself.

We have been trying for more than three years to make our officials at Washington see these dreadful things. If they will not see them now and if they will not search out the fundamental things that are wrong with the law itself, then this country and the people will have to pay a still more fearful price than they are now paying for the costly and disastrous privilege of trying to keep one-half of one percent of the American people from sometimes overindulging in stimulants.

We understand from press dispatches that the leaders of the dry movement who called the conference in Washington a few days in advance of your call for a meeting of the Governors—seemingly for the purpose of influencing the action of your conferences—are very much alarmed over the apparent breakdown of the Law Enforcement Department of the Government.

If these advocates now are so alarmed over the direful effects of their own prohibition law, where were they when we and other representatives of the brewing industry were trying to get some sort of honest enforcement of the law?

Where was the Anti-Saloon League when the Shipping Board was indulging in its eighteen months' spree on the high seas?

Where were these great moral forces when the Government was being corrupted, root and branch, and when millions of dollars were being collected from law violators for political purposes and when tens of thousands of people were holding school in their cellars in the art of making intoxicants in their homes?

Where were these advocates of prohibition when the bootleggers were learning and practicing their arts and craftiness and when the moonshiners were multiplying by the thousands and tens of thousands in the hills of every county in America and in every city?

We can only tell you, Mr. President, that they were not with us in our struggle covering a period of three years to get some sort of an honest and efficient administration of the law.

Mr. President, can it be that the Government has set aside all the established rules of conduct for public officials in connection with the operation of the Prohibition Enforcement Department? Quite recently there appeared in the newspapers of the country a series of syndicated articles under the name of Roy A. Haynes, Prohibition Commissioner of the United States. The articles bore evidence that they were written from official information gathered at great expense to the taxpayers. It is within our knowledge that they were offered to certain newspapers at $1,500 for the publication rights.

It is a matter of current knowledge that the Prohibition Commissioner received a large sum of money for the articles, which could have been written only from public documents in his possession. We are informed that newspapers not subscribing to the syndicated articles were denied access to the public documents.

If the Government permits the Prohibition Commissioner to capitalize the public information in his office for personal gain, has the Government any right to complain if the agents employed by this department sell protection to law violators for personal gain or political advantage?

We are presenting this memorial to you, Mr. President, as a plea for justice to an industry that has long been made the football of practical politics. Owing to the unfortunate political conditions with which we were surrounded and the demands made upon us through legislation and taxation, there were some evils that crept into the retail distributing system of our business. We stand ready and we think the entire industry stands ready to correct all those evils and to lend hearty and effective cooperation to the Government in the administration of any remedial law that will preclude the possibility of a reversion to the evils against which public sentiment had been directed in the past.

We believe that anyone, who will carefully weigh the results of the attempt to enforce the present drastic prohibitory law, must be convinced that the moral side of this so-called moral question has swung from prohibition, as it is administered, to anti-prohibition or modification of the present law to satisfy the great majority of the American people and at the same time create a temperance system that would approach the ideal.

Mr. President, we have always stood for law enforcement and real temperance. We realize that we labor under the disadvantage of having our motives misunderstood, but we hope that you will at least give us some credit for our interest in good citizenship and genuine temperance. When our experience in dealing with prohibition from a practical standpoint must have been somewhat similar to that of President Harding, who found it to be the most demoralizing factor in our public life, and the Attorney General, who became convinced from the facts that the law in practical operation constitutes the most tragic epoch in American history with respect to law enforcement, we think it must be conceded that its evil effects far transcend any possible benefits that could arise from it.

It behooves those in charge of administering the Government to consider whether the tragic conditions are not due to fundamental defects in the law itself and to use their power to bring the law within reasonable harmony with the wishes of the people so that it will command their respect.

An unpopular statutory control of individual habits can never be substituted for voluntary temperance, individual self-restraint and reasonable statutory regulation. The law should be written in terms of temperance and reasonable regulations; then the evils of the present system would disappear.

We stand ready at all times to lend you and other departments of the Government all our experience of a practical nature in perfecting a system that will reduce intemperance in America to an irreducible minimum and at the same time restore respect for law and order and purge the Government of the corruption that now threatens to undermine the Republic itself.

On the presentation of this letter to President Coolidge, he merely said, "Thank you" and did nothing.

Chapter XI

A NATION BEGINS TO

GET OVER ITS HANGOVER

FOLLOWING August A. Busch's almost singlehanded exposure of the operations of the United States Shipping Board, a rapidly growing public sentiment for a change in the Enforcement Act and outright repeal of the Eighteenth Amendment began to show.

Scores of anti-prohibition organizations sprang up, lived a short while, then died. Three—the Association Against the Prohibition Amendment, with headquarters in Washington; the Moderation League in New York, and the Constitutional Liberty League of Massachusetts, survived. These were joined by the American Federation of Labor, in which organization there was a strong sentiment for a change in the law to legalize 2.75 percent beer.

In January, 1924, these four formed a Joint Legislative Committee for Modification of the Prohibition Act.

In that same year, defying the all-powerful Anti-Saloon League, sixty representatives in Congress introduced bills for a change in the alcoholic content

152

of permissible beverages from ½ of 1 percent to 2.75 percent by volume. Their theory was that this mild beer was nonintoxicating; that, therefore, the Congress had power, under the Eighteenth Amendment, to authorize the change; that such a change would be a positive aid to the enforcement of the laws against the manufacture and smuggling of illicit liquor of higher alcohol content.

The Anti-Saloon League began to fight. And, while all sixty congressional members who introduced the bill were sincere, none ever had the slightest notion that the House Judiciary Committee would ever report out their bills. All knew that the bills would die in committee.

But their efforts had started a movement. The hearings before the full House Judiciary Committee opened April 24, 1924. This marked the official beginning of the nine years' fight either to modify the Prohibition Act or to repeal the Eighteenth Amendment.

Supporting the sixty congressmen's beer bill was Samuel Gompers, president of the American Federation of Labor. He said, " . . . in my judgment, passing of this bill would transform the people of the U. S. from a whiskey-drinking to a beer-drinking people. It is not merely the question of what amount of kick there is in beer, but the fact that it is drinkable. That which we have and called 'near-beer,' with less than ½ of 1 percent of alcohol, is *not* drinkable, it is *not* palatable, it is *not* good. It is no part of a meal, nor can it be made a part of a meal."

Mr. Gompers, as proof of his authority to speak for organized labor, produced the resolutions passed almost unanimously by the 1919, 1921 and 1923 American Federation of Labor conventions. All protested against the prohibition law and demanded the legalization of real beer.

The fight had begun, with these other voices joined to that of Mr. Busch. The others added volume and force to the protest. But the Busch strategy of "tell the people the truth" remained the spearhead behind the demand.

Time and again pamphlets, simply captioned "Face the Facts," were issued. Their purpose was solely to inform the public—and particularly members of Congress and the Administration—of the extremely vicious evils of prohibition and to fasten responsibility for these evils on the Anti-Saloon League.

The House Judiciary Committee had adjourned in 1924, but not dissolved. In 1925, several bills were introduced in the Senate . . . for the repeal or amendment of the Eighteenth Amendment . . . for the relegalization of beer . . . for modifying the restrictions on physicians' prescriptions for liquor . . . for a national referendum to test officially public opinion on the prohibition issue.

Senators Edge and Edwards of New Jersey, Wadsworth of New York, Bruce of Maryland and others were the authors.

———————

ANTI-SALOON LEAGUE PROPOSES
PUBLIC INDICTMENT OF COOLIDGE

This was the big black headline that streamed across the front page of the New York American and all other Hearst newspapers across the country on July 10, 1927. It was the first of a series of twelve full-page stories based upon the long secret records of the Anti-Saloon League.

Printed in large type on the first page, the story read:

The Executive Committee of the Anti-Saloon League of America addresses the following communication to the People of the United States:

There have been presented to the Anti-Saloon League at its biennial convention reports of delegates from various states and utterances from the platform which clearly indicate misfeasance and malfeasance in the executive branch of the Federal Government.

These reports and utterances include charges of appointments of incompetents and, worse, to positions of authority in enforcement, and of the issuance of permits for huge amounts of alcohol to those with a criminal record for violation of the prohibition laws.

The Anti-Saloon League solemnly asserts the obvious truth that these facts as reported constitute an indictment of the Federal Administration in respect to prohibition enforcement.

The Constitution of the United States specifically places the duty of enforcing the laws on the President of the United States. He is the only officer so charged in the Federal Constitution with responsibility for enforcement and it is impossible for him to shift this responsibility to any cabinet member or department official.

The Anti-Saloon League cannot do less than the Constitution does in recognition of law enforcement responsibility and it, therefore, calls upon Calvin Coolidge, the President of the United States, publicly to declare that past and present conditions which amount to a hindrance to the cause of enforcement do not represent the policy of his administration.

And, the Anti-Saloon League further calls upon the President to indicate his acceptance of enforcement of the law and the triumph of the Government over the bootlegger and his affiliated outlaws.

Actually, the indictment was never adopted. But it had been drawn up, debated and voted upon in a secret meeting of the Executive Committee of the Anti-Saloon League during its national convention in Chicago, November 8, 1925. The indictment was defeated by one vote—four ayes, five noes.

The League was now making tracks to "get out from under," since the people were making efforts to repeal the Eighteenth Amendment. Now Wheeler and the League were only too eager to shift responsibility to the President of the United States. Truly, as Lord Acton said, "Power corrupts and absolute power corrupts absolutely."

More was to come. On July 11, 1927, the Hearst headlines read:

DRY LEAGUE RUSHES TO COOLIDGE
DEMANDING ITS ORDERS BE OBEYED

MELLON ACCUSED OF WANTING LIBERAL
FLOW OF WHISKEY

A subhead read, "Secret Anti-Saloon League Records Reveal How Hayne's Appointment Was Forced on Harding . . . On His Death, New England League Superintendent Was Called to Use His Personal Influence with Coolidge."

This newspaper story said that from reports filed with the Reed Committee by Wheeler, the League had spent a total of $67,565,313.72 in its campaigns for ratification of the Eighteenth Amendment and its support up to the end of 1925.

Again, the secret minutes of the League attested to the unlimited power granted Wheeler, who pointed to an article in the North American Review, which he had written. There he told his Executive Committee, " . . . you will see it set out that the offender against a Wheelerized law is convicted by a jury selected by a Wheelerized marshal. After prosecution by a Wheelerized District Attorney, he is sentenced by a Wheelerized judge. Nor does the Anti-Saloon League's long arm stop there. It pursues the man to the penitentiary and sees that he is not let out."

A subsequent Hearst newspaper headline read:

DRY LEAGUE IN HANDS OF 19 CZARS

HANDLE $67,000,000; DIRECT 1,000 PAID WORKERS

LEAGUE HAS NO MEMBERS—ITS CLAIM TO

REPRESENT CHURCHES DISPROVED BY ITS RECORDS

Here is a briefing of the main charges brought out in detail under these headlines:

(A) Apart from its one thousand employees, the Anti-Saloon League is nothing but an Executive Committee of nineteen self-perpetuating members, some of them clergymen.

(B) In their executive meetings, these nineteen praise themselves as the chosen agency of the Almighty to keep the country dry.

(C) The League gets its money (1) by field days in churches, addressed by the League's paid spellbinders; (2) through solicitors and collectors who work on salary and commission; (3) by nationwide circularization of business concerns.

One of the League's spellbinders was William Jennings Bryan, who, on a four-month speaking tour, collected $700,000 for the Anti-Saloon League.

Nor was the printed word overlooked. The League's own record showed that, from the American Issue Publishing Company, owned and operated by the Anti-Saloon League, 182,500,000 copies of periodicals had been published.

THE ANTI-SALOON LEAGUE MUST GO
BEFORE THE COUNTRY IS MANY YEARS OLDER

Thus did the New York Post editorialize—saying:

The articles in the Hearst newspapers reveal a condition shocking to any American sense of democracy. They show a small body of men seeking, through undercover methods with amazing success, to have laws framed as they want them, administered by men they want, in the way they want and through courts and prosecutors they want. They paint a picture of the Anti-Saloon League which is bound to bring revolt, whether it involves Mr. Wayne B. Wheeler's downfall or not.

The shocking feature is the enormous assumption of power by a group of men holding no elective office and responsible to nobody. They bedevilled poor Harding. They had Attorney General Daugherty where they wanted him. They put constant pressure on Coolidge. They paid Senators and Congressmen vast sums as collectors and orators. They had their own Secret Service.

In the old days we had two evils. One the "liquor evil," the other the "saloon evil." Today we no longer have the saloon—we have the "blind pig" instead. "Regulated" liquor is gone—replaced by "bootlegged" liquor.

What all reasonable people want is something free from the evils of both old and new systems . . . something that can be attained by a sensible modification of the Volstead Act.

The exposure of their records threw consternation into the camp of the Anti-Saloon League and Wayne B. Wheeler. Following the exposure, Wheeler seemed to believe that he was lost . . . and with him, the prohibition cause also. Attempting a come-back, he prepared a press release which wound up picturing himself as "a poor man, with a salary of only $8,000 a year . . . who lives on that small sum, saves something from it and is supremely happy in doing his bit for a cause that no one doubts he would give his life for, if need be."

The newspapers did not publish it. He prepared another, a self-portrait in full length, giving his own estimate of what he believed would be, or should be, his place in history. That release, too, found its way into wastebaskets in newspaper offices all over the country.

The effects began to tell on Wheeler. In July, 1927, he went to Point Sable, Michigan, where he had a summer home, to rest and recuperate.

On September 5, 1927, the newspapers carried the news of his death.

Chapter XII

"AUGUST A. BUSCH HAS
SAID A MOUTHFUL"

IN JUNE, 1928, the Republicans nominated Herbert Hoover for President, and Senator Charles Curtis, of Kansas, for Vice-President. The Democrats nominated Governor Al Smith, of New York, for President and Senator Joseph T. Robinson, of Arkansas, for Vice-President.

Mr. Hoover was "dry" and the Republican convention adopted a platform satisfactory to the drys.

Al Smith advocated repeal of the Eighteenth Amendment. The Democratic convention failed to back him up with any declaration on prohibition. Instead, "enforcement of the law" was proposed.

Dr. Ernest H. Cherrington was secretary of the Executive Committee of the Anti-Saloon League. Cherrington charged that the former brewing industry was supporting Al Smith.

This was not true. What was true was that now, in 1928, Al Smith was advocating repeal and his stand naturally found sympathy with August.

Never one to seek the headlines, but aware of the need to keep the true facts of prohibition constantly before the people, Mr. Busch issued, on September 28, 1928, a 2,500-word press statement in reply to Cherrington's attack that the brewers were supporting Smith with ulterior motives. In the release, Mr. Busch reiterated the now familiar facts of the unscrupulous acts of the Anti-Saloon League and once more set forth his own convictions in these words:

> When the prohibition law was passed, in spite of its injustice, in spite of its attempt to substitute the authority of law for the virtue of man . . . I accepted it in good faith.
>
> Since July 1st, 1919, the organization of which I am the head has devoted itself to the establishment of industries that cannot be disturbed by every passing wave of fanatical legislation. Those industries are now on a profitable basis and they will continue to be operated, regardless of any changes that may be made in the prohibition law. I can, therefore, truthfully say that I have little or no financial interest at stake.
>
> I have always believed, however, that in making a pure, light beer . . . the world-famous Budweiser . . . I was contributing to the temperance progress of the nation.

Then Mr. Busch added:

> Dr. Cherrington seems to fear that the former brewers might support Governor Al Smith for President since the Governor has announced himself for "repeal." I have not the slightest idea—and have not conferred with other brewers—as to their voting preference. They certainly have as much right to support any candidate they like, as has the Anti-Saloon League.
>
> For my part, I am going to support Governor Smith. I am glad that he, as a great American, has had the courage to come out boldly against the sham and hypocrisy of prohibition. I shall support him, believing that by so doing I am exercising the highest duty of an American citizen, for by my vote I shall declare myself against the evils of prohibition.
>
> I believe his election will be regarded as a mandate from the American people to establish a real temperance system in this country. This I have always advocated, as my father, the late Adolphus Busch, also did throughout his life.

I would like to add that I have a great admiration for Mr. Hoover. I have had the pleasure of entertaining him in my home and consider him a great American and a superb administrator.

All the world knows that one of Al Smith's greatest appeals to the people was his famous slogan, "Let's look at the record." Time and again, he would demolish the specious arguments of his opponents with that simple tactic. He let the "facts" fight for him. Smart politician? Yes, but, like Busch, he trusted the common sense of the people . . . knew that facts, forthrightly presented, would win their support.

Despite the fact that Smith knew that the Democratic convention was going to straddle on the prohibition issue, he was not. Here is the telegram Smith sent to the Democrats at their convention in Houston, Texas.

> It is well known that I believe there should be fundamental changes in the present provisions for national prohibition, based, as I stated in my Jackson Day letter, on the fearless application to the problem of the fundamental principles of Jeffersonian democracy.
>
> While I fully appreciate that these changes can only be made by the people themselves through their elected representatives, I feel it to be the duty of the chosen leader of the people to point the way, which, in his opinion, leads to a sane, sensible solution of a condition which I am convinced is unsatisfactory to a great mass of our people. By the application of the Democratic principles of local self-government and state's rights we can secure real temperance, respect for law and eradication of the existing evil.

In his speech of acceptance of the Democratic nomination, Smith again came out on the prohibition question and said ". . . under modification of the Volstead Enforcement Act each state would have the privilege of fixing its own alcoholic standard on beverages; subject, of course, to the national standard. Under an amendment to the Eighteenth Amendment such of the states as desired might work out the problem of state control along the lines of the very satisfactory system (The Quebec Liquor Control System) adopted by our Canadian neighbors."

The Anti-Saloon League had high hopes for Hoover. In speech after speech, he described prohibition as a noble experiment intended to protect the home, the women and children.

The best evidence that Smith *could* do something to change the law is that 31 organizations and more than 5,000 professional propagandists worked like beavers against him. *They* knew that if he were elected their jobs and graft would be at an end.

As the campaign closed, the political forces favored Hoover. He won by a majority of over 6,000,000 votes. Having described prohibition as "a noble experiment," he was now assured of an opportunity to see what he could do to make it work.

On May 20, two months after his inauguration, Hoover announced the appointment of a Commission on Law Enforcement and Observance. With Mr. George W. Wickersham as chairman, the Commission consisted of eleven members. Wickersham said, "We are under no illusions . . . we know there is no short cut to the millennium . . . this commission is not to be the arbiter between the wets and the drys."

Eight months later the Wickersham Commission had accomplished nothing. Meantime, the main outlines of Hoover's prohibition policy had become clear. It was an attempt to persuade the public to accept prohibition (and all laws) as a duty of good citizenship. Harding had tried that approach—and failed. Coolidge had tried it—and failed. Hoover soon joined his predecessors in failure.

It was still true, as Lincoln had said, "No law is stronger than the public sentiment where it is to be enforced."

———

At 10:15 A.M., February 12, 1930, the Chairman of the House Judiciary Committee rapped for order. Outlining the scope of the hearings about to begin, he said, ". . . seven resolutions to amend the Constitution have been introduced in the House of Representatives. This Committee is to consider them. If we deem them meritorious and so report to the House, they must write a law which must be approved by two thirds vote in each branch of Congress. Then this new law must be referred to the States and, if ratified by thirty six of them, it becomes a part of the Constitution of the United States.

". . . The Eighteenth Amendment and the enforcement law have been tested for 10 years . . . we must remember that, under the slogan of 'down with the saloon,' churches were opened and opportunities given to those who advocated prohibition . . . what opportunity has there been given to the conscientious thinker and believer who is opposed to prohibition? . . ."

Mrs. Charles H. Sabin, chairman of the Women's Organization for National Prohibition Reform—an organization only a few months old but even then with an enrollment of 50,000 members and growing at the rate of 3,000 a day—told the Chairman:

> . . . I am here to refute the contention by dry organizations that all the women of America favor prohibition. Our organization, organized only eight months ago, I am proud to say, has a membership in every state of the Union. These thousands upon thousands of women from all walks of life . . . are convinced that the National Prohibition Law has failed.
>
> It is generally conceded that women played a large part in the enactment of the Eighteenth Amendment . . . they thought prohibition would strengthen man's weak nature. They did not realize that, if the spirit of temperance is not within him, legislation can be of no avail.
>
> . . . it was predicted that saloons would be closed . . . today in any speakeasy in the United States you can find boys and girls in their 'teens drinking liquor, poisonous or non-poisonous . . . the mothers of the country feel something must be done to protect their children.

The last day of the hearings was April 2, 1930. The House Judiciary Committee did *not* report the bills.

The presidential and congressional elections of 1932 made repeal a certainty in the near future.

On February 17, 1933, both the House and Senate sent the Twenty First Amendment—repealing the Eighteenth Amendment—to conventions in the states for action. The House voted 289 to 121 to initiate submission of a repeal resolution. The Senate voted 62 for submission, 23 against.

In a 1931 magazine advertisement devoted to the selling of some of his new products, August A. Busch parenthetically made the statement that, in his opinion, "the manufacture and sale of wholesome 4% beer would be a good thing, economically and socially, for the nation."

Immediately the drys sprang into action—challenging Mr. Busch to prove his opinions. Mr. Busch's reply was printed by nearly all daily papers.

The facts Mr. Busch used in his statement were especially timely because in the mid-summer of 1931, unemployment, which reached tremendous heights in the depression years of 1932 and 1933, was beginning to be felt all over America. The suggestion of reopening the breweries and thus revitalizing the industries that supplied them with materials of all kinds caught the imagination of the public.

Thousands of columns of editorials endorsing Mr. Busch's idea were presented. The New York Daily News said:

August A. Busch has said a mouthful about prohibition.

As President of Anheuser-Busch, Inc., whose Budweiser used to be one of the wonders of the world, Mr. Busch is naturally interested in the return of lawful beer . . . he deserves to be listened to with respect.

Mr. Busch digs up a couple of arguments used by the drys in the days of World War I and uses those arguments to clip the drys of this day squarely on the chin. Thirteen years ago the drys said they were outraged and heartbroken because the brewing industry used, in one year, 3,220,000 tons of coal, 527,000 barrels of oil and gasoline, 3,500,000 cubic feet of gas and required the use of 180,000 freight cars.

Mr. Busch wants to know whether, in these tough times, it wouldn't be a fine thing for the railroads, the coal, oil and gas industries to get back that business. So do we.

Another war time squawk of the drys was that, in 1917, American brewers used almost 4,000,000 pounds of grain and other farm products. Since prohibition, American near-beer breweries' grain consumption and the prices of grains American farmers grow have dropped out of sight. Busch thinks that could be revised—and should be. So do we.

Other editorials said, in part:

Lynn (Mass.) Telegram— . . . August A. Busch, after quoting the drys' own figures on farm and other products consumed by American brewers, shows that the legalization of brewing today would give work to 1,250,000 persons, yield the Government $400,000,000 a year in taxes and do much to restore business stability. We think so, too.

New York World Telegram— . . . There is undeniably a change in favor of the legal control of what has become a vast and well organized lawless business. Eventually this sentiment will make itself felt in Congress.

While the drys were trying to refute their own facts, the American Bar Association in convention at Atlantic City adopted a resolution demanding immediate repeal.

The American Federation of Labor also adopted resolutions demanding the legalization of beer and asserted that it not only would give employment to 1,500,000 persons, but send an electrical thrill through more than sixty industries supplying the brewers with materials.

The American Legion and the Royal Order of Hibernians also took up the refrain and made the demand for beer and repeal almost unanimous among their memberships.

The White House was deluged with letters demanding the immediate reopening of the breweries. The temper of the nation indicated that the end of the "noble experiment" was in sight.

Chapter XIII

SOMETHING MORE

THAN BEER IS BACK

On June 13, 1932, as the Republican National Convention gathered in the great Chicago Stadium, everyone knew that the big issue was prohibition.

Repeal bands trumpeted in the streets and hotel corridors. A repeal parade six miles long with 1,500 floats was one of the big spectacles of the convention. An empty jail was depicted on one float labelled, "What Prohibition Promised." It was followed by another showing a jail crowded with men and women and labelled, "What Prohibition Gave Us."

In the Resolutions Committee, Senator Wadsworth of New York, said: "We all know that this convention will not champion this thing (prohibition) nor be silent upon it. Nor can the most adroit mind conjure up words which can fool the people on this fundamental question. We cannot fool anybody with talk of modifying or revising the amendment. The public mind is too keen, too alert. If we try to dodge, we shall be caught instantly. Dodging on this question will pin the label, 'Prohibition Party,' on what is still the Republican Party."

166

The drys, of course, were given a hearing. They told the Resolutions Committee that they represented many millions of people who were unalterably opposed to either repeal or modification. And the one thing they bitterly opposed was the submission of any amendment, whether for revision or repeal, to conventions of the people. If there were no alternative they wanted the amendment sent to the state legislatures, obviously so that the people themselves would have no opportunity to vote directly on repeal or modification.

As already pointed out, as long as the drys could control thirteen of the forty-eight states the prohibition amendment could not be gotten out of the Constitution.

Repeal strength in the convention was powerful, but President Hoover would not consent to outright repeal. The Hoover plank, approved by a majority of the Resolutions Committee read, in part, as follows:

> The Republican Party has always stood and stands today for obedience to and enforcement of the law as the very foundation of an orderly government and civilization. . . The duty of the President and officers of the law is clear. The law must be enforced as they find it. To these courses of action, we pledge our nominees.
>
> Article V of the Constitution limits the proposals of amendments to two methods: (1) two thirds of both houses of Congress may propose amendments, or (2) on application of the legislatures of two thirds of the states, a national convention shall be called by Congress to propose amendments. Thereafter, ratification must be had by either the legislatures of three fourths of the states or by conventions held in three fourths of the states. Congress is given power to determine the mode of ratification.
>
> . . . We do not favor a submission limited to the issue of retention or repeal. . . The people should have an opportunity to pass upon a proposed amendment . . . which shall allow states to deal with the problems as their citizens may determine, but subject always to the power of the Federal Government to protect these states where prohibition may exist and safeguard our citizens everywhere from the return of the saloon and attendant abuses . . .

This Hoover plank won 681 to 472 on the floor of the convention. This was what the drys wanted—to throw the issue back to the legislatures.

Two weeks later, the Democratic National Convention delegates and visitors filed into the same great Chicago Stadium and everybody knew one thing . . . and believed a second. First, they knew that the Democrats would adopt an outright repeal platform. Second, they believed that, running on such a platform, their nominee would be elected in November. They were right.

Franklin Delano Roosevelt was their nominee. The outright repeal plank won in the convention. It read as follows:

> We advocate the repeal of the Eighteenth Amendment.
> To effect such repeal, we demand the Congress immediately propose a Constitutional amendment to truly representative conventions in the states called to act solely on that proposal.
> We urge the enactment of such measures by the several states as will actually promote temperance, effectively prevent the return of the saloon and bring the liquor traffic into the open under complete supervision and control by the states.
> . . . pending repeal, we favor immediate modification of the Volstead Act to legalize the manufacture and sale of beer and other beverages of such alcoholic content as is permissible under the Constitution and to provide therefrom a proper and needed revenue.

In his acceptance speech, Roosevelt accepted the platform one hundred percent, saying, ". . . I congratulate this convention for having had the courage, fearlessly, to write into its declaration of principles what an overwhelming majority here assembled really thinks about the Eighteenth Amendment. This convention wants repeal. Your candidate wants repeal. And I am confident that the United States of America wants repeal."

Roosevelt and a Democratic House and Senate were elected. Missouri sent to Congress a delegation of thirteen members all committed to repeal. Roosevelt's popular plurality was over 7,000,000 votes. His electoral vote was 472 to Hoover's 59.

The old Seventy-second Congress met in the first week of December, 1932. It still had to run out its term, as a lame-duck Congress, until March 4, 1933. Previously it had twice voted against bills to relegalize beer. What would it do between December and March? With the grip of the Anti-Saloon League weakened through the overwhelming public support for beer and repeal, would they propose a constitutional amendment to conventions of the people?

A week before they met in their last term, the Kansas City Star had sent one of its top reporters to interview Mr. Busch. Then, the day before the Congress opened, it printed that interview headlined as follows:

WITH CONGRESS ABOUT TO MODIFY

OR REPEAL PROHIBITION, AUGUST A. BUSCH

GIVES HIS VIEWS . . . INSISTS UPON ALCOHOLIC

CONTENT OF 4% . . . SAYS BEER MUST BE

SOLD AT LOW PRICE

By A. B. MacDonald

St. Louis, Dec. 3, 1932. . . "When do you think you'll get the right to begin making beer again?" I asked Mr. Busch.

"Probably within a few months. But I don't just want the right again; I don't want to start making beer unless I can make and sell a beer with a content of 4% of alcohol," he said.

"I've written a letter to every Member of Congress stating the fact that if we start up to make a beer with 2.75% content of alcohol, it will just be a farce.

"People won't drink it. I ought to know. We have been brewers here for many years. We should know what the people will drink and what they won't drink.

"The people want a beer that is in all respects satisfying, that will give them a warmth and a mild stimulating glow."

"What percent was your pre-prohibition Budweiser?"

"That was 4.50% to 4.70%. We built a world-wide reputation on that beer. Now do you think we want to start to cheapen that brand by making 2.75%? No. We want to make a beer that will be worthy of

Budweiser. It is not intoxicating . . . you give us the right to make 4% beer and we will give the people a wholesome, satisfying beer that will sell."

About local option, he said: "We want the right of local option to be rigidly observed. Our company will never put Budweiser on sale in any state, county, city or community that declares by vote that it does not want it."

The Collier Bill legalizing beer with an alcoholic content of 3.2% by weight with a tax of $5.00 per barrel was offered in the House December 21. In less than two hours of debate, it passed, 230 to 165. When the Collier Bill went to the Senate, a controversy developed over the alcoholic content. The Senate wanted 3.05% by weight. Debate raged on this point and led to the defeat of beer legislation in the Senate.

Now, what of repeal of the Eighteenth Amendment?

The Senate was tense with drama at 3 P.M., February 16, 1933.

Within half an hour, the vote to send the Eighteenth Amendment back to the people for reconsideration was cast, 63 to 23—five more than the necessary two-thirds majority. Then, on February 20, after forty-five minutes of debate, the House voted 289 to 121 to let the people reconsider the Eighteenth Amendment. That was fifteen more than the necessary two-thirds majority.

On the next day, February 21, 1933, Secretary of State Henry L. Stimson certified the joint resolution to the governors of all the states. That completed official action of the federal government on the repeal issue. Mr. Hoover was still President and would be until March 4, 1933. But his signature was not required on the joint resolution.

All this made history, because, for the first time, Congress had sent an amendment of the Federal Constitution back to the people . . . for repeal. Moreover, it decisively defeated the Anti-Saloon League which desperately wanted the question handled by the state legislatures.

On April 4, 1933, Wisconsin voted 648,031 for repeal, 141,518 against. Between April and November, 1933, thirty-nine states had authorized repeal elections. Thirty-seven states, one more than necessary for a three-fourths majority, voted for repeal. A total of 20,928,378 citizens went to the polls and 15,341,849 voted for repeal. With only 5,576,529 against, the majority for repeal was 9,760,320. Up to that time, that was the largest majority ever reported on any national proposal voted upon by all the people of the United States.

At 5:00 P.M., December 5, 1933, Washington was notified that the last state had completed ratification of the repeal of the Eighteenth Amendment. Within the hour, the Secretary of State certified that it had been repealed!

The honor of modifying the Volstead Act prior to the completion of the repeal procedure went to the Seventy-third Congress and President Franklin D. Roosevelt.

Roosevelt was inaugurated on March 4, 1933. He called the Seventy-third Congress into extra session. He had been President only nine days when, on March 13, he sent the following special message to Congress:

> I recommend the passage of legislation for the immediate modification of the Volstead Act in order to legalize the manufacture and sale of beer and other beverages of such alcoholic content as is permissible under the Constitution; and to provide, through such manufacture and sale, by substantial taxes, a much needed revenue for the Government.
>
> I deem action at this time to be of the highest importance.

The next day, the Democratic leader, Representative James M. Byrnes of South Carolina, introduced a bill providing for the manufacture and sale of nonintoxicating beer containing 3.2% of alcohol by weight. It passed, 316 to 97, in the House. Two days later, the Senate passed the bill without change, 46 to 30.

The President signed the bill on March 22, to become effective within fifteen days or at midnight April 7, 1933.

Anticipating the return of beer, the Federal Commissioner of Industrial Alcohol issued advance permits for production to reliable brewers. Thus,

Something More than Beer is back

Beer is back! In those three simple words a great American industry has gone back to **work**. Hands long idle have found new jobs. Faces empty of hope brighten to a new promise. Thousands have found honorable livelihood. A vast American market—a new frontier of industry reopens—bringing sorely needed business to farmers, transportation and to hundreds of other industries. And with it, a new fountain head of tax revenue has arisen to add its dollars gladly to a nation in need.

Beer is back! But is that all? No! To cheer, to quicken American life with hospitality of old, the friendly glass of good-fellowship is back. Sociability and good living return to their own, once more to mingle with memories and sentiments of yesterday. America looks forward—and feels better...*Beer is back!* Yes! More than that. Beer at its best is back—the brew that outsold any other brand of bottled beer on earth; brewed and fully aged in the largest brewery in the world.

BUDWEISER IS BACK
King of Bottled Beer

Anheuser-Busch · St. Louis

AMERICA WELCOMES **Budweiser** **KING OF BOTTLED BEER**

1876   1933

THIS FULL-PAGE ADVERTISEMENT IN NEWSPAPERS AND MAGAZINES MADE HISTORY

SOMETHING MORE THAN BEER IS BACK—Adolphus III, August A., Sr., and August A., Jr., select the first case of relegalized Budweiser for President Roosevelt.

250,000 barrels of Budweiser—fully aged—were ready to be released when the law became effective.

Mr. Busch had not intended to open his plant for distribution of Budweiser until the regular business hours on the morning of April 7. But it seemed that on April 6 all of St. Louis awaited the midnight hour to drink the first real beer . . . the first Budweiser offered for legal sale for more than thirteen years. So the plans were changed.

At 12:01 A.M., April 7, the whistles of thousands of St. Louis factories screamed out a welcome for the return of beer. All the streets in the vicinity of the great Anheuser-Busch brewery were filled with happy, singing throngs. The gates were opened and fleets of trucks delivered Budweiser throughout the city to licensed outlets. They were crowded to the doors with customers waiting eagerly for the cool, foaming glasses of golden Budweiser.

Mr. Busch and his two sons, Adolphus Busch III and August A. Busch, Jr., selected one of the first cases of Budweiser to come from the bottling line and sent it to President Roosevelt by air express.

The return of beer was celebrated in many other cities. After the first gala day of celebration and rejoicing in New York City, the New York Times said editorially:

> It was announced late last night at Police Headquarters that although 3.2% beer flowed freely throughout the city yesterday, there was not a single arrest for drunkenness resulting from it. No disorder was reported at parties at which the new brew was served exclusively, and no drivers of automobiles had been found who were intoxicated on the legalized beverage.

This and other editorials of like nature were important, because, still fighting, the Anti-Saloon League had threatened to challenge the constitutionality of the 3.2% beer law in the courts. They insisted 3.2% beer was intoxicating. Public reaction was so overwhelmingly against them that plans for the suit were dropped.

Prohibition was dead . . . killed by the vote of the people . . . as August A. Busch, Senior, had predicted all along.

Since it no longer was illegal to advertise real beer, nearly every brewer back in business published an advertisement on April 7 in one or more newspapers. Coincidentally, nearly every one proclaimed that Good Old This Beer or Good Old That Beer was back.

Anheuser-Busch waited until all this printed clamor subsided completely and then, in all metropolitan newspapers, published this full-page advertisement:

SOMETHING MORE THAN BEER IS BACK

Beer is back! In those three simple words a great American industry has gone back to work. Hands long idle have found new jobs. Faces empty of hope brighten to a new promise. Thousands have found honorable livelihood. A vast American market—a new frontier of industry reopens—bringing sorely needed business to farmers, transportation and to hundreds of other industries. And, with it, a new fountain head of tax revenue has arisen to add its dollars gladly to a nation in need.

Beer is back! But is that all? No! To cheer, to quicken American life with hospitality of old, the friendly glass of good-fellowship is back. Sociability and good living return to their own, once more to mingle with memories and sentiments of yesterday. America looks forward—and feels better . . . Beer is back! Yes! But much more than that. Beer at its best is back—the brew that everybody knew best—the King of Bottled Beer that outsold any other bottled beer on earth.

BUDWEISER IS BACK

Anheuser-Busch, Inc. . . . St. Louis

This advertisement was a reflection of Mr. Busch's trust of the American people, his good business judgment and his faith in the American way.

————

Space limitations make it impossible to include in this volume all of the data made available by Mr. Eads. His records contain the story of prohibition in great detail.

Chapter XIV

THE ROAD BACK IS
JOYOUS—BUT OMINOUS

With the relegalization of beer, the great Anheuser-Busch brewery pulsed with new life in all of the seventy city blocks over which it sprawled, but the man who had brought its life back knew that his own was in jeopardy. He was tremendously happy, terribly tired. The heart that never lacked for courage now lacked for vitality. For the first time since he had assumed the presidency, August A. Busch, Senior, felt that he could, he must, relax.

Adolphus III continued as head of the Yeast, Malt and Corn Products Division. August A., Junior, with a nose for hops, an eye for barley, a palate for beer and the know-how of production and sales, took over management of the Brewery Division. His father knew that "Gussie" would do a good job —and the son did not fail him or "the family."

In a newspaper interview a few years earlier, the father had said:

> I have a fine family. The boys will succeed to the business whatever drift it takes. They are good executives. They do not avoid work or responsibility.

176

Each helps the other and studies to be useful in any and all our enterprises, land holdings in many cities and manufacturing that ranges from powerful engines to ice cream. This is as my noble father would have had it. He trained me to get up early and stay up late if that were necessary to our work.

I am well along in my sixties but this very morning I was up before daylight making a few visits to bakeries. Our drivers find it helpful if an executive sometimes goes with them into the hot bake oven room to say a word about our yeast. Why shouldn't the President go? I do and like it. The public may get an impression that loafing comes with age and success. It doesn't down here.

To the older generation, the big name in beer always had been Budweiser, and the younger generation took its cue from the older. Moreover, Anheuser-Busch began to advertise heavily in newspapers, magazines and on posters all over America.

Budweiser was restored quickly to its former status—the biggest-selling beer in America. The demand for it grew at such a rate that obviously a large expansion program was essential.

The most optimistic views of this expansion program proved to be too conservative and another was launched.

Between 1932 and 1951, Anheuser-Busch spent $83,743,000 upon the improvement of its St. Louis plant. Expansion of facilities cost $66,321,000, cooperage and stainless steel barrels $14,661,000 and wooden cases, during the war when fiber cartons were restricted, $2,761,000.

Of the total sum, $37,318,000 was provided by depreciation and the remainder was retired from earnings.

We have seen how August A. Busch, Senior, brought his heritage from the brink of doom to the horizon of boom. Before exploring those booming years, let us get still better acquainted with the man whom we already know well and respect mightily.

Chapter XV

INDUSTRIALIST AND

COUNTRY SQUIRE, TOO

AN ELDERLY gentleman named Jacob Sonnen died in St. Louis in 1929. His estate amounted to $18,000. He willed it to August A. Busch, who had employed him for thirty years as a servant.

No orator or biographer or painter could provide a better picture of the character of August Anheuser Busch, Senior. Jacob knew that his wealthy employer didn't need the money, but he did know that it would find its way into some worthwhile channel.

August A., Senior—and that is the way in which all but his most intimate associates referred to him—spent a lot of money in his lifetime, his own money and that of the company he guided. Whatever he spent, he demanded that it bring a handsome return—but not necessarily to August A.

There was a lot of sentiment in his wallet. For example, he learned in 1933 that The Mohican, a 28-year-old steamer that had carried passengers around Lake Otsego, near Cooperstown, N. Y., was to be broken up for scrap. August

A., whose summer home, bought by his father, was on the shores of the lake, knew that the people who lived in the community were, as he was, sentimental about seeing the old steamer puffing back and forth on the water that James Fenimore Cooper had made famous in his novels as "Glimmer Lake."

August A. bought The Mohican, had it made shipshape and turned it into a cruising houseboat. The people had their beloved landmark-on-water, after all, and the investment paid a handsome return—in deeper friendships.

He loved children and wanted to be with his own as much as possible.

For the entertainment of his children and grandchildren and to instill in them his own love of animals, August A. acquired a sizable menagerie on one of his most prized possessions, his home on Grant's Farm on the Gravois Road in the countryside near to St. Louis.

The farm represented another of the series of failures that beset Grant before he returned to the Army as a Colonel in the Illinois National Guard. Grant had made a failure of a saddlery and leather business in Illinois and then had taken up farming on the Gravois Road just outside of St. Louis. He built with his own hands the humble two-room log cabin where he and his family lived for five years before he gave up farming, which was six years before the Appomattox surrender and ten years before he became President. He cleared the timber from his land, cultivated his crops and cut and hauled cordwood fifteen miles to St. Louis, but was unable to make the property pay. Grant retained ownership of the farm until 1883, when he lost it in the failure of some of his Wall Street banking enterprises.

Adolphus Busch had presented the site, on which stood the log cabin that once was the home of Ulysses S. Grant, to his son in 1903. August A. longed to live there, but it was too far for daily horse-and-carriage journeys and the motor car in 1903 had little reputation for reliability. By 1912 the horseless carriage had proved itself dependable and fast and on the farm was built a chateau-like house to which the owner brought his family from No. 2 Busch Place for real country living.

Before giving you a picture of the house and its environs, let us stay for a moment with August A. and his deeply sentimental nature. Among the animals which populated the farm was what was reputed to be the world's tiniest elephant, named Tessie.

A scout for the Ringling Brothers-Barnum & Bailey Circus had heard of Tessie. He convinced August A. that it would be a generous gesture to let Tessie join the circus and live with other elephants. Besides, think how youngsters all over America coming to the menagerie tent to see the world's largest animal would be bug-eyed with wonderment to see the *tiniest* of the world's largest animals. Tessie and her owner parted.

A few years later, the circus was in town and August A. took his grandchildren to see the show. When he visited the menagerie tent, Tessie recognized

GENERAL GRANT SLEPT HERE—This is the cabin on the family estate on Gravois Road just outside of St. Louis which General Grant built and lived in with his family while trying unsuccessfully to become a farmer.

him instantly and trumpeted her joy. August A. was so touched that he wept openly. It was too late to do anything about it. Tessie was such an attraction that the circus would not part with her.

Grant's Farm was and still is a place designed for gracious and luxurious living. That was the tradition into which August A. was born. If it appears to be a place where a man of means indulged his whims and hobbies, that is only a portion of the story. He had to have a handsome return on this investment, too, and what he did to get it made new friendships with important partners of Anheuser-Busch—the farmers.

August A. employed experts in agriculture and animal husbandry to experiment on his farm and make resulting helpful information available to the farmer. The farm had thirty-two beautiful Jersey cows of finest ancestry. There was a model dairy of glistening white tile and metal. There were five wild boar from the Black Forest of Germany, brought here to be crossed with the red Duroc to obtain a finer breed of domestic hog. There was a poultry department that was a model in every respect, and adding color to the feathered colony were golden pheasants, ring-necked and silver pheasants, white swans and wild turkey, geese and ducks.

When August A. learned that Missouri farmers had been losing $5,000,000 a year and the farmers of the United States $30,000,000 a year from hog cholera, he began a series of experiments to try to produce a strain of hogs which would offer resistance to the disease through natural stamina. He imported to Grant's Farm a European wild boar and crossed the animal with domestic hogs using Yorkshire, Berkshire and Poland China sows in the experiments.

The pigs resulting from these matings, twelve and thirteen to each litter, appeared to have retained all the powers of natural resistance to disease possessed by the wild boar and all the domestic qualities of their good-natured dams. In physical appearance, the pigs closely resembled the boar. They were lively, wonderful foragers and grew to maturity quickly. Many experiments were made to determine whether or not they could be infected with cholera.

They were put into pens with cholera infected hogs, ate from the same troughs and slept in the same houses.

The records showed that not one of the hybrid pigs became infected nor were pigs given to neighbors who conducted similar experiments infected. The experiments were terminated when the wild boar was accidentally killed just before the outbreak of World War I and August was unable to obtain another from Europe.

Farmer Busch was eminently successful with other hog breeding. At butchering time, he presided over what became a ham-smoking and sausage-making festival, no less. His sausage was of such excellent quality and flavor that he was pleased to make up a huge pile of gift packages and distribute them with sentimental messages to his many good friends.

The Department of Agriculture in 1919 estimated that the country lost a billion dollars a year in the waste of manure as a fertilizer. Farmer Busch and his agricultural staff devised an efficient method of salvaging valuable liquid manure as well as solid manure that resulted in his farm producing 80 bushels of corn to the acre as compared with the county average of 36 bushels, 30 bushels of wheat compared with the average of 14 and 75 bushels of oats compared with the average of 25. As a result, the Department of Soils and Bacteriology at the University of Missouri highly recommended his method of drainage and reservoir storage as a means of enriching the state's farms, and information was disseminated among Missouri farmers at August's expense.

The sausage and the agricultural and animal husbandry activities at Grant's Farm broke into print when a St. Louis Post-Dispatch reporter published this interview with Mr. Busch:

My hobby is the great outdoors with all that it offers. I love horses, dogs, cattle, fowl and wild game. My herd of deer I have raised on my own grounds. One of my principal hobbies has been the breeding of hogs, resulting in a new breed from which is produced as fine sausage, I believe, as can be made anywhere.

Tree life is also a hobby of mine. I recall the warning of my father that there would be a lack of nurtured sub-soil and a lack of water in nature's reservoirs unless our forests were preserved. Conservation of wild life is another worthwhile hobby. At St. Peter's (St. Charles County, Missouri) I have provided a haven for wild fowl.

On Grant's Farm, Kerry cows, imported from Ireland, small of frame and yielding milk abundantly, had their stalls beside the stately Jerseys. On the farm, at various times, were European and Asiatic deer, American elk, Shetland ponies, Jerusalem donkeys and two elephants.

The experimental station that was Grant's Farm returned a handsome profit on the investment—to Missouri farmers—in 1918, when war made the increased production of food for America and its overseas allies a vital necessity.

August A. had printed that year by the rotogravure process a 64-page, tabloid-size bulletin containing a variety of suggestions to farmers. The manual was intended to show farmers how to make their farms yield $350,000,000 more food values every year. On the first inside page were photographs of President Wilson and his cabinet members and a reproduction of Wilson's speech on July 14, 1928, at Washington's Tomb, Mount Vernon. The booklet was replete with photographs of horses, livestock, poultry and other subjects interesting to farmers. There was a page devoted to dairying and various ways of caring for and improving a herd.

Here are examples of headlines in the publication:

RATIONS FOR THE BREEDING EWES

Rough Feeds May Be Used to Replace More Expensive Crops

SHEEP NEGLECTED AT FAIRS

Eight Points to Be Followed in Arranging a Good Exhibit

SCRUB RAM OFTEN EXPENSIVE

Good Breeding Means Heavier Lambs and Higher Prices

FARMER BUSCH BECOMES A PUBLISHER—This manual, distributed free to Missouri farmers, was packed with information much of which was authenticated by successful agricultural experiments on Grant's Farm.

FLOCK OF SHEEP SURE TO PAY

Will Add to Profits of Every Farmer if Properly Handled

IF LATE FOR CORN, PLANT KAFFIR

Soil Preparation About Same—Crop Not Hard on the Land

There was another page on the subject of growing corn and making more valuable assets of sheep and orchards. Even the subject of dogs and their value to farmers was covered.

Nor did he, with his love of children, forget the farm youngsters.

One of the standouts of the publication was the results of "The August A. Busch Essay Contest." The page pictured the boy who won the grand prize and also the teacher who won the prize in the teachers' division.

The purpose of the contest was to encourage children to do their bit toward winning the war. August A. offered a thoroughbred White Yorkshire pig from his Grant's Farm herd to the boy or girl in each Missouri congressional district who wrote the best essay on the subject of saving garbage and feeding it to pigs. The offer was made in response to the demand of the government for a 50% increase in pork production in Missouri.

Eight thousand rural teachers were invited to have their pupils participate. A Shetland pony was offered the teacher whose pupils showed the best results.

The judges were the state Secretary of Agriculture, teachers, and a farm publication editor.

The grand prize—a pair of thoroughbred White Yorkshire pigs—was won by George F. Addison of the Sixteenth District. Because of its simplicity, directness and unintentional humor, his essay is worthy of inclusion here:

In raising my hog this year, I was particular to get a good pig. I picked her from my father's herd. And as I wanted to raise this hog independently, I paid $3.15 for it, being twenty-one pounds at 15 cents a pound.

A man near my home wanted a pile of lumber moved and gave me enough lumber to build a pen for my pig for moving same. And my mother agreed to give me all the table scraps and kitchen refuse as long as I kept the wood box filled in the kitchen.

After I got the table scraps, I fed my pig all it could eat and this way I used up all the sour and clabbered milk. In a short time, my pig began to grow and get fat.

I saved my money which I got for doing odd jobs and bought a sack of hog tankage and a sack of middlings. Then along with the table scraps, I made a slop of middlings and water with a little hog tankage mixed in. This made my pig grow fatter and fatter and she got larger through the hips and shoulders.

I pulled the weeds out of the garden and fence corners. These I fed to my pig. I heard about charcoal being good for a hog so I got some and fed it to my pig. I found out that a pig would grow better in a clean pen, so once every week, I cleaned out my pen. On November 20, I had my pig weighed and was offered 17¼ cents per pound and, as she weighed 311 pounds, I would have gotten $53.65, but as she was such a fine sow, I decided not to sell her but to keep her for breeding next year. My sow will have pigs soon and my Daddy says she is worth $100 and he says he will give me that for her and give me one of her pigs. I think I will sell her and buy two of the Third Liberty Bonds and then start out new with my pig. It will cost me more this year to raise a pig because my mother belongs to the Hoover Club, and there are not as many table scraps coming to me.

I paid out altogether for feed $16.42. My net profit is $83.58 and a pig.

August A. got many a chuckle out of this American farm youngster's pig diary and was as proud of it as one might be of a diploma. Certainly that letter reflected Father Adolphus's thinking and teaching on the subjects of endless ingenuity and enterprise.

Since Grant's Farm was its owner's permanent home, he wanted it to match his station in life and to it he imparted some of the elegance that characterized his father's surroundings. He wanted, too, to realize his ambition to live as a country gentleman, or, as some newspaper and magazine writers had it, as a country squire.

The estate covered more than 486 acres. The arch in the old stone wall that surrounded the house of the farm personnel and stables was very beautiful and the wall covered with wild grape and honeysuckle. The buildings had bright red tile roofs and there was a huge clock in the steeple of one building. The place combined Old World charm with the most modern that America had to offer. There was a stork's nest on another roof to give it that Old World touch. An ancient bell hung in the arch of the stone wall.

In the coach house were many beautiful carriages and vehicles. There were a park coach and three road coaches and an 8-passenger English brake and a hackney pony coach, a 2-seated rig, a French sailor wagon, an imported German hunting wagon, a pony phaeton, a French governess cart and numerous Brewster rigs. All the coaches were the last word in elegance, proudly painted and exquisitely made, lined with velours or velvet or pigskin and ornamented with brass fixtures and handsome carriage lamps.

Most of them were used for grand occasions such as Thanksgiving, New Year's Day calls, football games, steeplechase races, and occasionally for a drive through the deer park. To an Italian cart were hitched Sicilian donkeys. There were a 4-horse 8-passenger sleigh with jingle bells, a 2-horse sleigh, a cutter and an old-fashioned bobsled. Some of the coaches were forty-five years old, but in perfect repair.

In the tack room there was a collection of cups, trophies and ribbons and a revolving steel case which displayed every type of bit. Other cases contained harnesses, stirrups and whips. Also on display were hunting horns and other reminders of the colorful pageantry of the hunt.

August A. and his family had been identified with every horse show held in St. Louis since the first indoor show in the old Coliseum at Twelfth Boulevard and Clark Avenue in 1896. He had guaranteed the promoter against financial loss. Through the years, he was a member of the Deficit Committee for the horse shows in the Coliseum at Thirteenth and St. Charles Streets and the Coliseum at Jefferson and Washington.

In the kennels on the farm were retrievers, fox hounds, German springers and police dogs.

MANSION BUILT BY AUGUST A., SR., ON GRANT'S FARM

THE BAUERENHOF—THE FOCAL POINT OF ACTIVITIES AT THE FARM

COLLECTION OF HORSE-DRAWN VEHICLES—
One of the finest collections in the world was
in the Farm stables.

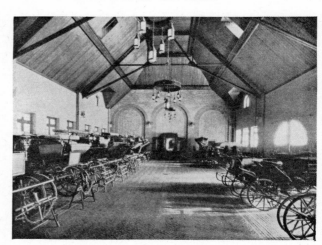

The deer park consisted of 175 acres, a magnificent forest preserve with riding trails and bridle paths with rail jumps and hurdles.

August A.'s herd of deer was perhaps the finest in the country at the time. In the deer park also were tropical and semi-tropical birds, wading birds, tall cranes, storks and flamingos.

As seen from the long windows of the drawing room of the house or from the flagged terrace just outside it, the scene was one of rare beauty. There was a long greensward that sloped gently down to a ravine through which a stream flowed. Rising up opposite was a steeper slope, a broad avenue cut through heavy woods. It was in this cleared pathway that the deer could be seen from the house. August A. spent years collecting his deer herd. It included species from all parts of the world. One of the most beautiful specimens was an Axis deer from India with spotted body and delicate antlers. Another from India was the Barasingha or swamp deer. There were deer from Japan, Siberia and Europe. The rarest species of all was the European roe deer.

American species in the collection were the elk or Wapita, second in size only to the moose, and the Virginia white-tail deer that frequents the northern part of this continent. There was also a group of prong-horned antelope from Canada.

The business of collecting this herd was greatly assisted by George P. Vierheller, Superintendent of the St. Louis Zoo, who was rewarded for his efforts by being presented with some of the specimens from Grant's Farm.

Included in the menagerie at the farm were two young elephants, Peggy and Tessie. August A. bought them principally for the entertainment of his grandchildren. They were trained to do many tricks by a trainer from Hollywood. In the stable was a tanbark ring and the white-washed brick walls were decorated for the children's pleasure with hobby horses and poster pictures of tigers, lions and bears. The elephants frequently gave performances when there was a family gathering. They were very attached to their owner, who would bring them special treats of sugar lumps and yeast.

SUMMER HOME OF AUGUST A. BUSCH, SR., COOPERSTOWN, NEW YORK

August A. spent many happy hours roaming through the woods and meadows of his acres. He was fond of carrying a huntsman's horn with him and sounding it from various spots in order to enjoy seeing his herd of deer come in answer to his call.

On his place in Cooperstown, his fish were his pride and pleasure. When he took over the tract for his summer home, he found a small stream flowing through a steep, narrow canyon that divided the property. He had several dams built in the canyon and stocked the resulting pools with trout. One of his daily diversions was to visit the pools and toss scraps of food to the darting fish. No one, not even himself, was permitted to catch them.

AUGUST A. BUSCH, SR., IN HUNTING CART AT HIS "SHOOTING LODGE" NEAR ST. PETERS, MISSOURI, LONG IDENTIFIED WITH GAME SHOOTING—It was here that Mr. Busch entertained sportsmen, family friends and world celebrities. In recent years his son August A. Busch, Jr., has devoted a large part of this estate to game conservation.

August A. was keenly interested in all sports. On one occasion, Sid Keener, sports editor of the St. Louis Star-Times, wrote an article about this interest, saying that August attended all major sporting events.

According to Keener, he found recreation in baseball, at race tracks, at boxing bouts and, of course, horse shows.

He was a regular attendant at baseball games at Sportsman's Park and Keener quoted the late Sam Breadon, president of the Cardinals Club, as saying: "I don't think anyone enjoyed a victory for the home team more than Mr. Busch. He was a regular dyed-in-the-wool rooter."

Keener said that August's interest in baseball was so great that several times he was reported to be interested in purchasing the Cardinals and also the Browns. For a number of years, it was his custom, according to Keener, to charter a special railroad car for the guests whom he invited to go with him to the Kentucky Derby. Keener said that August's interest in the Derby was of the greatest despite the fact that, with one exception, he had never entered a horse in a race.

Loving country life as he did, August A. was anxious to attract more St. Louisans into the open once the progress of the automobile was making such jaunts more feasible. He hit upon the idea of building Sunset Inn, about fifteen miles from the city limits. Its excellent cuisine, its indoor dining room and rooftop restaurant and its large swimming pool soon made it one of the most popular places in the community.

Sunset Inn finally became the member-owned Sunset Hills County Club and it, with one of the country's finest golf courses, prospers today.

It is not far from Sunset to Grant's Farm, where August A. lived happily with his beloved wife and children until marriage began to take the sons and daughters to their own respective homes. One of the daughters, Mrs. Webster Tilton, formerly Miss Alice Busch, in her book of memoirs circulated among relatives and friends, described some of the facets of life at the farm when all the family dwelt there.

Mrs. Tilton obviously found life most enjoyable in the large house of imposing French architecture, with its ballroom, eight large bedrooms, magnificent dining room, kitchen and pantries—the whole looking over a large terrace to the beautiful deer park and swan pond. It was in the ballroom in 1922, when she was chosen Queen of the Veiled Prophet's traditional autumn festival, that her father and mother had an American Beauty Rose ball in her honor.

Christmas and Easter were notable dates in the household. Mrs. Tilton wrote that Christmas dinner was traditionally always the same. It consisted of grapefruit baskets beribboned with red bows, delicious beef soup with plump

SUNSET HILLS COUNTRY CLUB—August A., Sr., built this beautiful place in the Ozark foothills and called it Sunset Inn. Its cuisine brought people from the city in the automobiles which were gaining daily in popularity. Later it was converted from an inn to a golf and country club.

marrow balls, hot cheese sticks, lobster a la Newburg, shoestring potatoes, cucumber salad, turkeys with snow-white paper cuffs on the drumsticks, turkey wings in wine, cream and broth, spinach rings with oyster plant Hollandaise, sweet potatoes with marshmallows, salad with a cheese platter, pumpernickel, homemade salt pretzels, cakes, chocolate truffles, snowballs of ice cream and plum puddings all afire.

"There are very few families such as mine," wrote Mrs. Tilton, "and so I must say it once again: The family, the family; you learn to give and you learn to take; it gladdens you, it saddens you, sometimes you feel it maddens you; but strongest of all and best of all is the pride and love you have for it, for each one that belongs to it. God bless and keep my family."

The family consisted of "precious Mama," who had been Miss Alice

Zisemann before she and August A. were married in 1890, and their five children: Adolphus III and August A., Jr., Marie (Mrs. C. Drummond Jones), Clara (Mrs. Percy J. Orthwein), and Alice (Mrs. Tilton).

Certainly, August Anheuser Busch, Senior, enjoyed good living as well as did his most spectacular father. Like his father, he felt that he need not apologize to anyone for his way of life. For what he had, he worked hard every day of his life. His generosity toward others was demonstrated over and over again.

The magazine, The Censor, on February 22, 1934, said of him:

> He was not a religious man in the general acceptance of the term, but he came nearer following in the footsteps of the Founder of the Christian religion than multitudes of proclaimers of their own righteousness. We have an illustration of this in the instance of his purchase of the former property of the Sisters of the Good Shepherd—a full block of ground between Seventeenth and Eighteenth Streets and Chestnut and Pine Streets. Mr. Busch, though he had no use for it at the time, bought the property from this religious order, saying merely that he might some time build a great hotel or business building on it.
>
> It was, in reality, a splendid benefaction. His purchase of that piece of property enabled the Catholic Sisterhood to come into possession of the splendid institution on Gravois Avenue known as the Convent of the Good Shepherd. Is it to be wondered at that the Roman Catholics of St. Louis honor the name of Busch?

The corporate contributions made at the behest of August A. were considerable, too. The substantial grants made by Anheuser-Busch to universities and hospitals for the furtherance of studies in the sciences of nutrition and medicine are dealt with in detail in a subsequent chapter. Besides, many man-hours of cooperation from the company's technical staff were given gratuitously to these studies.

Yes, on his own time, August A. lived the good life. The next chapter tells a bit about his working methods.

AUGUST A. BUSCH, SR.

Chapter XVI

AUGUST A. MAKES EVERY
HOUR EVERY DAY COUNT

IT IS WELL established that all small boys spend many hours gazing out of the schoolroom window, dreaming about the day when they will get out of the schoolhouse and seek greener pastures.

Fortune played a funny trick on August A. Busch, Senior. He never did get out of the schoolroom where he learned his three R's. The Lyon Public School at Ninth and Pestalozzi Streets in St. Louis was just across the street from the brewery. Adolphus Busch needed more office space and made an offer for the school building that the Board of Education was quick to accept. Then the building was remodeled for office use.

The big front room on the third floor, where young Gussie had knit his brows over math and rhetoric, became the office where he was to knit his brows over business problems for many a year.

It was the custom of August A. to stop at the Malt House across the street on his way to his office. Waiting for him in a pietin on a window sill near to the Malt House entrance was the most recent sample of sprouted and kilned barley. This he would sniff, crunch and taste, testing it for quality.

Then to his office, where his lifetime secretary, Mrs. Dora J. Schofield, awaited him with the day's agenda. "Mrs. Scho—"—or, if you knew her very well, "Schoie"—kept visitors moving in and out on schedule. Yet, with her tact and August A.'s polite nature, no one ever felt that he had got "the brush-off."

Much has been made of the fact that, compared to his father, August A. was somewhat shy of manner. That does not mean that his was a way of giving lip service while others ran the business. Quite the contrary. The Boss wanted to know at all times what was going on and, if he detected stupidity on the part of someone who should have known better, his wrath was instant and overwhelming—and quickly forgotten.

Once August A. Busch invested one of his staff with authority, that man was expected to take full responsibility for his department with the understanding that advice and counsel would be forthcoming for the asking.

Who hasn't at one time or another wished that he had more hands? August A. could well feel that he had a number of good right hands. One of them was Eberhard Anheuser, grandson of the co-founder of Anheuser-Busch. Before prohibition, Eberhard had been in charge of the City Department—that branch of the business which had to do with Budweiser sales in the whole St. Louis metropolitan area. His acquired knowledge and innate capacities were more than ample for the task.

During the lean prohibition years, his counsel was invaluable to August A., and when beer was relegalized that same counsel was to guide Adolphus III and August A., Jr., with such skill and competence that when the company moved into its hundredth year, Eberhard Anheuser was the chairman of its board of directors, still active, still canny, still kindly and still scrappy, as circumstances indicated.

August A., Sr., and "Ebie" were, in two aspects, kindred personalities.

MRS. DORA J. (SCHO) SCHOFIELD—One time secretary to August A., Sr., and successively secretary and loyal advisor to Adolphus Busch III and August A. Busch, Jr., "Schoie" occupied a unique place in American industry—a woman whose opinion was sought in many major decisions of management.

Each was eager for harmony and friendliness. Each was devoted to the business and all of the traditions that veined it. They made a real team.

Another good right-hand was the man who worked tirelessly behind a door whose small gilt letters said simply, R. Gull. That meant Dr. Rudolph Gull, brewmaster-genius whom Adolphus Busch had brought to St. Louis from an eminent brewery in Switzerland.

Bearded and somewhat apostolic of mien, Dr. Gull was tall, lanky and tireless. He was vague about many things — the time of day, just who was who on his appointment list, the sheaves of correspondence that gathered dust on his old roll-top desk—but he was not the least vague in the matter of brewing science.

Eventually, he would get around to his correspondence, much of which concerned the exchange of technical information with brewmasters abroad, much in the manner in which astronomers the world over exchange data on stars.

In the production of Budweiser and Michelob, he was a gentle tyrant supported to the limit by Adolphus Busch and August A. Busch. Equipment had to be just so and methods had to be just so. His technique resulted in the most expensive brewing process known, but one that paid off with the most famous beer the world has ever known.

There was another Rudy—R. A. Huber, a man whose small stature was deceptive to those matching wits with him. His title was vice-president, his job that of a roving ambassador. He knew everybody in the brewing industry and he knew and fended the machinations of prohibitionist and politician. He, too, lived to see the return of the product that he had protected and helped to make famous.

He had come to this country from Germany as a small boy. At the age of 14 he had been employed by Anheuser-Busch as a guide to show visitors through the plant. Adolphus Busch had taken an interest in him and encouraged him in his efforts to obtain an education.

Rudy Huber at first attended night schools and later obtained a diploma from the Benton College of Law. Although he did not practice law, his knowledge of it proved very valuable throughout his business career. He became a director in 1919 and for fifteen years was vice-president and treasurer.

Huber was to take a prominent part in the hearings of the House Ways and Means Committee in Washington in 1932, advocating the relegalization of beer and a code of practices. He was to become a member of the Advisory Commission named by Missouri's Governor Park for liquor control methods in the state. He was later to be first vice-president of the United States Brewers Association and one of the members representing that association on the Brewers' Code Authority.

Edward Magnus, a grandson of Adolphus Busch, was another vice-presidential right hand. Genial Eddie was by nature a hearty soul—and continued to be, despite the disheartening job of directing sales in the early prohibition years when what to make and how to sell it was a big problem. When Budweiser Malt Syrup became big business, he was well rewarded for his efforts in

EDWARD MAGNUS—Grandson of Adolphus Busch who stood loyally beside August A., Sr., and his sons in the dark days of prohibition and helped to get the great plant on its feet.

promoting it and he had acquired the stuff and the strength that a man needed to be a king-pin in the Busch-Sulzer Bros., Diesel Engine Company, when that organization virtually was turned over to the Navy Department in World War II.

Another of August A.'s old reliables was George A. H. Mills, who joined the company as secretary soon after the death of Adolphus Busch.

Mills had had a colorful career that fitted him for his position. He was born in 1871 in New York State. He was educated at George Washington University, where he received the degrees of LL.B. and LL.M. He was commissioned by President Cleveland as allotting agent for the Wichita Indian Tribe and affiliated Indian nations.

Upon settling in St. Louis, Mills became secretary of the Union Trust Company and later of the merged St. Louis Union Trust Company. Subsequently he was associated with the law firm of Nagel and Kirby. Upon the death of Adolphus, he took over management of his estate. He served Anheuser-Busch as secretary until his resignation on May 8, 1947. He was a member of the Board of Directors from which he resigned in 1950. During his active life, he served as secretary of other companies in which the Busch family was interested.

Charles Staudinger was advertising manager for many years until his retirement just before the return of beer. When not collaborating with the company's advertising agency in St. Louis, he spent much of his time touring the country, feeling the marketing pulse and visiting with wholesalers.

Charlie Staudinger would have been the first to agree that often he automatically became assistant advertising manager. That was when The Boss was having one of his ideas.

August A. inherited a generous measure of his father's flair for advertising. Indeed, Adolphus had made Budweiser one of America's first nationally advertised products. He had used newspapers extensively and his messages, some of which are reprinted in another chapter, had been aggressive and truthful.

Adolphus had been one of the first to use 24-sheet posters. He had been one of the first, also, to use electrically lighted "spectaculars." For years, Pacific Ocean travelers had been greeted at night by the name, Budweiser, in electric lights as ships approached San Francisco Bay.

In New York's Times Square, one of the earliest flashing electric signs pictured the A-and-Eagle trademark of Anheuser-Busch.

August A. was keenly interested in posters and poster art. He paid bonus prices to get the finest of pictures, on one occasion having the world-famous Ludwig Holwein of Munich paint a series for Budweiser Malt Syrup and Busch Extra Dry Ginger Ale. On another occasion, when motor vehicle accidents had the public press aroused, he created a sensation by devoting all of his poster space to a strictly non-commercial message. A mother and infant were pictured and the message read, "We love our children . . . Drive carefully . . . August A. Busch." The goodwill that was created was tremendous.

Another of his ideas provoked much head-shaking and some wringing of hands in the heyday of malt syrup. He announced that he wanted to put "Tony Cabooch" on a national radio network. Tony was played by a former vaudeville actor, Chester Gruber. In fact, by lightning-fast changes of voice and inflection, Gruber played all the characters in his skits. That was why he called himself "the one man radio show."

Tony Cabooch had been locally sponsored in St. Louis without too great success. When August A. announced his decision, protests came thick and fast from his staff and from his advertising agency. They were to the effect that the program was too much of a "cornball" for Anheuser-Busch. The Boss was adamant, contending that it took a certain "corniness" in one's make-up to produce and enjoy home-brew. Tony went on the air.

The response was immediate and tremendous. The stationery, the handwriting and the comments of fan mail showed that August A. had estimated his audience correctly. Then a radio miracle happened. The Boss suggested that listeners be invited to send in labels from Budweiser Malt Syrup cans to indicate their interest in the program. This, said a network spokesman, was sheer nonsense. All of the radio people's experience had proved long ago that people just wouldn't bother to soak off or scrape off a can label. Again, The Boss was adamant.

So, one evening Tony stepped out of character, pointed out that the only way in which Anheuser-Busch could afford to support such a show was through the sale of malt syrup and, therefore, he personally would appreciate evidence of sales. The result was that each mail brought in labels until a paper mountain of them was created in a basement storeroom.

August A. didn't say, "I told you so," but his wide grin did.

Sometimes the advertising and promotion ideas of The Boss went to extremes—as is told in a later chapter on the subject of advertising—but in every instance those ideas paid off in goodwill and patronage.

Other things often went to extremes, too. Among them were the demands of his work. In the last days of prohibition, when August A. taxed his mental and physical vigor to the utmost to maintain the momentum of approaching victory, his heart began giving him trouble steadily, and periodically he suffered intense pain.

He hung on doggedly, saw prohibition go out and Budweiser come in and saw his boys proving unquestionably their ability to manage the affairs of Anheuser-Busch with the stewardship that he expected, that his father would have expected. He decided too late to retire and lead a rested life.

Heart attacks were recurring with punishing regularity. He suffered excruciating pain. For August Anheuser Busch . . . for dear "Gussie" . . . for the beloved Boss . . . for adored Papa . . . the end came suddenly on February 13, 1934.

It was a sad, sad day for St. Louis. The citizens felt deeply the loss of one of their good neighbors, good industrialists and intrepid leaders and it brought the kind of deep hurt that is reflected in a very sober face and a very deep sigh.

In his will, August A. had asked that he be buried without ostentation. This request could keep the burial service simple, but it could not keep ten thousand persons from visiting Grant's Farm and passing silently before the plain casket in the great living room. Standing as a guard of honor, day and night until the burial service, were members of the Walter J. Hatsfeld Post of the American Legion. Thus they showed their appreciation of what August and his mother had done for war wounded with the family gardens in Pasadena, California.

The service began at 11 A.M. on Saturday, February 17. Two thousand persons, unable to enter the house, waited solemnly outside to join the funeral procession to a cemetery very near to the farm. The Reverend Hubert A. Woolfall, of St. Peter's Episcopal Church, read briefly from the Scriptures. Thereafter, Daniel N. Kirby, legal counsellor and lifetime friend, read the following eulogy:

It is not given to anyone to accurately or adequately judge his fellow man. Yet the intimate personal and business contacts in family and friendly relations give us some glimpses into a man's soul, some knowledge of the burdens he bore, of the problems he faced and solved and some conception of what manner of man he was, who so won our love, admiration and respect.

Few men have been called upon to bear more difficult responsibilities than was August A. Busch.

Upon the death, in 1913, of his distinguished and aggressive father, there was thrust upon August Busch the burden of taking his father's place in the management of great businesses here and of many properties scattered throughout the United States. Up to that time, the course of business had been one of continued and amazing growth under the dictatorship of Adolphus Busch as chief proprietor, but under general conditions in which industrial growth was the order of the day.

Even under favoring conditions, the task of trying to be official successor to Adolphus Busch would have discouraged most men at the beginning. Not so with August Busch. His pride in his father's character and accomplishments and his firm belief in the business traditions which his father had established, challenged his imagination and inspired in him a desire to follow as best he could the same policies and methods.

From the beginning, he faced handicaps to which his father had not been subject.

Owning but a minority interest, August Busch had the greater responsibility of acting as trustee for many families whose welfare depended on the success of his leadership. His task was primarily that of a leader, not of a dictator.

Within a year after he took charge, the inevitable consequences of the World War began to be felt. In due course, it imposed war prohibition, then national prohibition intended to be permanent, and caused substantial confiscation of the most profitable part of the family's businesses.

No one could then foresee how many and how difficult would be the problems to arise during the long period of uncertainty that followed. Many experienced and sagacious men gave up in hopeless despair, junked their equipment, sacrificed their plants and abandoned their businesses. But August Busch, believing that while national prohibition was inevitable, the American people would ultimately condemn it as an unwise experiment, planned for the long future, refused to surrender without a struggle for existence, courageously entered upon new and allied businesses which kept the plant and organization somewhat occupied and so saved that great enterprise until the day, in 1933, when its chief product again became legalized.

To his courage, firmness and competent leadership, not only those directly interested as proprietors, managers and employes, but all of South St. Louis will always be indebted for saving its greatest industry through a period the financial distress which has been unequaled in history.

Most significant of all, as revealing the character of the man—through the long years of fighting to ward off destruction he stood firmly for obedience to the law even though that law, in the harshness of its provisions and the inadequacy of its enforcement, made it almost impossible for him to survive.

His constant and firm principle was: "Obey the law, and if it be found unjust, change it."

So he extended his active leadership beyond the sphere of his immediate business cares into the realm of public opinion, and under his direction there was gathered a mass of historical, scientific and statistical information, made public from time to time, which had great influence in finally persuading public opinion that national prohibition had been a tragic error.

Such leadership evidenced a noble and stalwart citizenship and calls for genuine recognition.

But he fell victim to his task. When the struggle was over and the great stress became somewhat lifted, he found his health and strength gone beyond the hope of recovery. He had given all he had to win the rewards of a great success which he was not to fully enjoy.

A worthy son of a noble father, he was a great leader in saving the industry, as his father had been in creating it.

But, his distinguishing characteristics as a man were not those to attract the limelight of popular interest; on the contrary, he shrank from publicity and used it only to further the business in his charge.

His was a simplicity and a sweetness of nature which ripened with age and experience. His methods were open and direct, free from guile. He never did a mean thing. He was very human. Conscious of his own shortcomings, he was tolerant of the weaknesses of others.

Most pronounced was his intense love of his family. He loved Nature, lived close to Nature, and spent much time in the study of Nature's methods and moods and of the beauty of her handiwork.

One need only enter these grounds to know that he loved children and that by placing here and there the figures of elves, gnomes and other small peoples of folk lore and fairyland, he sought to please his small friends. He would show you these figures and explain that they were for the enjoyment of children, but one could see that he himself loved, as much as they, these gentle people of the dream world and was happy to think that they would feel safe near him.

The quality of his friendship was rare and true, his comradeship a delight. His friendly goodwill was so genuinely cordial and his quick sense of humor so free from any thought of giving offense that he won and welcomed the abiding affection of many hundreds of people in all walks of life.

His own friendship, once given to others, was loyal, understanding and unselfish.

Today, as we bid farewell, no one of us can forget the love, the affection, the friendship, the courtesy in word or deed that each of us in varying ways has received as the generous gift of his heart.

As we dwell upon the greatness of his simple and sweet nature, each one of us, whether family, friend or acquaintance, will reflect with gratitude that we were privileged to know and to love August A. Busch.

From strings in another part of the house came the overwhelming beauty and the overwhelming sadness of Ave Maria—and sudden silence that said all that could be said.

A great heart had ceased to pulse, but the rhythm of its beat remained with the people and the business that had been rescued by that heart from ruin.

Chapter XVII

ONCE AGAIN "THE
FAMILY" HAS TO RALLY

ONCE AGAIN there had to be a rally—and again the rally was around "the family."

The third president of Anheuser-Busch was Adolphus Busch III.

By his side stood wise Eberhard Anheuser, well tested in the crucible of adversity and finely tempered by the experience. And, beside the two, stood The Third's brother, August Anheuser Busch, Junior—"Young Gussie."

Had it not been for that feeling for "the family," things might have been very much "otherwise." These brothers differed greatly in temperament.

Adolphus was shy and retiring most of the time, but when tradition had to be upheld, he could come out swinging.

There could have been—but there wasn't—disagreement with Brother Gussie, whose approach to any problem, whether a business matter in a Board of Directors room or a stone fence on a steeplechase course, was and definitely is strictly let's-have-action-now.

210

ADOLPHUS BUSCH III—The new president took over at a time when the rejuvenated business was facing multilateral problems, and he came out beautifully.

There could have been jealousy.

There could have been conflict and chaos.

There wasn't.

The family.

Adolphus went sagely about the business of management of the overall operation and left to the one time kid brother the business of making the Brewery Division hum. It was just the sort of assignment that August A., Jr., was cut out for—and he gave it a certain yip and zip that could be expected only from a happy extrovert who feeds on ebullience and optimism and has only a mild curiosity about frustrations.

Observance of business tradition made it essential that Adolphus Busch III and August A. Busch, Jr., be addressed in the second person as "Mr. Busch," but that family touch led all Anheuser-Busch personnel to refer to them in the third person as "The Third" and as "Gus."

After the first elation and excitement over making and marketing Budweiser had faded, Gus had to deliver gloomy reports to his brother-president. True, Budweiser had caught on with consumers to such an extent that demand exceeded supply and expansion of facilities already was under way. With sales zooming, there not only were no beer profits for Anheuser-Busch, but actually the Brewery Division was in the red.

Why, when other brewers were making tidy profits? The reasons were several. Gus, remembering what Grandfather would have done, demanded and got quality in every respect. The old practice of paying premium prices for the best ingredients was adhered to religiously. That policy wasn't paying off at the moment, but it was destined to pay off in a big way. (Incidentally, during World War II, when the authority of the Federal Office of Price Administration made it illegal to pay higher than "ceiling prices" for materials, Anheuser-Busch continued to get the pick of the barley crop, because the growers knew that when the OPA controls were dropped the company again would pay the premium prices.)

There were 700 breweries in the United States in the year 1934 and not a few of them were turning out beer of sorts with neither too much know-how nor too good ingredients. (In 1951 there were fewer than 500 breweries.)

Nor had the consumer acquired much know-how in judging quality. Beer was beer, he thought. The Third and Gus were convinced that the consumer would change his mind and become quality conscious. He did, obviously, but it took a bit of time.

Selling costs, bucked by the competition of more cheaply made beers that many consumers found acceptable at the time, were immense. Advertising had a long-haul job to do, because Anheuser-Busch had to scatter its shot with smaller newspaper space all over America, while sectional and regional brewers could concentrate their advertising dollars in big space in limited areas. Fortunately, there were the national magazines in which full pages in color could do the long-haul job for Budweiser all over the land.

Fortunate, too, was the fact that the Yeast, Malt and Corn Products Division which August A., Sr., had founded, now had grown to a little giant under The Third's guidance. This profitable enterprise supplied stamina and strength when the in-fighting might have dealt lethal corporate body blows. Adolphus III bade his brother to stick it out in the struggle for quality and supremacy more than mere survival. And that is exactly what Gus did— with gusto.

The Brewers' News of July 18, 1935, published an article about Anheuser-Busch in the course of which it said:

> But beer is not the most profitable of Anheuser-Busch's products today as it was in 1914. In fact, it is doubtful whether beer is profitable at all. It may be in time when the beer industry settles down: when brewers and dispensers agree among themselves what are fair trade practices and what are not: when the public decides what kinds of beer it likes and how much and what price it will pay.
>
> Meanwhile, so keen is competition in the trade that many brewers simply do not make beer of the same quality that they made before the

war without taking a loss. Already since repeal, more than seventy-five U. S. breweries have gone out of business. Others hang on, cutting corners where they can and relying on the fact that people who have grown up since the war don't know good beer when they taste it.

Anheuser-Busch prefers to take a loss on beer. Anheuser-Busch can afford to take it, because from those other products which were tried during prohibition as temporary catch-penny substitutes for beer, Anheuser-Busch now draws a substantial profit.

Specifically, it is one product that nets Adolphus and his brother, August, more than enough to compensate them for any losses they may take on the nostalgic brewery their grandfather bequeathed them and that product is yeast. Now yeast is not the highly competitive business that beer is today. And though Anheuser-Busch's share of the trade is small, it is still big enough to earn a substantial and dependable profit every year.

In spite of its losses on beer and various minor products, in 1933 Anheuser-Busch managed to clear $325,000. Last year it cleared $907,000 —the first really substantial profit since the $600,000 of 1926. But the productive Busches have a long row to hoe yet before they can equal the great profits beers used to bring before the war when $3,500,000 was not an uncommon income.

There were other headaches, too. All the foes of alcoholic beverages were not gone from state legislatures or municipal governments. Regulations of different communities were so varied and often conflicting that a special staff had to be set up by Anheuser-Busch to keep matters straight. For example, certain states demanded then, as they do now, that the bottle crown top have a specific design.

With inventory what it is in a big industrial operation, a change ordered in that design could leave Anheuser-Busch holding the bag overnight for thousands of dollars' worth of crown tops.

As indicated by the Brewers' News article previously quoted, the brewing industry was in a fluid and often fidgety condition in the several years following repeal. There was, for example, the matter of packaging.

A significant innovation was introduced with the advent of the can. The American Can Company designed, developed and introduced a beer can shortly after repeal. Much of the preliminary testing of this package was done by Anheuser-Busch in conjunction with the technical staff of the American Can Company. Early pioneer work had to be done on several features of this container, including the type of liner and the choice of flat top versus cone top. Budweiser did not appear in cans until the new containers were proved perfect.

Still another problem faced the industry. The time-honored wooden barrel and half-barrel were reaching the end of their existence because of increasing scarcity of oak staves. What would provide a satisfactory replacement was a big question. It became increasingly urgent to find the right answer before heavy investments were made in new cooperage.

One of the first packages submitted for testing was a laminated wooden barrel in which other woods besides oak could be used except on the inner lamination. These packages did not completely meet the rigid requirements and the interest of Anheuser-Busch was directed more to metal. Aluminum packages were tested extensively. One outstanding advantage of these barrels as compared to the wooden type was their light weight. Anheuser-Busch decided to use aluminum half-barrels and had approximately 100,000 packages of this type in service at one time. However, the company still was looking for a package even better than aluminum.

The search turned to stainless steel. In conjunction with The Firestone Company, a stainless steel half-barrel was designed, fabricated and tested. This package was a double wall half-barrel with the inner wall being stainless. It was also considerably lighter in weight than the wooden half-barrel. When exhaustive tests showed this package to be practical, many thousands of them were purchased and put into service.

Since the aluminum half-barrel was a single shell package and very light in weight, both Anheuser-Busch and Firestone were vitally interested in perfecting a single shell stainless steel half-barrel comparable in weight to the aluminum package. In time this was accomplished and the company policy was to use exclusively single shell stainless steel containers as older cooperage of other types was replaced.

Still another problem. During the years of prohibition, farmers in the barley growing areas of the United States virtually had ceased to grow grain suitable for malting. When repeal came, the old time Oderbrucker type of barley formerly used by maltsters in the Middle West had been abandoned by farmers and a new variety known as Wisconsin 38 was the predominant variety.

The new variety was used extensively by the maltsters, although it was not considered ideal. In 1936, the Middle West suffered one of the worst droughts in its history. The barley crop was nearly a complete failure.

Maltsters and brewers were faced with finding other sources of supply. Much European barley was shipped in and malted. Also, Pacific Coast barleys were available. Anheuser-Busch found a way to use considerable six-row California barley, although it was quite unlike the six-row Middle West types.

Out of these experiences an organized effort to improve the Middle West malting barleys was set up. The Malt Research Institute with headquarters at the University of Wisconsin was organized. This group, composed of a limited number of maltsters and brewers and representatives of the U. S. Department of Agriculture, undertook to sponsor and study new varieties of malting barley. Since its inception, the Malt Research Institute has been increasingly active in this work. Considerable progress has been made as indicated by the new varieties of good malting barleys that have been developed and produced commercially.

At Anheuser-Busch, both in the laboratory and in the brewery, extensive work went on in testing out the malt produced from the new grains.

During all this time, Anheuser-Busch malted a very considerable amount of two-row Western barley grown chiefly in the Tule Lake region near Klamath Falls, Oregon.

From inception of the Malt Standardization Committee in 1933, members of the Anheuser-Busch laboratory staff were active in the American Society of Brewing Chemists. Two of the laboratory staff have served as presidents of this organization—G. C. Bratton from 1938 to 1940 and B. H. Nisson from 1944 to 1946.

Another technological advance in beer production was made in 1937 when the process was developed for removing some of the constituents of hops which contribute to a lingering bitterness in beer. Under the direction of Dr. Gull, an entirely new type of fermentation tank was designed and constructed. It incorporated certain patented features that facilitated the removal of the bitter precipitate that forms during the early stages of fermentation. This development culminated in the construction of the Bosari type of fermenter cellar, the first of which was the "Gull Cellar."

Concurrently with the experimental work leading to the de-bitterizing process, an extensive operation was carried on to improve upon the standard procedure of cooling wort. Out of this came new improved stainless steel wort coolers and aerators with filtered and sterilized air. The Bosari settling and starting tanks were part of this new system. (U. S. Patent—2359876—by Anheuser-Busch, Inc.)

In the year of repeal, 1933, Anheuser-Busch produced and marketed 607,511 barrels of Budweiser. Before the year was over, the previously noted agitation from many wholesalers and branch and district managers for a change in the taste of Budweiser began to be heard. When August A. Busch, Sr., flatly refused to change the taste on the grounds that it was the taste that finally won over the sophisticated palate, he could not have dreamed how right he was going to be proved. In the next year, sales soared to 1,093,222 barrels and, in 1935, only the fact that expanding facilities had not been expanded enough kept the output from going past 1,136,776 barrels.

Once again Budweiser was booming, destined to count its output in the millions of barrels instead of one million plus. Then, in 1937, the national calamity which repeal had helped to squelch—economic depression—threatened again. President Roosevelt chose to call it a "recession," but, by whatever name it was called, it did manage to thoroughly frighten employer and employee alike.

Many economists, in trying to explain how it started, managed only to add to the confusion. One thing emerged clearly. The public at large had lost confidence, had succumbed to an instinct to hole in and wait for something to happen.

Adolphus—The Third—gave his sanction to a bold move, indeed. It was to devote the company's entire 1938 national advertising campaign to a series of advertisements calculated to quiet alarm and restore public confidence. Some of these advertisements are reproduced on adjacent pages and a glance will show that the only mention of Budweiser was in the words, "Live life . . . every golden minute of it . . . Enjoy Budweiser . . . Every golden drop of it." The trademark was used as a signature and the product was pictured. That was all.

In introducing this campaign, The Third issued the following message, which was widely quoted:

WHAT IS THE MOST IMPORTANT JOB IN AMERICA TODAY?

To sell a calm assurance of the future of America and its generous offer of rewards to each and every American who has confidence in himself.

To sell confidence in the foundations laid down by our pioneer forefathers.

To realize that we have comforts and conveniences beyond the reach of peoples of other nations; that other nations listen enviously as America continues to tell us "there is opportunity for all."

To sell America to Americans.

To me this is our Challenge, more important than selling beer—more important than making profits. For only when we contribute our confidence in the soundness of the foundations upon which those forefathers built America will factories hum and provide jobs for more Americans on our pay rolls and families be provided with the needs and comforts of life—

only then will we as American businessmen find a normal and enduring market for our products.

Advertising may be used to sell a product, idea, a service, or an institution. Heretofore, we have devoted our advertising to an informative, educational story about Budweiser and America has shown its confidence in what we have said in the product we have made—a confidence so outstanding that we repeatedly have not been able to fill all orders. Certainly we must be deserving of such public confidence. Yet, there are very few ways by which a business institution can show its appreciation.

We could have prepared advertisements which talked only about our product or our institution—our age, our size, the taxes we pay, our position in the industry. We could have prepared a campaign of widespread benefit to the brewing industry at large. In many ways, all of these ideas would have been helpful to the stimulation of business.

But, it is impossible for me to sit at my desk in intimate daily contact with the problems of each community and with the general sentiment throughout America without becoming conscious of a definite need—bigger than our product, bigger than our institution, bigger than the brewing industry.

America is made up of people—people as you and I—each confronted with problems and, in the minds of millions of our fellow Americans, their major problem is economy, with a feeling of lack of security, which stimulates a widespread fear of tomorrow.

Our advertising campaign is designed to reflect Anheuser-Busch's confidence in the future of America. It is designed to help Americans re-evaluate our America. It is Anheuser-Busch's investment in America's tomorrow, a confidence born of the philosophy and faith of over eighty years of active business relations with our fellow Americans. It is designed to help quicken the return, not of the prosperity of the late '20's, but of the time when every man in America is on a pay roll.

Here is the first series of advertisements that are going to be read in 930 newspapers and in magazines by literally millions of people. Let us work together so that this campaign will help those millions of fellow Americans to translate their hope of tomorrow into sunshine for today.

Here again was the spirit of Grandfather Adolphus, aghast at the San Francisco 'quake and fire, alive to public need.

The response to this series of messages was amazing and, considering the temper of the times, the resultant goodwill as indicated by soaring sales of Budweiser, was more amazing still. The brewery's output in 1938 passed the two-million-barrel mark for the first time by 87,185 barrels.

The London Economist took cognizance of the messages and editorially asked why no advertiser in the British Empire followed the example of the St. Louis company.

Public response to Anheuser-Busch's bid for courage was such that the company produced a motion picture built around the messages and it was shown to millions of viewers.

Letters of praise and gratitude from industrialists, bankers, business men and public officials poured onto the desk of The Third.

Public confidence began returning because of a number of factors and Anheuser-Busch could well feel that it was one of them.

Yes, public confidence was bolstered despite the fact that for the second time the peace of all Europe was threatened by a Little Corporal, Austria's Hitler, an outlander in Germany just as the Napoleon whom he sought to emulate was a Corsican Corporal before he dubbed himself Emperor of the French.

When Hitler threw his Sunday punch and America began re-arming, Anheuser-Busch people wondered if they were going to live 1918-1932 all over again. Would the prohibitionists seize upon the war threat to base a claim that grain was needed for food? Would they repeat the breast-beating about "protect our boys" from alcohol?

They tried, as usual, but didn't get to bat, much less to first base.

Faced with the threat of another world war, the people were in no mood for a repetition of the prohibition farce. Nor was G.I. Joe. The soldier soon made it known that he wanted beer. He knew that rigorous training and obstacle courses couldn't be tackled with a hangover and that beer gave him temperate satisfaction. The Army was to see to it that he got his beer all through the ensuing war.

When the United States entered World War II on December 8, 1941, it was to bring about great changes in the world's largest brewery, just as it brought changes to every business and every family the country over.

Six months after Pearl Harbor, Gus became Major August A. Busch, Jr., Ordnance Department, United States Army, in which capacity he was to "pioneer a new type of coordination between industry and Army Ordnance, establishing precedents and procedures that were of primary importance in organizing the nation's industry to work as a unit" and to win a citation for the Legion of Merit and a colonel's commission before he was honorably discharged in peacetime.

One of Gus's last acts as a civilian was to approve, as his brother had approved, a decision to devote the company's advertising appropriations first to an institutional campaign showing Anheuser-Busch's stature and fitness for participation in the war effort and, secondly, a campaign devoted 95 percent to messages which the federal government wished conveyed to the people. Examples of both campaigns are shown on pages 348-355 and 360-371.

Chapter XVIII

IN THE FAMILY TRADITION,

ADOLPHUS BUSCH III

IN ITS LIFETIME, Anheuser-Busch had experienced staggering changes and learned to roll with the punch. That toughening-up process stood management in good stead in the brewery's ninetieth year, because the changes wrought by World War II were enough to crack a crystal ball.

Who would have dreamed that a brewer would be called upon to manufacture glider fuselages and wing assemblies? Or parts for guns and field kitchens?

Anheuser-Busch was called upon to produce—and produce it did. Prosit!

Who would have thought that a brewer would be asked to supply enormous amounts of nutrients not only for the rations of the armed services but for civilian populations abroad as well as at home?

Anheuser-Busch was asked—and did.

Who would have dreamed that the government would "suggest" that the brewer relinquish his lush Pacific Coast market—with other brewers, of course—so that more freight cars with war material could use the rails to the coastal

222

embarkation points? Anheuser-Busch responded instantly, although there was no compulsion behind the "suggestion" other than one of patriotism. The company was the only one to comply. Indeed, other brewers increased their shipments of beer in order to gobble up big mouthfuls of that market. Just one of those things.

Adolphus—The Third—found himself with plenty to think about and plenty to do, with more than a few of his key men in military service as his brother was. It would have been a task doomed to failure without the loyal spirit of "the family" of Anheuser-Busch people.

The Third questioned the personnel of the Refrigerator Cabinet Division about their ability to produce glider fuselages and wing assemblies. They said they could do it. The cabinet business was discontinued for the duration of the war, the equipment largely shoved aside and the place retooled for the new operation. Exactly what the Air Force called for it got and in jig time.

Meanwhile, Washington informed the Brewery Division that tin cans for beer for the armed services would be forthcoming, but tin and steel for bottle crown tops was something else again. And, the hard-working civilian population was demanding beer in its moments of leisure.

Somebody remembered that the food processing companies were being allocated large size cans for preserved food—known as No. 10 cans—and decided that the metal could be salvaged, flattened, cleaned and made into crown tops. Thereafter, everyone connected with the distribution of Budweiser—including friendly retailers—conducted a national scavenger hunt that actually became a treasure hunt. Budweiser reached not only military personnel but the thirsty civilian worker as well but never in quantities to keep people satisfied.

Anheuser-Busch had no choice but to curtail its service to some retailers for the reason that manpower and gasoline shortages made delivery to many points impossible. The resentment that this move provoked was augmented by resentment from those dealers who still were being rationed Budweiser. Each felt that he ought to get more, that his competitor was getting much more. Of course, the rationed consumer added his gripe to the chorus when forced to accept other beers. The entire situation paralleled that in the Army, wherein many grumblers vowed they would beat the second lieutenant to a pulp once both were back in peacetime. Fortunately, the joy of peace healed all those wounded feelings eventually.

The call for Anheuser-Busch to participate in a food enrichment program for the armed forces and civilians as well was a natural one when it is remembered that the company had acquired an enviable reputation for its work in nutrition and medicine.

In the late twenties, the company's technical staff had worked with the scientists of the pharmaceutical house of Mead-Johnson to produce a special strain of yeast with a high ergosterol content. Ergosterol is a compound, which, when irradiated, becomes vitamin D (viosterol). At that time, it commanded a price of $250 a pound. The work of the scientists had proved successful and greatly reduced the cost.

The Army wanted its K-1 ration for combat troops to contain the maximum of health and energy-giving nutrients in the most compact package possible. Anheuser-Busch was called upon to furnish many hundreds of thousands of pounds of food yeast for the ration. Other huge quantities went to allied countries to supplement the diet of fighting man and civilian alike.

A more comprehensive report of the work of the company in nutrition and medicine is given in another chapter.

In January, 1943, an official suggestion from Washington was made that Anheuser-Busch and other national brewers volunteer to withdraw from the Pacific Coast states. When the St. Louis company agreed, it published in West Coast newspapers a farewell message explaining why the step was taken. That message prompted a Portland, Oregon, competitor to publish a salute giving Anheuser-Busch high praise for its concept of business ethics and public duty. Both messages appear on an adjacent page.

Pages could be written about the difficulties of guiding a huge operation like that of Anheuser-Busch through the war years, but no such account of corporate and individual headaches is included. After all, who didn't have headaches and heartaches during World War II?

The campaign to sell bonds for the Fourth War Loan was conducted in January and February of 1944. Representatives of Anheuser-Busch employees arranged with the War Finance Committee to earmark the bonds bought by the employees for the purchase of an Army Air Force bomber, a B-17, the most powerful bomber then known and, at that time, the most costly. When the campaign was only half concluded in the brewery, the response had been so great that the slogan sprang up, "Let's make it two—one for the Nazis and one for the Japs." Another surge of bond-buying skyrocketed the grand total for the campaign to a bond maturity value of $879,350—more than enough for two of these flying fortresses.

The Anheuser-Busch people requested that one B-17 be named "Miss Budweiser" and the other "Busch-wacker" in tribute to the spirit which made the campaign a success. Not only was the request granted, but the Army sent photographs of the two planes.

As the war drew to its end, Adolphus III could look back with the satisfaction that the tradition of, "What would Grandfather have done?" had not been breached. Public service had been performed with distinction and Budweiser had gone to the consumer with its high standard of quality unsullied.

More beer, but not true Budweiser, could have been produced with dilution and substitutes. There had been on the market a substance loosely called "manioc." It was a type of starch extracted from a root cultivated in the tropics. When properly treated, it could be converted into something somewhat resembling the maltose sugar in a barley malt.

Substitute.

Not for Budweiser.

The eagerness of the consumer to get Budweiser during the years of war and rationing was multiplied many times with the coming of peace. Productive

A GREAT COMPLIMENT FROM COMPETITORS

When Anheuser-Busch withdrew from the west coast, in February 1943, the company declared publicly . . . .

To the many friends of Budweiser

It is our privilege and desire to cooperate in the relief of the rail traffic problem on the Pacific Coast

While shipments of Budweiser constitute but a fraction of the total rail traffic load on the Pacific Coast, we have decided to withhold all such shipments until such a time as the present rail traffic emergency is relieved,—and we have so informed the War Production Board

This decision applies to all shipments of Budweiser scheduled to leave our plant in St. Louis for California, Oregon and Washington, after January 31st

We know that all who are identified with Budweiser on the Pacific Coast,—wholesalers, retailers, and our many other friends,—will consider it a privilege to share in this temporary sacrifice to hasten the day of Victory.

For over fifty years we have been proud of your selection of Budweiser as a symbol of your famous hospitality, and we join with you in looking forward to the day when this companion of good taste will again be available.

In the busy meantime, we commend to our friends the many fine beers now being brewed on the Pacific Coast.

ANHEUSER-BUSCH
SAINT LOUIS

A competitor acknowledged the move with a fine tribute in this unusual newspaper advertisement

To Budweiser...
and its many friends:

It is unfortunate that famous Budweiser Beer will temporarily not be available on the Pacific Coast. We mean this sincerely. Not only because you are one of the truly great beers of America; not only because you have for years been a national institution; but because in all the past years your competition has been clean, fair, honest. Your last statement, *"We commend to our friends the many fine beers now being brewed on the Pacific Coast"*, is evidence of your good sportsmanship.

This statement and the unselfish action, that prompted your announcement, is typical of public responsibility which, we like to feel, our industry has and will continue to have ever in mind.

We, as one of the Pacific Coast's oldest breweries, will do our utmost to see that the thousands of folks in this area who attach a special value to their right to enjoy a truly fine glass of beer as a *beverage of moderation* . . have that opportunity.

BLITZ-WEINHARD COMPANY
PORTLAND, OREGON

capacity was stepped up as fast as the increases of ingredients, other raw materials and personnel permitted.

V-J Day—Victory over Japan—came on August 14, 1945. Then came demobilization, the tearing up of ration cards, the hunt for a new car, the plans for a new home, the hurry to overcome obsolescence—the boom that follows in the wake of victorious arms. People had money to spend and a great desire to enjoy life fully again. With every facility taxed, Anheuser-Busch could not meet the immense demand for Budweiser.

Gus, out of the Army with tributes far exceeding an honorable discharge, pored over blueprints with The Third. The blueprints were plans for an Eastern brewery on a site in Newark, New Jersey. The plans had gathered cobwebs during the war. In these booming postwar days, the time for expansion seemed ripe. True, there were dour prophets warning daily that bust was bound to follow boom, but they didn't know then that our lend-lease ally, Russia, was going to give us a long-term lease on fear of a third world conflict and that re-arming would bolster the national economy.

Prophets of glory or gloom notwithstanding, The Third and his brother persuaded the Board of Directors to proceed with the Newark brewery.

Meanwhile, the decision was made to expand greatly the facilities in St. Louis. New buildings and new equipment began appearing with miraculous speed. To the two enormous chimneys that had been a South Side landmark for decades was added a third that signified that a great new power house was in operation. By 1949, the expansion program had cost $66,000,000 and still was not ended. Sales of Budweiser kept abreast of the expansion . . . amazingly so.

Still, it wasn't so amazing, after all. The costly expansion was necessary because The Third and Gus were determined that the kraüsening and lagering that gave Budweiser its high-light of quality would not be abandoned. That process required vast storage facilities. Other large brewers had given up lagering as too costly. They preferred to give their product a primary fermentation, meanwhile recapturing the CO_2 to be pumped back into the liquid when fermentation ceased. Thus, they were able to market beer after "ageing" it thirty days or even less time, while Budweiser required months to reach mellow maturity and be enriched with natural carbonation. Toward the middle of the century, about seven percent of the beer produced in America was true lager beer and Anheuser-Busch produced more than half of it.

Once again the world's largest brewery was humming and optimism made the air crisp and good to breathe in. And, once again a bolt came out of the blue.

The Third underwent a routine physical check-up in the summer of 1946, including X-ray examination. His condition was pronounced excellent. Yet, his health began to fail suddenly and rapidly. The X-ray, as often happens, had failed to detect the presence of cancer.

One year and fifteen days after the end of the war through which he had guided his company so surely, Adolphus Busch III died.

So ended a lifetime of achievement of which his forebears could be proud. His father had been determined that "my boys" would not be dawdlers. The Third had been a good scholar, being graduated from Smith Academy. Immediately after graduation, he was put to work in the brewery and exhibited such adaptability and resourcefulness that his election to the Board of Directors and to the third vice-presidency in 1911 was a matter of course. Three years later he was chosen second vice-president and, four years after that, he became first vice-president, which position he filled until voted president at the first board meeting following the death of his father in 1934. He was the company president for twelve years.

Although his fiber was tested over and over again, one of the severest trials came in the midst of the jubilation over the return of beer in 1933. The federal government decided that the banks of the country needed an examination. One of the first chosen was the Lafayette-South Side Bank & Trust Company, not far from the brewery, in which The Third was a director. It was ordered closed.

Some defenders of the Lafayette-South Side contended bitterly that the institution had been made a guinea pig; that its policies differed little from those of other banks with good reputations; that other banks got an opportunity after the closing to clean house. Nonetheless, the bank was closed.

The closing was defined in the gossip that went around as a "failure" and it was a blow to Anheuser-Busch, not because the company owned even a penny's worth of stock in the institution, but because many South Side residents supposed the bank was "an Anheuser-Busch institution" since members of the Busch family owned some of the stock.

There was a very, very gloomy meeting one evening in The Third's home and the unanimous opinion was that, whether the public supposed rightly or wrongly that Lafayette-South Side was "an Anheuser-Busch institution," the company's reputation had to be protected at any cost.

On December 2, 1933, there appeared in the Post-Dispatch a paid announcement by the committee for the reorganization of the Lafayette-South Side Bank & Trust Company. The committee consisted of Adolphus Busch, III, Walter L. Freund, William J. Jones, Joseph L. Rehme and A. E. Wright. The announcement said that the plan of reorganization, dated October 9, 1933, had been completed. It was expected that the new bank would open at the old location no later than December 20, 1933. The new bank was to be called the Manufacturers' Bank and Trust Company.

The reorganization plan required that $716,000 cash be raised by the sale of common stock of the new bank. This was accomplished because of the efforts of the old and new directors and because Anheuser-Busch, Inc., the Busch family and the Busch interests in South St. Louis either bought or by lending made it possible for others to buy the common stock of the new bank which had a par value of $20 a share, but was sold for $33.33 per share.

The announcement in the Post-Dispatch said:

> The Busch interests, by actual purchase of this stock and by lending money to others to buy it, supplied $636,000 of $716,000 required by the plan, and others interested in the bank's success supplied the other $80,000 of cash.

Neither Anheuser-Busch, Inc. nor any other Busch industry owned a single share of the stock of the Lafayette-South Side Bank and Trust Company. Members of the Busch family owned together about eleven percent of the Lafayette.

Thus, while neither the Anheuser nor the Busch families were ever anything more than owners of the minority of the stock of the Lafayette and although neither Anheuser-Busch, Inc. nor Mr. Busch owed the bank a dollar when it closed, nevertheless, they have always felt that South St. Louis should have good banking facilities and they have realized that a host of friends and employees have done business with the Lafayette-South Side Bank and Trust Company under the impression that the Busch interests either owned or controlled that bank, when as a matter of fact, they never did.

The statement said that completion of the plan made available about $400,000 for reorganizing the South Side National Bank, an associate of the Lafayette.

According to the Globe-Democrat, the opening of the Manufacturers' Bank and Trust Company was a gala occasion with light standards on Broadway being decorated with gay bunting and flags and printed signs announcing the opening and congratulating the institution on its reincarnation.

The Globe-Democrat added that after being closed ten months, the bank would release about $8,500,000 to depositors at once.

The same paper on December 21, 1933, carried this one column headline:

NEW BANK REGISTERS

GAIN ON FIRST DAY

South Side Institution Shows
$275,000 Deposits Over Withdrawals

The news story went on to say that the bank remained open until 5:00 P.M. to accommodate the large number of persons who visited and made the usual 2:00 P.M. closing hour impossible. The newspaper reported that all of the depositors seemed to be imbued with confidence in the new institution.

The Post-Dispatch of March 9, 1934, reported that reorganization of the South Side National Bank in St. Louis freed deposits of about $3,000,000.

The Third was chairman of the board of the Busch-Sulzer Brothers Diesel Engine Company, president and a director of the Dallas Hotel Company (Hotel Adolphus), chairman of the board of the Manufacturers' Railway Company, chairman of the St. Louis & O'Fallon Railway Company, a director of Adolphus Busch Estate, Inc., chairman of the board of the Manufacturers' Bank and Trust Company and a member of the board of trustees of the St. Louis Refrigerator Car Company.

In addition to his many Anheuser-Busch problems during the war years, Adolphus was compelled to devote much time to the diesel engine company. It was, as is told in another chapter, engaged in 'round-the-clock production of complex ammunition hoists for the Navy and engines of various sizes for the armed forces and allied countries.

The news of his death was published prominently in all the metropolitan newspapers. The New York Herald-Tribune carried the story under a two-column headline with a portrait and said in part:

> St. Louis, August 29—Adolphus Busch, III, fifty-five, President of Anheuser-Busch, Inc., brewers of Budweiser beer, died in Barnes Hospital here today after a short illness.
>
> (The story went on to recount the history of Anheuser-Busch and then it made the following comment.)
>
> It was when the company entered the yeast manufacturing field that Adolphus III displayed the business acumen that made his succession to the presidency inevitable. Starting from scratch, he personally stumped the country to contact large buyers and it wasn't long before he was one of the largest manufacturers of yeast in the business.
>
> Never a playboy, Adolphus III, like his father, entered the business early and learned it from the ground up. He disliked publicity and kept his private life to himself.
>
> When not out of the city, he went early and stayed late at the main

building of the vast brewery which covers 142 acres. He limited his annual vacation to two weeks.

His multiple activities denied him in his last years what The Third, like his father, enjoyed to the utmost—regular excursions into country life and the company of birds and animals. He was an expert judge of horses and served as president of the St. Louis Horse Show Society. He was noted for riding ability and won many prizes at horse shows. Being interested in the sport only for sport's sake, he always gave his winnings to charity.

The Third was especially distinguished for driving four-in-hand coaches and he also won many awards with singles, tandems and high steppers. The publication Bit and Spur described him on one occasion as "the greatest 19-year-old horseman in the world today."

His love of animals was great: A personable, small fox terrier named Sunshine was his constant companion, attending all board of directors and staff meetings with becoming gravity. Sunshine slipped out of the house one evening and took off to see the sights, ultimately becoming lost. Her master's concern was so great that a friend called several radio stations, which took the stand that a dog which attended directors' meetings should be found. The news went over the air and in almost a matter of minutes the wanderer was returned to her home by a man who had heard the broadcast and recognized the dog.

There is more than meets the eye in what the Herald-Tribune said about The Third having been no playboy, having disliked publicity and having wished to keep his private life his own. Like his father and grandfather, Adolphus had, when provoked, a flaring and subsiding wrath, but no capacity for grudges. Anger and reproach came from him rarely and then only under extreme provocation.

His bearing was a blend of gentleness and poise with an evident eagerness to be friendly. Office boys may be universally addressed as "Hey, you," or "Say, boy," but to The Third they were always "Son."

Subordinates in the business never stood awesomely before a forbidding desk and faced an austere president. He had a huge leather couch in his office and liked to seat his visitor and himself there and make the conversation as informal as possible, however pointed it might be.

Anyone who knew Adolphus III will remember his habit of being a very, very good listener and his way of saying, "Yes, yes," and, "Please go on," to encourage the speaker to tell his whole story. Nor will they forget that, although he was a flawless dresser, his first act upon arriving in his office was to shed coat and tie and open his collar. It wasn't a craving for comfort, but a tacit way of telling one and all, "I'm no stuffed shirt."

When the war was ended, The Third wisely elected to stay at his home in Huntleigh Village for a few days after the pressure of work had gone too far. If need be, members of his staff with pressing problems were invited to bring them either to the friendly living room or the shaded patio. Often, when a decision pleased him, he would call, "Kitty . . . Can you come here for a moment, please?" Then Mrs. Busch would hear the good news and praise for the bearer of the news. Again, "the family."

To attempt to describe the sorrow of The Third's associates over his death would be to overwork words. They, who would have liked to come in numbers to pay tribute at his burial, understood the gentle, shy nature which prompted him to ask for a simple, private service.

Members of the Busch and Anheuser families and a few very intimate friends gathered at the residence on Saturday afternoon, August 31, 1946. The Episcopal service was read by The Reverend Charles D. Kean, rector of Grace Church, Kirkwood. Burial was close to the grave of his beloved father.

Chapter XIX

GUS AND GRANDFATHER

SEE EYE-TO-EYE

AUGUST A. BUSCH, JR., became the fifth president of Anheuser-Busch at the first meeting of the Board of Directors after his brother's death. How, under the tutelage of his father and grandfather, he had been prepared for his place in the business has been told on other pages.

For the record, the following dates and data concerning his service are included.

He was born March 28, 1899, and entered the employ of Anheuser-Busch, Incorporated, on January 1, 1924. He was made general superintendent on May 20, 1924, and continued in that position until December 7, 1926, when he was elected sixth vice-president and general manager.

He was elected as a member of the Board of Directors for the first time on December 7, 1926, and has served continuously as a director.

He served as sixth vice-president and general manager until June 23, 1931, on which date he was elected second vice-president and general manager and continued as such until his election as first vice-president and general manager on February 22, 1934.

He was elected president on September 5, 1946.

He received a commission as Major, U. S. Army, and left St. Louis to report to the Department of Ordnance in Washington, D. C., on June 22, 1942.

His record in the service is as follows:

Major   June 22, 1942—January 1, 1943

Lt. Col.   January 1, 1943—November 8, 1944

Colonel   November 9, 1944—discharge June 12, 1945

     Awarded Legion of Merit October 21, 1946

He returned to assume his duties as vice-president and general manager of Anheuser-Busch, Incorporated, on June 12, 1945.

Many a man feels that his hitch in the Army was wasted years, but Gus is not one of them. His Ordnance Department assignments kept him jumping by plane, train and motor to spots where knotting-up and bottlenecks called for one slugfest after another. It was an excellent post-graduate course for the man who was to direct the shaping of Anheuser-Busch destiny.

This is what the Army thought of him:

CITATION FOR THE LEGION OF MERIT

Colonel August A. Busch, Jr., rendered exceptionally meritorious services, successively as Industry Engineering Officer, Chief of Industry Integration Unit, and Chief of Industry Production Branch of the Ammunition Division, Office, Chief of Ordnance, from June 1942 to July 1945. He pioneered a new type of coordination between industry and Army Ordnance, establishing precedents and procedures that were of primary importance in organizing the nation's industry to work as a unit. Through his exceptional resourcefulness and ability, Colonel Busch contributed greatly to the continued production of material for overseas operations.

AUGUST ANHEUSER BUSCH, JUNIOR—The fourth Busch to be president of Anheuser-Busch quickly demonstrated that he had a scrappy and progressive interpretation of "what would Grandfather have done?"

FIFTH ARMY
MISSOURI MILITARY DISTRICT

Colonel August A. Busch Jr.   April 9, 1948
President, Anheuser-Busch, Inc.
721 Pestalozzi Street, St. Louis 18, Mo.

Dear Colonel Busch:

Records of my office indicate you are entitled to receive one or more of the following campaign medals for your service in World War II: (1) American Campaign, (2) Asiatic-Pacific Campaign, (3) European-African-Middle Eastern Campaign.

General distribution of these medals will not be made until after June 1. However this office has been given a small advance allotment from which I will be very glad to issue you the medals for which you are eligible. All that is necessary is that you complete the enclosed receipt form and mail it to my office. The medals will then be delivered to you promptly.

Eligibility requirements are summarized in the enclosed memorandum, but should you have any question as to your eligibility, please feel free to write or call my office for further information.

Yours sincerely
s/ Glen R. Townsend
Colonel, Infantry, Executive

HEADQUARTERS FIFTH ARMY

Office of the Commanding General, Chicago, Illinois

This is to certify that Mr. August A. Busch, Jr. has this day been appointed a member of the Army Advisory Committee for the Fifth United States Army in St. Louis, Missouri. The Army Advisory Committee's purpose is to cement the close and continuing relationship between the Army and the people it serves.

For the Commanding General
T. J. Marnane, Lt. Colonel
Adjutant General's Department
Adjutant General
10 October 1947

He is a life member of the Army Ordnance Association.

While Gus was in the Army, the St. Louis Democratic City Committee paid him the honor of requesting him to become the party's candidate for mayor. Under the headline

BUSCH DECLINES

TO BE CANDIDATE

IN MAYOR RACE

Says he feels it is his duty
to continue service as Colonel
in Army Ordnance Office

the St. Louis Post-Dispatch of February 8, 1945, published the following dispatch from Washington:

Col. August A. Busch, Jr., vice-president of Anheuser-Busch, Inc., now on duty in the Army Ordnance Department, announced today that he declined to become a candidate for the Democratic nomination for Mayor of St. Louis, in the primary March 9.

In a formal announcement, Col. Busch stated that he was declining "the request of several organizations" to enter the mayoralty contest. He stated that he felt it his duty to continue his service in the Ordnance office.

His announcement said:

St. Louis and its people have made an enviable record in the war. In addition to those serving their city and country overseas, many public-spirited citizens have shown their patriotism by their outstanding services.

With unbounded faith in the future of America, and in the important place of St. Louis in the postwar world, I again thank you for the high honor conferred upon me, which I must regretfully decline at this time.

To be requested to become a candidate for Mayor of this city is a high honor of which any St. Louisan may well be proud. I am deeply appreciative of such requests made by many individuals and organizations.

Several years ago, however, I made the decision to serve my country during the grave emergency which faced it, by accepting a commission in the Ordnance Department of the Army. I was granted leave of absence by my company and have been continuously on such duty since that time.

No one could have participated, as I have, in production activities in that department without being inspired to contribute his every energy to meet our national objective of producing vitally needed munitions.

None of us can afford to forget the fact that the war is not yet won, and I, personally, cannot be unmindful that my first and continuing duty is that of furthering the interest of the Ordnance Department in its production efforts. In doing so, I feel that I am serving St. Louis in the capacity which circumstances now indicate to be the most urgent.

To his postwar task, Gus brought not only his abilities but a steel, not iron, constitution. He keeps that steel tempered by enforced relaxation at regular intervals and plenty of outdoor exercise. A man, who, in his fifty-third year, can take a high-spirited jumper over stone fences in the field and canter away with prize after prize at horse shows isn't doing too badly.

Even in his frequent staff meetings the boundless energy appears. These meetings are picturesque to say the least.

As did his brother, Gus gives coat and tie a pitch and succeeds in keeping proceedings informal. There are no smug salutations of, "Mr. President." Rather, it's, "It's this way, Boss," or, "Gussie, don't forget so and so." And, often in a fast-paced debate, Gus will say, "Just a moment. . . Let me finish and then *you* can blow your top."

Yes, Gus believes in encouraging his co-workers to blow off steam.

One of Gus's closest business associates in 1952 described him thus:

August A. Busch, Jr., to those who know him well and who knew Adolphus, see in him many of the characteristics of his grandfather, known for his force of character and spontaneous reaction to problems of the day.

August A. Busch, Jr., possesses these same characteristics in a high degree. He is aggressive, a keen observer of human nature, has a retentive memory and does not hesitate to come to a decision, once he makes up his mind that he is right. Also, like his grandfather, he travels a great deal and enjoys visiting with the trade. He is democratic and likes people . . . a trait that contributed much to the success of Adolphus Busch.

August A. Busch, Jr., is a man of dynamic personality and action. He pursues his business activities wherever he goes. When he visits Hot Springs, Arkansas, for three weeks each year, which has been his custom for years, he takes his secretarial staff with him and conducts the affairs of the business from there. This frequently calls for visits by the key men of the company to Hot Springs for conferences and final decisions.

When he travels to other parts of the country, he is in constant touch with his office and all the departments of the business by long distance so that he is never out of touch with what is going on.

In his relations with labor, he recognizes the rights of labor as well as the interests of the company and is respected for the fair attitude he takes with respect to the rights of both.

No President of Anheuser-Busch has ever taken his duties more seriously than does August A. Busch, Jr., but he also welcomes his hours of relaxation and takes them. He loves the outdoors and spends his weekends riding, driving and enjoying the wonders of nature at Grant's Farm and St. Peter's, Missouri, where he has a hunting lodge. Here, as well as at Grant's Farm, he spends his leisure hours with his family and other relatives, who gather together for a good time.

Wildlife has a great attraction for August A. Busch, Jr., who was instrumental in having his mother establish the wildlife conservation area for use by the public at Weldon Springs, Missouri, in memory of his late father, August A. Busch, Sr.

Production records of the brewery were blown galley-west in the second year of Gus's presidency when the four-million-barrel mark was passed.

That was the result of the expansion program that was getting into full stride when he assumed the presidency. In Frank Schwaiger, he knew that he had a brewmaster of rare attainments—a man of great technical skill and possessed of the imagination to visualize the plant requirements to implement that skill.

A year and a half after his discharge from the Army, Gus found himself in another war—a fight to recapture first place in the brewing industry which, traditionally, had been held by Anheuser-Busch. The Schlitz Brewing Company of Milwaukee announced in 1947 that its brand then was the biggest-selling beer in America. Obviously, this was a hornet sting to the pride of everyone concerned with Budweiser.

Obviously, too, the solution was easy if recapturing first place were the only consideration. All that was necessary was to turn out a greater volume of beer—not Budweiser, but just beer—and ship it in quantity to wholesalers, who never since the middle thirties had had all the Budweiser they could sell.

What would Grandfather have done?

Just what Gus did.

He resolved that there would be much greater production of Budweiser —genuine Budweiser. Since lagering, which was the heart and soul of the process, called for immense storage facilities and a great volume of near-freezing refrigeration, any expansion program aimed at first place in the industry would have to be of titanic dimensions.

From the discussions between the president, his brewmaster and the architects emerged a mountain of blueprints and, from the blueprints, began an emerging of huge additions, brick by brick, girder by girder and tank by tank—truly an undertaking of tremendous magnitude that had to pay off. Three years after the fateful decision of 1947, the St. Louis brewery reached an all-time production high with five million barrels of delicious, thoroughly aged Budweiser.

Work on the new plant in Newark, New Jersey, began in 1950 and by June of the following year it was in production.

ANHEUSER-BUSCH BEER SALES

1876 through 1919

Year	Barrels	Year	Barrels
1876	38,413	1898	782,002
1877	56,532	1899	824,548
1878	74,687	1900	939,768
1879	105,234	1901	1,006,490
1880	141,163	1902	1,090,834
1881	201,053	1903	1,171,761
1882	247,069	1904	1,335,722
1883	303,584	1905	1,375,791
1884	320,704	1906	1,543,407
1885	318,107	1907	1,599,918
1886	379,290	1908	1,378,481
1887	456,511	1909	1,368,145
1888	505,370	1910	1,479,253
1889	582,443	1911	1,527,831
1890	702,346	1912	1,517,781
1891	612,366	1913	1,530,085
1892	712,258	1914	1,307,784
1893	714,707	1915	1,078,204
1894	704,757	1916	1,083,026
1895	681,948	*1917	978,516
1896	739,951	1918	699,645
1897	767,356	1919	218,073

*United States entered World War I in April, 1917.

ANHEUSER-BUSCH BEER SALES

1933 through 1950

After Repeal, April 7, 1933

Year	Barrels
1933	607,511
1934	1,093,223
1935	1,135,776
1936	1,376,692
1937	1,839,960
1938	2,087,185
1939	2,305,984
1940	2,462,209
1941	3,089,954
1942	3,492,343
1943	3,569,031
1944	3,692,352
1945	3,529,469
1946	3,026,413
1947	3,608,738
1948	4,042,181
1949	4,526,115
1950	4,888,732

In this connection, it is interesting to note the increases in wages, taxes and raw material costs in the ten-year period from 1941 to 1951. The cost of living increased eighty-four percent, wages went up one hundred seven percent, the sales price of 12-ounce returnable bottles up thirty-seven percent, draught beer sales price up seventy-one percent, Western barley up ninety-five percent, Midwestern barley malt up one hundred fifty-eight percent, rice up ninety-five percent, imported hops up eighty-one percent, 12-ounce returnable bottles up one hundred twenty percent, federal tax up thirty-three percent.

After one hundred years, the Anheuser-Busch picture looked like this.

The Brewery Division was producing Budweiser in 12-ounce returnable bottles, 12-ounce non-returnable bottles, 7-ounce returnable bottles, 32-ounce returnable and non-returnable bottles and in 12-ounce flat top cans. Budweiser draught beer and Michelob draught beer were marketed in stainless steel half-barrels of 15½ gallons capacity.

The Yeast, Malt and Corn Products Division produced bakers' yeast, frozen eggs, malt syrup, pharmaceutical yeast, corn syrup, corn oil, starches, dextrines and table syrup. The Refrigerated Cabinet Division manufactured and sold ice cream cabinets and frozen food cabinets. The Feeds Department disposed of beer and corn residuals consisting of brewers' dried grains, broken barley and barley screenings, malt sprouts, corn gluten feed and corn oil and cake meal.

The yeast, first produced in St. Louis in 1926, and its output augmented by a second plant completed in Old Bridge, New Jersey, in 1931, was highly esteemed by the baking industry. This department was the second largest producer of bakers' compressed yeast in the world. Bud Brand Frozen Eggs, a very high quality product, were sold to the baking and food industries.

Budweiser Malt Syrup and Dri-malt were sold to the baking and pharmaceutical industries.

A-B Brand Corn Syrup, a crystal clear, viscous product, sometimes known as glucose, was used by the candy and table syrup industries.

A-B Brand Starches—pure food, powdered, pearl, chlorinated and thin boiling—were used extensively by the textile, paper and food processing industries. The oil industry was using industrial starches in the drilling of off-shore oil wells.

A-B Brand Dextrines, unique in their highly specialized field, were used by the adhesive, textile and paper industries.

Unrefined corn oil was being sold to refiners for use in salad dressings and vegetable cooking oils and also for use with gluten feed and cake meal for the animal feed industry.

Table syrups—Bud Waffle, Bud Crystal White, Bud Golden and Delta—were marketed through grocery stores for home consumption in eight southern states. They were packed in New Orleans, Louisiana.

The great importance of the company's pharmaceutical yeast has been thoroughly described in another chapter.

Manufacturing buildings numbered 60 covering 94 acres.

The power plant could generate electricity for the household needs of a city of 150,000 persons, and the water works had a daily capacity of seven million gallons.

The St. Louis Globe-Democrat of Friday, October 19, 1951, published a story under a two-column heading which read:

BUSCH WATER PLANT ADEQUATE

FOR CITY IN CASE OF WAR

The story said that water treatment facilities at the Anheuser-Busch brewery could provide the city's emergency water needs in the event that enemy action disabled the municipal water plants at both Howard's Bend and at the Chain of Rocks, according to Raymond R. Tucker, Director of Civil Defense for St. Louis.

Tucker spoke at a meeting of the Engineers Club and outlined the structure of the civil defense organization.

On this and the following 2 pages are some of the distinguished members of the Anheuser-Busch family of products.

ANHEUSER-BUSCH was the first company in America to produce nonfermentable, dried yeast for nutritional purposes.

Answering a question, Tucker said that investigation of the water treating plant at the brewery revealed that it was adequate to serve the city on an emergency basis and under strict rationing.

He called the plant "our ace in the hole."

The water plant at the brewery filtered and purified water, not for brewing purposes, but for washing and sluicing and also for boilers. While it was pure in every respect, the brewmaster preferred to use city water.

Anheuser-Busch used more than seventy-two thousand freight cars to ship in supplies and equipment and to ship out Budweiser and its own products.

The company was selling Budweiser in every state, every county and every city of the United States except prohibition areas. In addition, foreign markets had been re-entered since the war. Budweiser could be bought in twenty-two countries or territories throughout the world and new markets were being opened regularly. The geographical conditions of Budweiser's market and the income levels of Budweiser's consumers were variable to the extreme.

Budweiser was being shipped to 930 distributing points operated by independent wholesalers. These points ranged in area from one to fifteen counties. In addition, the brewery-operated sales branches were located in sixteen key cities.

The Sales Department was being operated on a territorial basis. There were eight domestic sales regions and one export division. The work was correlated closely with the company's advertising and merchandising departments. Each of the sales regions was supervised by a sales manager who travelled extensively, checking wholesaler operations and the work of the brewery's divisional and district managers and salesmen.

Anheuser-Busch merely suggested wholesaler prices (price from wholesaler to retailer). Virtually all wholesalers realized that the margins suggested by the brewery were fair and that it was good business not to over-price Budweiser. There were no price cuts or free deals offered to wholesalers.

There was only one f.o.b. St. Louis price on each package. To this the wholesaler added his freight, state tax and profit margin. The f.o.b. price on beer was adjusted occasionally to reflect the current cost of raw materials, bottles, taxes, labor and other expenses.

There was no preference given orders. The only stipulation made by the brewery was that carload orders be large enough to meet the minimum weight requirements of the railroads.

Very little warehousing was done for two reasons. One was that the orders were so numerous that many packaged and draught beer shipments were loaded directly from the filling units. The other was that it would be too costly to warehouse beer in packages in any quantity. A million cases would be only a few days' supply even in winter, and that sort of warehouse storage space was not available.

Ground was broken on February 13, 1950, for the erection of the No. 2 Home of Budweiser beer at Newark, New Jersey. The plant had an initial productive capacity of 1,250,000 barrels annually. The 51-acre tract across the highway from the Newark airport permitted erection of buildings to treble the initial output.

The decision to build was made after exhaustive investigation of many existing breweries. In all cases a study of the plants, their physical layout, and the type of equipment, indicated a rehabilitation program of about 80 percent to convert the plants to Budweiser specifications . . . practically an entire reconstruction and re-equipment project. The purchase price of a brewery plus rehabilitation costs and the time required to complete conversion of an existing plant was about the same as building new.

The Newark venture proved a wise one. Sales of Budweiser continued to soar. On July 10, 1952, ground was broken for an addition to the Newark brewery so that its productive capacity could be increased from 1,200,000 barrels to 1,600,000.

In that same month, it was announced that a 65-acre site in the San

Fernando Valley of Los Angeles County, California, had been purchased for erection of a 750,000-barrel brewery.

When, in August of 1951, production of Budweiser climbed to 607,000 barrels, a historic record was established. That was more beer than ever before had been turned out by a single brewery in one month. It began to look like the struggle for the traditional first place was going well.

In August of 1952, the president had news for the company's shareholders. His report, in part, follows:

To the Shareholders of Anheuser-Busch, Incorporated

Despite a 12-day work stoppage at St. Louis and a 17-day work stoppage at Newark during April and May, accelerated shipments after full operations were resumed at both plants on May 15th, indicate that the Company will achieve its sales goal for the year. Beer sales for the first half of year were 2,861,149 barrels versus 2,606,239 barrels last year, an increase of 10%. The yeast-malt-corn products division, which comprises a wide diversification of products, while not up to 1951 volume, produced satisfactory results. The refrigerated cabinet division sales were necessarily off . . . steel and other metals being in short supply, its sales volume was down about 11%.

Earnings for the first half of 1952 were $5,548,319 ($1.24 per share) as compared with $6,619,158 ($1.48 per share) last year. It is important to note that pre-tax earnings present a more favorable picture . . . for the first six months of 1952, they were $2.95 per share versus $3.05 per share last year. Income taxes increased from $1.57 per share in 1951 to $1.71 per share in 1952.

The funds provided in the first half of 1952 from operations, depreciation, disposition of property, and deferred charges totaled $9,050,718.

These funds were used for the following purposes:

Improve working capital $4,640,694
Additions to property 2,082,385
Miscellaneous assets acquired   90,139
Dividends paid to shareholders 2,237,500

Total $9,050,718

At the Board of Directors meeting, held on July 9, 1952, the Directors declared the regular quarterly dividend of 25c per share, payable September 2, 1952, to shareholders of record August 5, 1952.

———

THE NEW ANHEUSER-BUSCH BREWERY IN NEWARK, N. J.—It was so built that it could be expanded as the need for expansion arose—and it arose quickly. In 1952 the expansion program at Newark was well under way and a site had been purchased near Los Angeles for a third Home of Budweiser.

ANHEUSER-BUSCH, INCORPORATED AND SUBSIDIARY COMPANIES
CONSOLIDATED BALANCE SHEET, JUNE 30, 1952 AND 1951

	June 30	
ASSETS	1952	1951
CURRENT ASSETS:		
Cash	$ 12,863,907	$ 11,246,602
United States government securities....	549,750	898,600
Receivables, less reserves............	11,812,739	11,964,770
Revenue stamps..................	2,295,562	3,967,058
Inventories	22,542,888	22,731,849
Total current assets..............	$ 50,064,846	$ 50,808,879
MISCELLANEOUS NON-CURRENT ASSETS	$ 259,714	$ 322,600
TREASURY STOCK 25,000 shares in 1952 and 15,000 shares in 1951, at cost (15,000 shares reserved under an option agreement with an officer) ..	$ 598,375	$ 356,250
PROPERTY (Depreciated value):		
Plant and branch property...........	$ 68,431,563	$ 41,335,543
Construction in progress............	3,663,528	26,374,685
Real estate other than plant property....	619,989	1,015,236
Cooperage and drums..............	2,003,077	3,239,602
Net property..................	$ 74,718,157	$ 71,965,066
DEFERRED CHARGES..............	$ 1,917,082	$ 2,367,546
TOTAL	$127,558,174	$125,820,341

	June 30	
LIABILITIES	1952	1951
CURRENT LIABILITIES:		
Notes payable		$ 5,000,000
Accounts payable	$ 2,015,147	3,425,700
Accruals:		
Salaries and wages	2,083,551	1,098,711
Miscellaneous taxes and expenses	2,938,893	2,165,249
Dividends payable		1,121,250
Federal and state income taxes—Estimated (less tax notes $350,000 in 1952 and $3,641,000 in 1951)	10,318,198	8,261,434
Total current liabilities	$ 17,355,789	$ 21,072,344
NOTES PAYABLE, 2¾%, due serially 1954-1961	$ 15,000,000	$ 15,000,000
CAPITAL STOCK — Authorized and outstanding 4,500,000 shares of $4 each	$ 18,000,000	$ 18,000,000
SURPLUS— Earned	$ 77,202,385	$ 71,747,997
TOTAL	$127,558,174	$125,820,341

NOTE: Contractual obligations for equipment and construction amounted to $1,264,254 at June 30, 1952.

ANHEUSER-BUSCH, INCORPORATED AND SUBSIDIARY COMPANIES

SUMMARY OF CONSOLIDATED INCOME FOR THE

FIRST SIX MONTHS OF 1952 AND OF 1951

	Six Months Ended June 30	
	1952	1951
Net sales including beer taxes..........	$128,144,924	$109,924,705
Beer taxes.........................	29,769,474	25,015,016
Net sales.........................	$ 98,375,450	$ 84,909,689
Cost of sales, advertising, selling, general and administrative, research and development, and employees' retirement and group benefits expenses.............	84,639,465	71,756,638
Profit from operations................	$ 13,735,985	$ 13,153,051
Other income charges, net (1951 net income credits include $443,851 agent's adjustments to 1947-48-49 taxable income)	525,702	511,603
Income before provision for income taxes..	$ 13,210,283	$ 13,664,654
Per share.......................	2.95	3.05
Provision for income taxes (see note)....	7,661,964	7,045,496
Per share.......................	1.71	1.57
Net income......................	$ 5,548,319	$ 6,619,158
Ratio to net sales..................	5.6%	7.8%
Per share.......................	1.24	1.48
Dividends paid or declared............	2,237,500	3,371,250
Income reinvested in the business.......	$ 3,310,819	$ 3,247,908
Surplus, January 1st................	73,891,566	68,500,089
Surplus, June 30th..................	$ 77,202,385	$ 71,747,997
Provision for depreciation included in operations	$ 2,695,608	$ 2,240,371

NOTE: The income shown above is subject to adjustment of inventory values to the Life valuation method employed since the year 1941. The amount of this adjustment cannot be determined until the close of the year. The provision for 1952 estimated income tax shown is based on the effective rate under the 1951 revenue act calculated on the estimated income for the year 1952.

In the year of 1952, the Japanese peace treaty had been signed, but there was fighting in Korea and threats that there might be Communist aggression elsewhere. The nation was engaged in its greatest armament and defense program of peacetime. Taxes and labor and material costs had soared in dizzy spirals and there was much talk in the air of further inflation. Pessimism was part and parcel of business—but not with Anheuser-Busch. An organization that had been floored so often—but not flattened—doesn't scare easily.

Asked in the company's centennial year if he cared to make some profound pronouncement for posterity, Gus grinned broadly and said, "Not profound, just factual. You remember the old saying, 'The first hundred years are the hardest'? Well, from now on it should be a breeze. With the facilities we have, with the products we have, with the family we have and with the friends we have we would have to really struggle to lose out."

And, in the hundredth year, this was the roster of key men in The Family that were helping the company's fifth president, August A. Busch, Jr., to do the job—a whale of a job.

OFFICERS OF ANHEUSER-BUSCH, INC.

Name	Office
Eberhard Anheuser	Chairman of the Board
August A. Busch, Jr.	President
A. von Gontard	Vice-President
L. Busch Faust	Vice-President
John L. Wilson	Vice-President
R. W. Upshaw	Vice-President
F. H. Schwaiger	Vice-President
Adolphus B. Orthwein	Vice-President
Edwin Kalbfleish	Comptroller
K. Siebert	Secretary
Reid McCrum	Treasurer
C. E. Ehrhardt	Assistant Comptroller
J. E. Ritter	Assistant Secretary
E. T. Moberg	Assistant Treasurer

DIRECTORS OF ANHEUSER-BUSCH, INC.

Eberhard Anheuser
William S. Anheuser
August A. Busch, Jr.
David R. Calhoun, Jr.
Emmet T. Carter
L. Busch Faust
Horace C. Flanigan
A. von Gontard

Andrew W. Johnson
H. Norris Love
Percy J. Orthwein
Curt H. Reisinger
Ethan A. H. Shepley
John L. Wilson
Sam E. Woods

Eberhard Anheuser, grandson of the founder of Anheuser-Busch, was chairman of the Board of Directors, a position which he filled actively and ably after a brilliant career with the company. It was his function to preside at all meetings of the directors and to be an ex-officio member of all standing committees. In the absence of the president he performed all of the latter's duties. Other functions were to carry out all directives of the Board and of the Executive Committee and to perform the work of a vice-president as defined by the by-laws.

However, Ebie for years had had another position that no by-laws prescribed. He was the right-hand man to three presidents. August A., Sr., Adolphus III and Gus never made a major decision without consulting him. That represents quite a climb up the ladder for a kid of fifteen who did his first work for Anheuser-Busch during the school vacation months in summer.

After finishing his public school studies and attending Washington University, Ebie came to Anheuser-Busch on a permanent basis as a clerk. He worked in the busy City Department, which had charge of all Anheuser-Busch sales in St. Louis. Ebie soon demonstrated his talents as a salesman and diplomat, an ability that was to make him a trouble shooter in future years for any sales problem that arose anywhere in the country. Sometimes the solution of some particularly vexing problem would keep him on the scene for months.

His missions were not confined to important people. When a company salesman reported no progress with a certain retailer who was disgruntled, Ebie would visit the customer and talk things over with a couple of friendly bottles of Bud between them. Many a lifelong loyal friendship for the company resulted because the dealer could tell his patrons that he had a personal call "from Mr. Anheuser, of Anheuser-Busch."

In addition to his duties in the City Department, of which he became manager, Ebie was placed in charge of the Commercial Livestock Feed Department in 1919. This became a very profitable operation. Indeed, Anheuser-Busch, through acquisition of the European Heckscher Patent, did much of the pioneer work in converting the spent grains of brewing into feed for animals and poultry.

One of the toughest nuts that Ebie had to crack came when the company decided during prohibition to produce malt syrup. There were many competitive brands in the St. Louis market, but one in particular dominated the field. The makers of home-brew swore by this brand—had done so for several years. Budweiser Malt Syrup got off to a slow start in St. Louis, but Ebie and his sales force kept at it and kept at it until finally their product moved off of dealers' shelves at an inspiring pace.

When repeal brought back Budweiser beer, Ebie's City Department went to work with a will and soon had the famous beer back to its place of prestige in St. Louis. This does not mean that all of his activities were Anheuser-Busch activities. Through the years, Ebie had won a fine reputation for his work in civic affairs.

He was given much of the credit for having made the Liberty Loans of World War I a success in his native city. Also, he was active in the founding and maintenance of the Sunset Hills Country Club.

On Thursday, August 1, 1940, The Censor, a weekly magazine published in St. Louis, paid Ebie an unusual tribute. It published a portrait of him on its front cover and on an inside page said:

> As one watches the progress and growth of Anheuser-Busch, Inc., from year to year, one cannot help being impressed by the fact that not a little of this success is due to the enterprising ability of those men who are directing its destinies. One of those who has contributed his share to this success is Eberhard Anheuser, who, besides being privileged to carry on an honored name and family reputation, has proved that he himself is a worthy business executive in his own right.
>
> During the years that Anheuser has been associated with the Anheuser-Busch brewery he has molded for himself a highly successful business career, which has been partially responsible for his being recognized as one of the outstanding representative citizens of St. Louis.

After tracing the origin of the company and explaining that the grandsons were carrying on its business, the article continued:

> In considering the tremendous increase that has been made in recent years in the volume of sales of Budweiser beer and other Anheuser-Busch products one can appreciate the fine work that Anheuser has done as head of the sales department and why his services are considered invaluable and indispensable to the success of the brewery.
>
> He has given generously of his time and his effort in the work that is his and has even devoted himself at other times to various civic and charitable causes, which have all gone in the direction of establishing him firmly in the estimation of the people of this city.
>
> One might also say that Anheuser's social life is one that may be attributed a success, which is fully understandable when one realizes that he is capably assisted in his social efforts by the charming and capable Mrs. Anheuser. From every standpoint it must be agreed that his success in life is a substantial one and one which demonstrates fully his right to carry on the fine name and reputation of the Anheuser family. Indeed, St. Louis could well afford to have more men of the outstanding and worthwhile ability of Eberhard Anheuser.

To Ebie's business and social reputation must be added his reputation as a sportsman. For many years he was a breeder of fine hunting dogs and did much to further the propagation of quail. He was for long a member of the Missouri Conservation Commission. His expert game of golf was something that the years might have slowed up but could not dim.

Another grandson of Eberhard Anheuser to serve the company with perception and perseverance was Ebie's cousin, W. Fred Anheuser. He entered the company in 1897 and made his work so varied that he was familiar with just about every phase of the business. Fred knew the brewing process backward and forward, so much so that, with the help of the laboratory staff, he helped to prepare literature to be given the many tourists who visited the huge plant and wanted a sort of prompt book to take home with them to help in explaining to friends what they had seen in St. Louis.

Dear Ebe -

     I know of no better place to pay the
tribute that is in my heart for you than in the
History of Anheuser-Busch.

     I never knew your good grandfather and
my great grandfather, Eberhard Anheuser, but from
all I have heard through the years, we all owe him
our thanks and gratitude for the fine and memorable
part he played in the establishment of the business,
whose 100th Anniversary we are now celebrating.

     As to your good self, Ebe, I want to pay
you the well deserved compliment you have so justly
earned for your never-failing and constant loyalty
to the business that is so close to both our hearts.

     I value my long association with you, not
only as a dependable business associate, but as a
warm personal friend.

Gussie.

WHAT GUSSIE THINKS OF EBE

In 1914, Fred was elected fifth vice-president, in 1918 fourth, in 1934 third and in 1946 second vice-president. In the next year, the company adopted new by-laws which established the custom of identifying vice-presidents' rank by seniority instead of number. Since Fred was second in years served he thus became the second vice-president under the new system. It was in that capacity that he was serving when he died in December, 1948.

Adalbert von Gontard, 52, a grandson of Adolphus Busch, was director of sales and advertising for all departments of Anheuser-Busch. In addition, he was vice-president, a member of the Board of Directors and director of production for the Yeast, Malt and Corn Products Division.

Adie joined Anheuser-Busch well schooled for the positions he was to occupy successively. Born July 20, 1900, in Germany, he was graduated from the high school at Kathrineum in Lubeck. From 1919 until 1923, he attended the Institute of Technology at Karlsruhe, Baden, and there received his master's degree in engineering. He returned to the Institute in 1938 and prepared himself for a Ph.D. degree in engineering.

In February, 1923, Adie came to America and started his career in November, 1923, as assistant technical director. In 1926 he was made chief engineer and remained in that position until 1947 when he was made director of sales and production of the Yeast, Malt, and Corn Products Division.

Adie's new position as chief engineer in 1926 was to prove no sinecure as he well knew when he took it. The bold venture of August A., Sr., into the bakers' yeast business, began showing great promise in the next year, 1927, after having had a very shaky beginning. The president ordered a yeast plant of large proportions built. From the mass of plans, specifications and estimates a final draft emerged and each approved sheet bore a signature that was to become a sort of trademark of the Engineering Department—"A. von Gontard."

So well did this plant function and so fast was its product sold that in the depression year of 1932 a $2,000,000 yeast plant was erected at Old Bridge, New Jersey, under the supervision of A. von Gontard.

FRED ANHEUSER—Long identified with Anheuser-Busch, Inc. as a vice-president and director. His responsibilities included management of the extensive real estate holdings of the company.

In the twenty-one years in which he served as chief engineer, A. von Gontard was responsible for vast changes and tremendous improvements in the whole Anheuser-Busch plant.

Steam utilities were revamped on a huge scale. A. von Gontard introduced pulverized coal in the interest of economy and increased efficiency. In 1930, three huge boilers were installed to replace fourteen small, nearly obsolete units. In 1934, with Budweiser again in production, a fourth mammoth boiler was installed. In 1938-39, when St. Louis was setting the pace for other cities in smoke elimination, mechanical ash collectors were put to work. In 1947, a fifth big boiler was put into operation, making the plant's steam utilities one of the biggest operations of its kind anywhere.

The refrigeration utilities also got an A. von Gontard going-over. In 1931, a 250-ton motor-driven ammonia compressor replaced a 165-ton steam-driven unit. In the following years, one 350-ton, three 500-ton, one 600-ton, one 900-ton and one 1,400-ton compressors were installed. Tons, in this instance, means not weight but refrigeration output.

New ice plants on Ninth Street and Seventh Street were built in 1931 and 1940 respectively, so that the obsolete establishment on Second Street could be abandoned.

The water purification plant was revamped in 1939 with the installation of new pumping and filtration equipment. Its capacity was stepped up to seven million gallons a day, enough water to meet the normal demands of a city of 125,000 persons.

Electrical facilities, too, were improved and greatly expanded during the A. von Gontard regime. In 1930, diesel generators were abandoned for two 500-kilowatt motor-generator sets. A similar unit of 400-kilowatt capacity replaced old steam-driven generators. Between 1930 and 1948, five immense turbo-generators revolutionized the plant's facilities for current output.

While all of these A. von Gontard changes were being effected, the demand for Budweiser was increasing by leaps and bounds. The need for new cellars

ADALBERT VON GONTARD—A grandson of Adolphus Busch, who in the midst of a brilliant career as vice-president in charge of engineering, elected to try his hand at salesmanship with such success that he was placed in charge of all sales of all divisions.

became pressing. Adie supervised the construction of new stock houses containing much equipment built to the company's own design. The first new cellar was a paragon of efficiency and beauty and, to the brewing industry, became a showplace. It was named the Junior Cellar in honor of Adie's cousin, Gus. When a second building was completed the honor was reversed and the structure was named the von Gontard Cellar.

The following telegram from Adolphus Busch III is self-explanatory:

Thanks for your message advising that beer went into the new cellar at 9:15 this morning. Naturally, was very happy to receive this good news and want to extend my heartiest compliments to you and all who had a part in this outstanding accomplishment on the splendid and able job that was made of bringing this new cellar to completion at this particular time when it is so vitally important to our operations. Again my sincere compliments and congratulations.

The Third followed this two days later on July 18, 1941, with this letter:

There is no doubt that you and all the members of your department have done a fine job on the new cellar and that it was finished and filled at a time when we needed it badly is a tribute to your and their conscientious performance of duty, which I am happy to acknowledge and compliment. Under all the circumstances I feel that this new cellar should and appropriately be known as the von Gontard cellar and you have my full approval to so designate it.

I know that we are going to be as proud of this cellar as we are of all its predecessors and that it is destined to be another strong link in our plant facilities. Again my congratulations on a job well done.

In the midst of these activities, A. von Gontard managed to launch the starch business, which was destined to become a highly profitable enterprise, and to plan and install the necessary facilities.

In April, 1951, he was made director of sales and advertising of the entire Anheuser-Busch organization and continued as director of production of the Yeast, Malt and Corn Products Division. Adie was elected to the Board of Directors in January, 1933, and elected vice-president in December, 1934.

In October, 1942, he entered the United States Navy as a lieutenant and was on active duty until August, 1944. In May, 1950, he was commissioned a lieutenant commander in the Naval Reserve. In August, 1951, he was honorably discharged.

Adie, after World War II, organized the Junior Executives Training Program. Those key men chosen to be junior executives attended the school for two years and fifteen weeks. It was a school recognized and accredited by the federal government and brought Adie much praise.

Adie was married to Miss Susanne Schilling von Canstatt, of Karlsruhe, at the home of Mrs. Edmee Greenough, his aunt, in New York on July 31, 1924. The von Gontards had three children: Adalbert, Jr., now associated with the Manufacturers Trust Company, New York, Paul Victor, Assistant Brewmaster, Anheuser-Busch, and Clara Hazel.

———

Leicester Busch Faust, grandson of Adolphus, was vice-president in charge of purchases in the company's centennial year. He was the son of Edward A. Faust and Anna Busch Faust.

Leicester was born in St. Louis in 1897. He attended Smith Academy in his native city and then the Lake Placid School in New York. Later he went to Yale, after which came a hitch in the Army during World War I.

In 1918 he began his business training in his father's boat building company. In 1935, he joined Anheuser-Busch and went to work in the Grain Department, whose traditional responsibility it was to see to it that Budweiser beer got the best barley that premium prices could buy. In this department, too, purchases of rice for brewing and corn for the company's corn products were consummated.

Leicester's father, Edward, was a son of the famed restaurateur, Tony Faust. It will be remembered that Adolphus was at first a patron of the historic restaurant and later Tony's fast friend. When Edward, who had been well

LEICESTER BUSCH FAUST—Vice-president in charge of purchases of Anheuser-Busch, Inc. He started his career with the company in the Grain Department.

trained in his father's business, sought the hand of Anna Busch, Adolphus gave his blessing happily.

Adolphus keenly evaluated Edward's capacities and induced him to join Anheuser-Busch, where the promise of the future had a larger potential.

It was not long before Edward became a vice-president in charge of all grain and raw material purchases. He so conducted himself that Adolphus stipulated in his will that, in the event of August A., Sr., dying prematurely, Edward was to assume charge of the brewery and other Busch activities.

When Adolphus decided to build the Adolphus Hotel in Dallas, he chose Edward to superintend all incident details.

August A., Sr., was with his father when the latter died in Europe in 1913. To Edward fell the great task of meeting with the press, dignitaries planning to pay homage and others involved in legal matters or concerned with the funeral.

In 1916, Edward was nearing the half-century mark in age and could give a very good account of his stewardship for Anheuser-Busch. He always had loved boating. Reluctantly, he severed his connection with the brewery staff to become affiliated with the St. Louis Boat and Engineering Company. He remained in this happy atmosphere until his retirement and ultimately his death in 1936 when he was sixty-seven years old.

Always interested in civic progress, he had been a member of the Board of Directors of the St. Louis Art Museum and of the St. Louis Symphony Society.

Adolphus Busch Orthwein, great-grandson of Adolphus, was made a vice-president on August 14, 1951, being placed in charge of the company's Engineering Department, Industrial Engineering Department, Material Control Department, the Newark Brewery, Plant Protection and Sanitation and the Beer Packaging and Shipping Department in St. Louis.

Dolph's affiliation with Anheuser-Busch began in the traditional way—at the bottom. That was in March, 1946, when, after attending a training course, he took a job as unloading foreman in the bottle shop basement. After working through various foremen's jobs, he was made director of foremen's training.

Prior to joining Anheuser-Busch, Dolph got his business feet wet in the Industrial Sales Department of the Shell Oil Company. When war clouds began their overcast, he joined the Navy, being commissioned an ensign on June 22, 1941. After four years of active duty, he was detached from active service as a lieutenant commander and placed in the Naval Reserve.

Back in civilian life and with his early indoctrination as foreman behind him, Dolph's ascendancy toward a key position in management was rapid. He became assistant to the manager of the Beer Packaging and Shipping Department, then a member of the staff of the vice-president in charge of the Brewery Division and, successively, assistant production manager and production manager in charge of beer packaging and shipping. And finally came the vice-presidency and its multilateral jobs.

Another great-grandson of Adolphus with a varied career both before joining the company and while in its service was Walter Chalmers Reisinger, son of Walter Busch Reisinger. "Bud" Reisinger was born in New York and reared in Greenwich, Connecticut. His schooling followed the pattern of so many youths of his generation—study in Greenwich Country Day, Fessenden in Massachusetts, Taft in Connecticut and, finally, because of the war threat, the Roosevelt Aviation School at Roslyn, New York.

Young Reisinger joined the Army Air Force, Air Transport Command, and served it for thirty months, with ten of them being duty in the Azores. He was given his honorable discharge in February, 1946, and applied for a job with Anheuser-Busch.

Two years were spent in the Junior Executives Training Program, which encompassed study of all phases and operations of the three divisions of the company—Brewery, Yeast, Malt and Corn Products, and Refrigerated Cabinet. The course culminated in sales training in the field.

Thereafter, Bud Reisinger was a salesman for two years in the Westbury, New York, and St. Louis branches. After service in the Sales Promotion Department in St. Louis, he was appointed assistant advertising manager.

Another great-grandson in the service of Anheuser-Busch was Paul Victor von Gontard, Assistant Brewmaster and son of Adalbert von Gontard. Born in St. Louis on August 2, 1926, Paul attended the Rossman and Maryland Schools and then spent eight years at the St. Louis Country Day School, where he received a letter for football, baseball and soccer.

He enlisted in the Navy during World War II and served for two years, part of the time as a petty officer on an LSM of the Seventh Fleet Amphibious Force.

Paul began work for Anheuser-Busch in 1946 as a plant inspector. Naturally, this sort of job took him around the property a lot and led to his decision to become a brewmaster. So, in 1949, he studied at the Seibel Institute of Technology with all of the emphasis on its course in brewing. Two years later, he became assistant to the brewmaster, Frank H. Schwaiger. He was a member of the Master Brewers' Association of America.

Still another great-grandson to see a good part of the world before being able to follow in the footsteps of his forebears was John Flanigan, son of Mr. and Mrs. Horace C. Flanigan, of New York.

After attending Portsmouth Priority School in Rhode Island, John went to the Massachusetts Institute of Technology in 1940 and subsequently to Princeton, which he left in 1942 to join the Army. He spent the remaining years of the war in the United States, then journeyed to Tokyo as an aid to Joseph Keenan, Chief Prosecutor for War Crimes Trials in the Far East.

John was discharged with the rank of first lieutenant in the Army Air Corps in 1946. Next year he went to work in the Sales and Purchasing Departments of Anheuser-Busch. The Sales Department was his final choice and he served it with diligence and distinction, so much so that in 1952 he had become regional manager of the Pacific Coast and Western Area.

Frank H. Schwaiger, vice-president and chief brewmaster in 1952, had brought to Anheuser-Busch in April, 1933, technical skill enriched with a colorful background in Europe.

Frank was born June 13, 1908, in Freising, Bavaria, Germany. He entered the malting and brewing business after completing a business and high school education in the spring of 1924. He served his apprenticeship in his father's malt house in Freising, in the Hacky Brewery, Freising, and in the Versuchs Und Lehr Brewery, Weihenstephan, Germany.

Upon completing his apprenticeship, he worked as a journeyman, a brewer and maltster in the Hofbrauhaus, Munich, Citicens Brewery, Pilsen, Czechoslovakia, and the Union Brewery, Dortmund, Germany. He matriculated in the autumn of 1927 at the College of Agriculture and Brewing, Weihenstephan.

Frank Schwaiger was graduated in 1929 as a brewmaster and in 1930 as a brewery engineer. During intermissions at school, he took temporary positions in breweries in Dresden, Saalfeld, Bayreuth and Freising, Germany, as either chemist or assistant brewmaster.

He was employed at the Karlsberg Brewery, Homburg, in the Saar, as assistant brewmaster and head of laboratory, from the time of his graduation in 1930 until the spring of 1933.

Seeing the trend in the United States away from prohibition, he applied for a position with Anheuser-Busch shortly before repeal. His experience and qualifications made it a certainty that Anheuser-Busch would welcome him into "the family," and he came to work as brewmaster and assistant to the technical director, Dr. Gull, in April, 1933. In 1938, he became a citizen of the United States. Since 1939, Frank has been head brewmaster in charge of beer, malt and malt syrup wort production for Anheuser-Busch. He was elected an officer of the company on March 12, 1947, and became a vice-president on June 14, 1950. Since February, 1952, he has been in charge of the newly created Brewing Research Department.

With the expansion of Anheuser-Busch business as well as facilities, Gus felt the need of additional personnel in management. He invited John L. Wilson, president of the St. Louis Public Service Company, the transportation utility of the city, to become a member of "the family." John accepted and on May 24,

1951, he was elected vice-president and financial officer and also a member of the Board of Directors of Anheuser-Busch.

A well-rounded-out career gave John Wilson a certain fitness for his new post. After attending Wittenberg College, Ohio, he became a salesman for the Mack Truck Company, an experience which was to lead him into the transportation field. He joined the St. Louis utility in 1944 as president. Under his administration, the system was completely modernized, new streamlined busses and trolley cars purchased, shops and offices remodeled extensively and the bonded indebtedness of the corporation completely retired.

In his new post with Anheuser-Busch, John Wilson was given jurisdiction over the Treasury Department, the Industrial Relations Division, Research Department, Quality Control Division and Traffic Department. He headed the Plant Committee and served on the Salary, General Administrative and Contributions Committee.

Thus ends the narrative of 100 years of Anheuser-Busch.

And yet it doesn't end.

The following chapters are unrelated one to another and, therefore, lacking in continuity. They are included because they contain a wealth of information without which this chronicle would be incomplete.

Chapter XX

WHAT IS THIS THING
CALLED BUDWEISER?

WHEN A PRODUCT has such a personality that it becomes the pivotal factor in building an industrial empire and shapes the future and fortunes of many men, that personality is deserving of close scrutiny.

Just what was there about this new Budweiser beer of 1876 that destined it never to see a year when supply could meet demand?

Well, for one thing, Budweiser had some very distinguished ancestors. In the twelve years before, Adolphus Busch had produced a number of types and brands of beer. That they were of increasingly good quality is shown by rocketing sales, as noted in an earlier chapter. These years served as a prep school for Adolphus and the staff that he gathered about him. A staff of men can profit immensely from twelve years of trial and error.

Adolphus knew in 1876 that he and his business family were well schooled and ready for the venture he had dreamed of—making the finest beer, in America surely and perhaps in the world.

How he collaborated with Carl Conrad, advisor and friend until parted by death, has been told. They agreed that the start would be made with the costliest ingredients available—barley malt from the finest grain, hops from the Saaz district of old Bohemia (now a part of Czecho-Slovakia).

Adolphus introduced two-row barley from Europe and persuaded American farmers to cultivate it.

Adolphus's decision in later years to rely upon rice as a supplementary ingredient had much to do with the fame of Budweiser. Other brewers had begun to use corn grits as a source of extra starch to compensate for the high protein content of American barley. Rice, as an adjunct, produces a finer, more distinctive flavor in beer than corn grits can. Moreover, the oil content of rice usually is less than that of corn grits and the oil in the rice is less apt to turn rancid.

The next step was to standardize the various phases of the malting, brewing and lagering techniques. The small breweries of the era long had operated on a happy-go-lucky hit-or-miss basis. Generally favorable rather than optimum conditions were the rule. The part that even minor temperature fluctuations played in affecting the character of beer was not fully comprehended.

Standard procedure was a must for Budweiser. Each purchase of ingredients had to match the last. There was no deviation from barley cleaning methods, steeping, sprouting or kilning. Proportions were established and adhered to. Primary fermentation proceeded under ideal conditions and lagering (ageing) was long and complete.

Budweiser quickly acquired a reputation for its distinctive taste and the uniformity of its quality. Consumers, by constantly upping the sales, may have felt that Budweiser was just about perfect, but Adolphus was constantly eager to improve his product, while keeping the basic identity which brought it popularity, and he was equally eager to improve his facilities until they were second to none.

The hundredth anniversary of the Anheuser-Busch brewery coincides with the end of the hundred years in which the most rapid advance in science and technology has been made in the history of mankind. Enzyme chemistry and micro-biology explained many problems in brewing and fermenting that existed in the days when the first brew was made on the site of what was to become the Anheuser-Busch brewery.

In his search for ways to advance on the technological front in brewing, Adolphus found in Bohemia the yeasts he wanted and successfully brought the cultures to St. Louis.

Adolphus was one of the first brewers to test out an ammonia compressor for producing mechanical refrigeration. This new development in refrigeration and making artificial ice was first tried out in this country in a New Orleans brewery in 1869. Very shortly after that Adolphus purchased from a German firm a small ammonia compressor which was soon replaced with larger units.

(Incidentally, this small compressor was purchased from Adolphus by another brewer and was still in service in a small brewery in Central America when last heard of in 1950.)

The development of mechanical refrigeration has done more perhaps than any other modern invention to make large scale brewing a reality. The output of beer by Anheuser-Busch increased tenfold during the first ten years after installing the first refrigeration machine.

Another discovery of world wide importance a few years after the refrigeration machine had tremendous importance in the shipping, storage and merchandising of beer. It was Louis Pasteur's proof that perishable products could be preserved by means of applying heat after filling and sealing the container. Several publications in the eighties gave Anheuser-Busch credit for having been the first American brewers to pasteurize beer successfully.

In the nineties, another invention important to brewing made its appearance. It was a closing device known later as the "Golden Gate" valve for beer barrels. Adolphus immediately started tests with this valve and as soon as he was convinced of its merits he had all the cooperage owned by the brewery equipped with it. The valve was more costly than other closure devices, but it was so superior in point of protection, both for beer and for the empty package, that it has remained standard equipment to this day.

The endless quest for perfection soon resulted in the Anheuser-Busch brewery becoming a showplace and it was necessary to have a corps of guides to conduct visitors through the plant. Literally millions of persons have toured the brewery since the practice was begun.

As each year saw the demand for Budweiser reach fabulously higher levels, Adolphus realized that his brewery was going to be a behemoth and the finest of brewing skill that he could obtain would be cheap at nearly any price. He canvassed the best breweries of England, Germany, Bohemia, Holland, Denmark and Switzerland and, from the latter, obtained Dr. Rudolph Gull.

Dr. Gull and his new employer quickly made the happy discovery that they saw eye-to-eye. Soon after his arrival in 1894, the Swiss scientist was firmly entrenched as Budweiser's technical boss. To his skill in brewing was added the faculty of transforming relatively minute operations into gigantic mass operations—and always under strict quality control.

Early records indicate that Anheuser-Busch laid claim to the distinction of having had the first brewery laboratory. In any event, as the brewery grew larger to meet the enlarging demand for Budweiser, laboratory substations began to appear in different departments to make sure that there never was any deviation from Budweiser beer quality.

In 1933, the ageing brewmaster, Dr. Gull, told management that he wanted a competent man to be trained as his successor and the result was that Anheuser-Busch obtained the services of Frank Schwaiger, who, in 1939 became head brewmaster and in 1950 was made a vice-president.

Just how should Budweiser be described?

In the words of Frank Schwaiger, Budweiser has taste appeal without an off-taste, without a sour or bitter aftertaste—just good taste—clean, clear and crisp. Budweiser has something for the eye, too. It is noted throughout the industry for its sparkling appearance and its excellent white foam. In addressing the company's annual sales convention in January, 1952, Frank made the statement that Budweiser was "aged in wood" but hastened to explain that this meant neither wooden vats nor wooden kegs. Wooden vats, because of their porosity and tendency to shrink and their sap content, are not conducive to good tasting beer. When vats were used in past years, they always were coated with some sort of lining.

"Aged in wood" meant a step used in the secondary fermentation by Anheuser-Busch, a step formerly used by other brewers but discarded as too expensive and time consuming. In the Budweiser process, sterilized neutral beechwood chips are placed in pressure-tight glass- or ebon-lined tanks. The chips provide a large neutral porous surface area to act as a clarifying and ripening agent. The yeast is permitted to settle on these wooden shavings in thousands of thin layers and work from them instead of all that yeast forming a heavy sludge at the bottom of the tank. This placement of the yeast and the ability of the porous wood to attract haze-forming material results in naturally matured and clarified beer that has been given plenty of time.

Anheuser-Busch did not reduce the specific gravity or strength of Budweiser at any time despite the difficulty in World War II years of getting raw materials. The company brewed Budweiser from the traditional malt, rice, hops, water and yeast only. At all times the traditional ageing time was maintained.

Management was insistent that the beer be not diluted or its quality tampered with in any respect. Such dilution was practiced by some brewers. These brewers, unable to get as much barley malt as they needed, used substitutes such as cassava, tapioca and molasses.

Obtaining good hops was a major problem. The quantity of domestic hops was restricted through manpower shortages and other factors. European imports were shut off. Long before this hops crisis, the brewmaster and his staff made it their business to try every type of domestic hops from every district. They made many test brews to determine the best blending and processing and to establish the most suitable quantity for Budweiser. They worked closely with leading hops producers to follow up in the growing and curing end of the hops business, so that they might have the most desirable types cultivated or increased as quickly as possible.

Another accomplishment resulted from the problem presented by malt. This basic ingredient in brewing is derived from barley. The brewmaster and his staff had made the barley grain the outstanding subject of their tests ever since repeal. Long before the war emergency, they had developed successfully a means to use a considerable amount of a Western barley type, which produced higher extract yields than the ordinary types. By increasing the percentage of the high extract type during the emergency, they got more malt extract out of the allotted poundage of malt than would have been possible with the standard type.

Rice was exempt from rationing, but the possibility that it might be rationed presented another problem. If rice had been rationed, it would have been necessary to use another ingredient. The most likely choice would have been corn grits, although from the days of Adolphus Busch on, the thought of using corn grits in Budweiser was always abhorrent to management. If rice were rationed, using corn grits to stay in business obviously would have been imperative. Then, too, there was the possibility that corn might be rationed.

In this situation, a first, second and even third alternative would have to be obtained. The technical staff made an exhaustive study of the whole field of possible adjuncts. Since "the proof of the pudding is in the eating," they had to do a lot of sampling from the tests made and, as Frank Schwaiger put it, "this wasn't always fun."

Still another possibility had to be faced. This was that a dilute brew might become mandatory through government directive. As a consequence, exhaustive small scale and large scale tests were made to arrive at a type of yeast for

and its treatment in dilute brews. Naturally, the yeast would have to be especially treated and re-evaluated in order to protect the flavor of such a dilute brew.

Fortunately, none of these expediences became necessary. Anheuser-Busch was able to produce 3,492,343 barrels of beer in 1942 and comparable production was maintained in the following years through 1946. At no time, however, was there enough Budweiser to meet the demand.

The history of lager beer goes back about two hundred years when bottom fermenting types of yeast began to replace the top fermenting kind in the brewing of beer. This new kind, or as it became known, Bavarian beer, produced during the cold weather months could be stored up to early summer in deep caves without artificial refrigeration. It was much preferred by consumers to the beer produced during summer and called "summer beer" or "young beer." This summer beer had to be consumed without a prolonged ageing period in order to keep it from spoiling.

The public demand for aged or lager beer the year 'round was insistent, and the introduction of mechanical refrigeration in breweries made fulfillment of this demand gradually possible.

In addressing the 1948 general sales convention of Anheuser-Busch, Frank Schwaiger answered the question, "What are the advantages of a lager beer system?" with these words:

1. It provides possibility of having a ready stock of beer on hand for use during peak demand.

2. It allows time for natural clarification of beer.

3. A prolonged moderate secondary or after-fermentation at cold temperature will produce a finer and richer flavor due to formation of esters and so-called "higher alcohols." Due to expulsion of raw volatiles, reduction of fermentable matter to proper degree and other changes of certain organic matters as time goes on, the taste and the quality are increased.

4. This period allows for natural super-saturation of beer with the carbon dioxide produced during the cold, slow after-fermentation.

In order to get the fullest possible advantages out of our lagering period, Anheuser-Busch still follows the time honored, but costly, practice to conduct this secondary fermentation in the presence of wood chips or wood shavings. These shavings offer a tremendous surface to the beer in ageing, thereby stimulating the desired actions. I agree with the majority of brewers that as far as point 1.,—availability of stock, is concerned—modern equipment in the brewhouse and up-to-date planning to a certain extent eliminate the original advantage. I agree with them on point 2.,—that is clarification—that modern filtration methods will solve the problem fairly well without the need of prolonged storage for clarification.

On points 3. and 4.—that is the necessity of prolonged lager or storage from the standpoint of taste, quality and natural super-saturation with carbon dioxide—we are at odds with most brewers in this country. Maybe the words "at odds" are not exactly right; I believe that the more capable and conscientious brewers are in agreement with us, anyway deep down in their hearts. Their excuses for deviation from the true principles of lager beer production can be summed up as follows:

a.) Storage capacity is the most expensive item in a brewery; that is, for a given investment the output is low, if you age properly.

b.) The lager process requires a rather intricate knowledge and is quite a bit of work.

c.) The opinion,—"Oh well, most people can't tell the difference anyway."

At the company's general sales convention in 1950, Mr. Schwaiger cited some facts that prove the high quality of Budweiser year in and year out, as follows:

Approximately 2,200,000 bushels of the 1949 crop of choicest Western premium barley were purchased against tough competition. The quantity purchased was close to 50 per cent of the best brewing barley available in America.

Anheuser-Busch bought more than 2,600,000 pounds of the choicest European hops of the 1949 crop—the cost of which was double that of domestic hops. Total imports of the 1949 crop of European hops into the United States were between five and six million pounds. In other words, the company bought about fifty per cent of the best foreign hops available in America. These, blended with the small amounts of the finest domestic hops, imparted the rich, mild hops aroma and snappy taste found only in Anheuser-Busch beer.

After Repeal, Anheuser-Busch, for a number of years, did all its own malting as it had done before prohibition. However, the vast expansion program made it necessary to buy a good quantity of this commodity from commercial malt houses. In the past, these maltsters made malt as they thought it should be made for the brewer. This was changed due to closer cooperation between the maltsters and Anheuser-Busch, through the latter's demand for special barley types, grades and flavors of malt.

We maintain our nine principal processing steps—against the five normally employed by ordinary brewers—after the brew leaves the brew-house. This means that our brew is transferred nine times under controlled conditions, such as air elimination, decanting, and so on. If we ship 20,000 barrels of beer per day during summer, we have to move nine times 20,000 or 180,000 barrels of beer per day under exacting schedules.

In regular production, all of our beer is now fermented in new tanks of our own design. We are the sole owners of the patents involved. One of our licensees now advertises this as the exclusive "de-bitterizing" process.

The aged and naturally clarified beer is filtered through pads of pure cotton fibre to obtain the high brilliance of Budweiser. At our suggestion, a new automatic press has been designed to shape these filter pads. Thus, we expect to produce a great improvement in the uniformity of structure of the filter pads, resulting in better filtration of the beer.

During the last two years, all of the bottling equipment has been replaced with more efficient and larger units, which give better results. After being capped, the bottles move through pasteurizers of our own design and then to the latest type labeling equipment. All parts of the packaging are constantly under test, and we continue our investigations to see where additional improvements can be made. This includes work on standardizing the type and color of the bottle glass, as well as improvements on labels, crowns, cartons and inspection of bottles.

In a 1951 report, the Anheuser-Busch technical staff emphasized the following ten points regarding the superiority of Budweiser:

1. *Barley:*

   We brew with a high percentage of the Western two-row barley malt because it makes for a milder and more pleasant beer. Western two-row barley malt is considerably more expensive than the six-row Midwest barley malt, which is the standard in this country.

2. *Malting:*

   Make much of our own malt. Being maltsters as well as brewers, we are in a position to know exactly what we want when we buy malt.

3. *Rice:*

   As stated on our label, Budweiser Lager Beer is brewed with choicest hops, rice and best barley malt; no corn products, milo maize, manioc, syrups or sugar, etc., are added to the brewing of Budweiser. It never has a syrupy character or a bitter or acid after-taste. In a side-by-side comparison against other beer, you will like Budweiser because of its clean and pleasant odor and taste. You also will enjoy its unsurpassed quality of being most agreeable.

4. *Hops:*

   We are by far the largest purchasers of Central European hops, which are the mildest and highest priced in the world.

5. *Equipment:*

   In every undertaking we strive for perfection. No piece of equipment, process or material can ever be too good. Much of it is of our own design and of highest quality. Not a piece of iron in contact with wort or beer anywhere. Copper and stainless steel in Brew House and Wort Cooling Tower; glass-lined or Ebon-lined tanks in fermenting and lagering cellars.

6. *Brewing Process:*

   Anheuser-Busch are the owners and patentees of a process to cool and prepare the wort for fermentation. We are also the owners and patentees of a special fermentation process. (This is sometimes called a "de-bitterizing" process.) This puts us in the position to uniformly produce a pleasantly mild, tasty, true lager beer of fine hop character. Instead of using the "quick" method of pumping-in carbon dioxide gas, we conduct a second fermentation under pressure, known as Krausening, which naturally supersaturates the beer with carbon dioxide. This is the lager beer process which is similar to the method for producing fine champagne.

7. *Temperature, Pressure and Sanitation:*

Temperatures and pressures are accurately and definitely controlled. Every piece of equipment and the buildings are designed for ease of cleaning and maintained in the most sanitary manner. Cleanliness is watched every minute of the day.

8. *Air Elimination:*

Air elimination by specially designed equipment, constantly controlled, from all bottles and cans of Budweiser.

9. *Stainless Cooperage:*

All our cooperage is manufactured exclusively of the finest stainless steel. These half-barrels are the finest obtainable and much higher in price than any other type of cooperage. They do not require pitching. They are thoroughly washed and sterilized before filling.

10. *Lager Valves:*

All our cooperage is equipped exclusively with the ever-sealed lager valves. Our barrels are never open in the trade. They are always sealed when returned to us.

Chapter XXI

MICHELOB, A FINE

BEER BY ANHEUSER-BUSCH

HAVING PERFECTED the world's finest bottled beer, Anheuser-Busch decided in the year 1896 to produce an unusual draught beer. The word "unusual" is used advisedly. Budweiser beer on draught was, of course, highly esteemed and tremendously popular. It was brewed and lagered in such a way that the trade could dispense it without too elaborate indoctrination in its proper handling.

The new draught beer was to be a more delicate beer in the sense that it was intended not only for connoisseurs, but actually had to be dispensed by connoisseurs, who were willing to go to extreme pains to maintain its very exquisite aroma and superb taste.

Michelob was an all-malt beer. To put it another way, the barley malt was very carefully chosen for its protein-to-carbohydrate ratio so that it was not necessary to add a supplemental carbohydrate such as rice. Moreover, the hops were entirely of the imported variety, giving the beer a flavor that captivated people capable of judging an unusual brew.

286

The nature of Michelob was such that it could not be bottled because pasteurization would work to the disadvantage of its elusive fragrance and taste. The laboratory worked for years on the problem of bottling Michelob, but by the centennial year had been unable to come up with a satisfactory solution.

Michelob in barrels was released only to carefully screened retail outlets. It was much in demand in exclusive clubs, restaurants and taverns of the better sort. No outlet was permitted to have Michelob until those involved with the dispensing of it had been given a special training course by brewery representatives.

Michelob was never heavily supported by advertising. In fact, point-of-sale signs, both illuminated and unilluminated, were virtually the only advertising effort behind the product. This draught beer was of such character that it could depend upon word of mouth advertising to keep its popularity sustained.

Anheuser-Busch never intended that this should be a mass production beer. The brewing process was such that it could not lend itself to very great mass production. Its sole purpose was to be one of the finest draught beers known in the world and thus add to the company's prestige.

In 1951 the total production of Michelob was 145,336 barrels.

Chapter XXII

AIDING MEDICAL SCIENCE

AND NUTRITION

IT IS A STRANGE and even wondrous thing that in its fight for survival with yeast, Anheuser-Busch followed a path that was to help many a human being in his own fight for survival from disease. The people who once had been brewers and, because they were brewers were fermentologists, too, found themselves through their vast research suddenly and closely allied with the pharmaceutical industry and subsequently the science of nutrition.

Anheuser-Busch interested itself in the medication potentials of yeast in 1927 and in the years that followed added chapter after chapter to its success story. By 1951, it had attained such stature that it was mentioned prominently in an article which created a national sensation when it was published in the September 1 issue of Collier's Magazine.

The article was entitled, "Has Science Found the Spark of Life" and was written by John Lear. It described the work of scientists, whose conclusions were that life could not exist without a mysterious substance known as adeno-

288

sine-5-triphosphate, commonly called ATP. Experiments tended to indicate conclusively that when properly administered, ATP could be used not only to combat disease but actually to prolong life and increase the usefulness of human faculties.

The "mother" of ATP is adenylic acid, found in muscle tissue and in certain types of yeast. If a person's supply of ATP is reduced and if adenylic acid is injected into living muscle, then the muscle will add footloose phosphorus to it and pass it along to the blood supply as ATP.

The article mentioned that the demand for more ATP was snowballing and that Anheuser-Busch was one of the scientific groups that had been asked to participate in the yeast research essential to furthering the program.

Not bad recognition for a company whose competitors were amused when its president announced, "We are in the yeast business to stay."

Anheuser-Busch's entry into this field of science was not the result of an accident, but the result of being alert. In 1928, a Swiss-born chemist named James D. Veron was employed by the company as a bakery service man and salesman. He visited bakers throughout the country, offering technical advice on how to improve their products.

Veron was conversant with the fact that Europeans had discovered the nutritional value of dried yeast and had put the discovery to work. He expressed surprise to Homer Ziegler, vice-president in charge of yeast sales, that no American manufacturer in general and Anheuser-Busch in particular had made use of the discovery on this continent. Together they recommended to August A., Sr., that commercial use be made of the residual yeast that resulted from brewing.

Veron pointed out that, just as the muddy water of the Mississippi could be purified through chemistry to make it fine for brewing, so could residual brewers' yeast be converted into food of great nutritional value. August A. agreed that the company should begin at once to explore the possibilities.

A few days later, Veron's work took him to Evansville, Indiana. While there, J. B. Murray, the Anheuser-Busch branch manager, told him that Mead-Johnson & Co., a local manufacturer of special baby foods and pharmaceuticals, was using bakers' compressed yeast.

Veron had an interview with Dr. Charles E. Bills, the research director of Mead-Johnson, who told him that bakers' yeast was being used to extract ergosterol, a compound which, when irradiated, becomes vitamin D (viosterol). It is very helpful in the prevention and cure of rickets. Veron, being a chemist, knew that Anheuser-Busch bakers' yeast contained an appreciable amount of ergosterol and suggested that Dr. Bills analyze it.

Within the next few months, Veron and Mead-Johnson worked closely together and they developed a special strain of yeast and methods to increase greatly the ergosterol content. Mead-Johnson used this new strain of yeast in large quantities. This was the first chemical use made of Anheuser-Busch yeast. The cost of ergosterol was lowered greatly.

It should be pointed out here that this yeast was a special bakers' type compressed yeast, not dried yeast. This development, however, was the step that led to the formation of the Dried Yeast Department in 1928, when Anheuser-Busch sold to Mead-Johnson the first fifty pounds of non-fermentable dried yeast commercially produced in America.

Veron was established as head of this department. From an output of 15,000 pounds the first year, production grew until in 1951 five large driers were in operation, producing annually millions of pounds of dried yeast with considerable profit.

In 1952, Anheuser-Busch was producing three different kinds of dried non-fermentable yeast:

Primary Dried Yeast grown for yeast production, exclusively, without reclaiming alcohol or any other by-product. This yeast is used in medication and nutrition.

Brewers' Dried Yeast, the residual by-product of beer brewing. When dried as is, it retains a bitter hop taste and is used for feeding animals and poultry.

Dried Debittered Brewers' Yeast, which is the residual brewers' yeast with most of the hop taste removed by a process developed by Anheuser-Busch. This dried debittered yeast complies with the United States pharmacopoeia specifications in regard to vitamin and protein contents, total ash, moisture, bacteria count and mold count. It is for human consumption, either as a medication or in processed foods.

From these three basic kinds of yeast, Anheuser-Busch, Inc., produced and sold many, many different kinds of products: in powder form, granular form and in liquid extract form. About 75 percent of the dried yeast and derivatives produced by Anheuser-Busch was used by food processors to increase nutritive value. Dried yeast was used in virtually all baby cereals and many baby and junior foods and in many processed foods for adult consumption. Large quantities of Anheuser-Busch dried food yeasts were being exported to countries whose agricultural production was not sufficient to meet the needs.

The Army's K-Ration, designed to give the most nutrition and energy in a small package, contained dried food yeast in its crackers. The fact that the addition of even 1 percent of dried yeast would increase the nutritional value of nearly any processed food to an astounding degree was the basis for the opinion that, some day in the future, dried yeast would be an ingredient in the majority of foods. A great many scientists and food processors were convinced of yeast's nutritional value, but the *extent* of its use in commercial foods would depend on its recognition by the mothers and wives of America. When they begin to look for yeast listed as an ingredient on the labels because they know of its health-giving value, dried food yeast may truly become the great factor in big business that many predicted it would.

The other 25 percent of the dried non-fermentable food yeast and derivatives produced by Anheuser-Busch was sold to pharmaceutical manufacturers. A small percentage was used for still another purpose—as an ingredient in the media or "soil" used to grow micro-organisms, such as bacteria and molds. The growing importance of yeast digests (autolysates) as a nutrient in the production of desirable micro-organisms, such as the then new antibiotic-producing molds, was of significance.

Anheuser-Busch, Inc. was the only manufacturer in America regularly publishing a scientific journal on the history, chemical composition, nutritional value and uses of dried non-fermentable food yeast. Anheuser-Busch has made large financial grants to schools and hospitals to conduct yeast research. The Anheuser-Busch staff of more than fifty research scientists devoted much of its work to yeast research and development. The little yeast is a remarkable chemical factory, containing many compounds that are of nutritional and chemical interest. Anheuser-Busch was experimentally extracting and testing these compounds such as nucleic acid, adenosine triphosphate, adenosine diphosphate, inositol, guanosine, and trehalose. As uses were found for them, they were made commercially available.

Yeast's primary function once was regarded by the world as merely a factor in the brewing of beer and the baking of bread.

By 1952, it had been recognized that dried non-fermentable food yeast was the harvest of the most efficient form of indoor farming. A fertile "soil" was prepared—wort—upon which to grow genetically pure and vigorous seed yeasts. Sterilization removed hazards of contamination, air conditioning guaranteed optimal weather for growth and hourly analysis assured continued fertility of wort. Crops matured daily. Yields in protein, minerals, vitamins and poundage could be foretold accurately.

This precision growing of dried non-fermentable food yeast, though simple in principle, required a compounded knowledge of engineering, bacteriology and biological chemistry. It was a new and growing concept, a new and potentially unlimited source of food whose nutritive quality was second to none and man-made abundance promised to yield a rich reward in better nutrition for all.

As noted previously, Anheuser-Busch, besides keeping a staff of fifty research scientists busy in its own laboratories, has made generous grants to various centers of learning for a generation.

These included the University of Southern Illinois, Rutgers University, Northwestern University, Washington University, the University of Texas, Textile Institute, Mellon Institute, Malting Institute, Corn Industries Research Foundation, U. S. Brewers Foundation, the University of Arkansas, the University of Cincinnati, Hillman Clinic, Birmingham, Alabama; Cornell University, LaWall Harrison Consulting Laboratory, Indiana University and the University of Alabama.

In the files of the Anheuser-Busch laboratories is a mass of technical information, difficult for the lay reader to comprehend, that indicates breathtaking progress since the day when August A. Busch, Sr., flung down the challenge, "We are in the yeast business to stay."

The technical information on file is too massive to attempt here more than a highlighted account of the amazing ramifications of an enterprise that began with a very small brewery in 1852.

What has been told briefly in this chapter teems with evidence of what leaders in the sciences of medicine and nutrition think of the brains and the products of Anheuser-Busch.

It is interesting, after one hundred years, to speculate upon what a better-fed and healthier posterity will think of the spade work done in St. Louis by men and women who starved neither for imagination nor initiative.

Chapter XXIII

SYRUPS AND CORN PRODUCTS

PROVE PROFITABLE

IN 1921, after extensive laboratory work, Anheuser-Busch placed malt syrup on the market for the special requirements of commercial bakers. Introduced under the name of Budweiser Malt Syrup, this new product quickly earned a leading position in the baking industry and in 1952 was one of the most important items sold by the Bakery Products Department.

The three primary types of malt syrup produced for the baker were:

Light Colored Diastatic Malt Syrup

Light Colored Non-Diastatic Malt Syrup

Dark Colored Non-Diastatic Malt Syrup

The dark colored non-diastatic malt syrup was used principally in dark baked goods, such as rye bread and pumpernickel. The light colored malt syrups were used more widely for all types of white bread, soda crackers, rolls and other yeast-raised baked goods.

Malt contributed to the quality of baked goods in several ways. However, it

294

was particularly important to the baker, because of the job it did in improving keeping qualities as well as flavor and taste.

The biggest portion of Budweiser Malt Syrup was sold in 55-gallon drums. It was available also in 30-gallon drums and 5-gallon pails.

In 1923, small containers of malt syrup were sold through grocery stores and other outlets for household use. Two package sizes were offered—2½-pound and 3-pound cans. Both plain and hop-flavored malt syrup were offered in these smaller containers, which enjoyed national distribution until 1933, when they were discontinued after repeal.

In 1935, Anheuser-Busch introduced a dried malt syrup for commercial bakery use. It was welcomed by the baking industry because of the advantages it offered in handling and storage. Malt in powdered form could be scaled quickly and accurately and many bakers preferred it as a regular ingredient in place of malt syrup.

Other specialty malt syrups were introduced during the same year. These were designed for use in the breakfast cereal and specialty food markets. The leading Anheuser-Busch syrup in this field was Type "J," which enjoyed a wide acceptance.

Many leading firms in the pharmaceutical field also purchased large quantities of specialty malt syrups from Anheuser-Busch. The greatest demand was for Types "E," "EG," and "HD," which were developed in 1939 to meet the exacting requirements of pharmaceutical houses that maintained a national distribution program, selling prepared tonics, cough syrups and other products.

In 1940, the company perfected another syrup for commercial bread baking, which was marketed under the name of Anheuser-Busch Bakers Syrup. An important characteristic of this product was the special method of processing which gave the baker free-flowing characteristics to assure speedy and accurate scaling. As a regular ingredient in yeast-raised sweet goods, bakers' syrup also provided definite sales advantages for the baker by improving the keeping qualities, taste and flavor of the finished baked goods.

In 1946 Anheuser-Busch perfected a type of syrup designated as "DM." Bakers, plagued by war-born material shortages, welcomed the new product as a virtual life-saver. When the materials situation was eased, the syrup was discontinued.

Here are some of the things which "DM" did for the baker:

It added tolerance to dough by supplying readily fermentable sugars. It converted some of the starches of the flour to needed additional sugars as the yeast consumed sugar. The syrup supplied dextrines, which increased the moisture retaining capacity of the loaf. Through its mineral salts and amino acids, it aided in stimulating fermentation. It helped produce a uniform loaf of silky fine texture with a more palatable flavor. It was the best source of soluble proteins which are the finest organic yeast food available. It gave the baked loaf that richer golden brown bloom and tender crust so much in demand. It enhanced the nutritional value of the bread. It was the most dependable source of proteolytic control for mellowing the dough without tearing down of the flour. Each batch of Budweiser Malt Syrup was rigidly tested by actual baking tests before shipments were made, thereby resulting in absolute uniformity.

Table Syrup Department

When it was decided in 1933 to abandon the manufacture and sale of crude corn sugar, preparations were made to establish a table syrup blending and packing operation in New Orleans to market various table syrups under an Anheuser-Busch label.

The South was chosen as the logical territory, as the per capita consumption of edible syrups was much greater there than in any other part of the country. New Orleans was selected for the location of the plant, because of favorable transportation, labor and rental conditions and also because the greater portion of the output would be sold F.O.B. New Orleans.

The business started in late 1934 with several salesmen, no customers, no established labels or brands, no advertising or promotional work, nothing but a syrup of excellence with a competitive price.

In 1935, approximately 3,000,000 pounds of mixed syrup packaged in tins ranging from 12-ounce to 10-pound capacity were sold. In 1936, additional salesmen were hired and coverage expanded to include all of Louisiana, Texas and Oklahoma. The following year saw further expansion of territory, sales personnel and customers. By 1951, the company was operating in Georgia, Florida, Alabama, Mississippi, Tennessee, Louisiana, Arkansas, Texas and Oklahoma.

The company then was producing and marketing approximately 15,000,000 pounds of table syrups yearly and was the second largest producer of table syrups in the South. The products were truly representative and worthy of the Anheuser-Busch label. They were distinctive in flavor. The raw materials used were unmatched in quality. The products were attractively packaged.

Delta Brand led in consumer preference, being a southern-type syrup. Approximately 70 percent of the sales volume was on this grade of syrup, the balance being four other types marketed under the "BUD" label: Bud Crystal White, Bud Golden, Bud Waffle and Bud Pure Honey Flavor Syrup. Sales were made to leading wholesale grocers, chains and supermarkets in the territory in which Anheuser-Busch operated.

Corn Products Department

In 1923, during the early days of prohibition, in a further endeavor to diversify the company's business, Anheuser-Busch went into production of corn syrup unmixed (glucose). This was very desirable, since the company had grain storage facilities, buildings and other equipment available. The corn refining industry was a closely held one, the leader in its field having just been cited for monopolistic practices and ordered to sell or abandon several of its existing plants. The wet corn refining business had proved stable through the years and seemed attractive as a diversification over a long period.

While at first only corn syrup unmixed was manufactured, crude corn sugar was added later. Approximately 70 to 75 percent of the corn syrup manufactured in America was used by two industries, the confectioners and table syrup manufacturers.

Operations continued on a comparatively small basis until the repeal of prohibition in 1933. Then it was decided to discontinue manufacture of crude corn sugar and add starch and dextrine products to increase the corn grinding volume. As the manufacture of table syrups constituted a major outlet for corn syrup, a table syrup plant was established in New Orleans in 1934.

In 1937, Anheuser-Busch was established in the production and sale of various starches and in 1939 began producing dextrines. Corn starches were used in scores of industries for multiple industrial and food purposes. The textile and paper industries were large consumers. Laundry starches and food starches for salad dressings, baking powders, pharmaceuticals and confections were being produced. A new usage for starch was developed in oil well drilling and ore refining. Production of this type starch was started during 1951.

Corn syrup, utilized by the confectionery and table syrup industries, was used also in baked goods, bread, rolls, pies and cake icings. It was used in processing tobacco, in the manufacture of adhesives, ice creams, jellies and preserves. A new and large usage was coming into being in the fruit canning industry, particularly for packing peaches. Corn syrup has its own characteristics and is used generally in conjunction with cane or beet sugar. In candy, ice cream and fruit canning, it produces a product of finer texture, prevents graining—which is a problem when all sucrose is used—holds flavors, delays staling and is in no way a diluent.

Glucose, the name by which corn syrup formerly was known, was in ill repute for many years prior to the thirties. Since then, medical science disclosed so many beneficial uses for this product that in 1952 it was accepted readily by food producers and consumers for its true characteristics, which gave certain products a plus value.

Corn syrup requires little or no digestion. In its manufacture, it is virtually pre-digested and one of its component parts, dextrose, is a blood sugar, used for intravenous injections when food cannot be taken by mouth.

As by-products, the company produced and marketed corn gluten feeds and crude corn oil. The feeds were sold through wholesale channels to feed dealers throughout the country, but mostly in protein deficient areas, such as dairy cattle country.

Crude corn oil was sold in railroad tank car lots of 60,000 pounds each to edible oil refiners where, in turn, it was refined and resold to food processors for such products as mayonnaise, cooking oils and deep-fry products, such as doughnuts and potato chips. Oleomargarine and numerous other products in which vegetable oils were an ingredient were made with crude corn oil.

Another by-product of wet corn milling was steepwater, which was the water in which the hard corn kernel had been soaked prior to processing. Steepwater was used in the manufacture of antibiotics, such as penicillin, for use by human beings and employed in animal and poultry feeds.

From a capacity in grind of approximately 5,000 bushels of corn per day, the company in 1952 was processing 17,000 bushels daily. The year of 1951 saw the largest tonnage sold in various bulk corn products, representing a total of 5,500,000 bushels of corn.

New uses and outlets for corn products were being developed constantly and the company was keeping pace with the yearly increase in volume of the entire industry.

Chapter XXIV

WHAT A BIG FAMILY

IT HAS BECOME!

IN THE YEARS just preceding Anheuser-Busch's centennial, the personnel had expanded to such an extent that creation of an Industrial Relations Division became essential. Here are some of the functions of that division and a brief outline of the benefits to employees. For the unorganized office workers, a policy was set up that a new employee, after six months' service with the company, had an interview with the supervisor, at which progress, or the lack of it, was discussed. At the end of a year, a similar meeting took place and the recommendations in the matter of salary were made by the supervisor. Thereafter, each year the employee's progress and the salary were reviewed by him with the supervisor in an effort to give that employee steady advancement.

Among the organized employees, 55 separate labor contracts were negotiated each year, stipulating wages for the coming year. In general, the regular work week consisted of five days for both plant and office employees. The regular work day consisted of eight hours making a 40-hour week. In the plant there were various shifts and quitting times depending upon manufacturing conditions and other factors. Overtime compensation was paid both hourly and salaried employees equal to or in excess of rates provided in the Fair Labor Standards Act and varied depending upon conditions under which the overtime was worked.

In 1947 Anheuser-Busch established a retirement income plan to provide an employee with a monthly life income beginning with his retirement. The benefits were to be paid in addition to those provided under the Federal Social Security Act.

Every regular full-time employee became eligible for the plan after completing three years of continuous service and after attaining his thirtieth birthday. Deductions were made monthly from his paycheck, as the plan called for contributions by both the participant and the company. For example, the employee contributed 3 percent of the first $250 of his monthly earnings and $4\frac{1}{2}$ percent of his monthly earnings in excess of the $250.

Also provided for employees was a group insurance plan which gave them life insurance, accidental death and dismemberment benefits, accident and sickness weekly hospital expense, surgical, medical care, maternity and ambulance service benefits. It provided dependents with hospital expenses, surgical, maternity and ambulance service benefits.

Anheuser-Busch maintained a modern, well-equipped dispensary on the first floor of the bottling plant. It operated on a 24-hour basis, seven days a week, with a staff of registered nurses at all times ready for prompt and efficient medical care. In addition, a doctor was in attendance two days each week for treatment of serious cases. Moreover, the company maintained an ambulance in readiness around the clock. These precautions were taken despite a most enviable safety record.

In order to make certain that no employee was placed in a job for which he was not physically suited, a physical examination was provided for all new employees in certain types of work.

A constant effort was made to make working conditions as attractive as possible. A new and modern cafeteria was built on the first floor of the bottling plant, where employees had a variety of quality foods from which to choose for their daily luncheon. Adjacent to the cafeteria was a canteen, operating 24 hours a day. Packaged foods were dispensed there with a minimum of time required for service.

All employees of Anheuser-Busch were eligible for membership in the Anheuser-Busch Employees Association, designed primarily to promote sociability among all of the workers. Control and administration of the organization were in the hands of the employees themselves, entirely independent of company direction. However, the company consistently followed a policy of fostering and assisting in every worthy project sponsored by the association.

The highlight of the social season was the Coronation Ball, where the queen of Anheuser-Busch was chosen by popular vote and crowned "Miss Budweiser" for the current year. Other social functions included the employees' annual picnic, scheduled seasonable parties, barbecues and book reviews, organized teams of baseball, softball, cork ball, tennis, golf and a bowling league. The dues were small and membership entirely optional.

Another activity was the Anheuser-Busch Employees Credit Union. The primary purpose was to promote thrift among the workers by allowing them to purchase shares of stock in the credit union and to make loans to fellow employees at minimum interest rates. The union offered a dividend rate based upon the earnings of the credit union. The benefits of the organization were made available to members of the Anheuser-Busch Employees Association and members of their immediate families only.

The union was a cooperative effort governed by a board of directors elected annually by the members. It was incorporated as a separate entity and operated under the Missouri state laws.

Another activity was the Service Award Program. This program took recognition of the years of service contributed by various employees. Each year there was a Service Award Banquet at which the wives or husbands of the interested employees were the guests of the company. Lapel pins were distributed for 5, 15, 25, 35, 45 and 50 years of service.

Employees who had completed 35 through 49 years of service within the calendar year received a standard gift of a prestige brand American-made watch of either the pocket or wrist type. Employees with 50 or more years of service within the calendar year received a special gift, the cost approximating $250. This gift was chosen with consideration for the employee's mode of life, personal interest and likes. For example, when television was beginning to zoom in popularity, most of the employees in this bracket received handsome television sets and were mightily pleased to get them.

Chapter XXV

A TOY-TOWN RAILROAD

BECOMES BIG BUSINESS

THIS CHAPTER is the story, in brief, of the Manufacturers Railway Company—a story not about an Anheuser-Busch activity, but about another of the exploits of Adolphus Busch and the men who surrounded him and succeeded him in this undertaking.

Although his contemporaries gave Adolphus all the credit for making the original little railway into something that mattered, credit for its emergence from a one-horse operation goes to August A. Busch, Sr. Once Adolphus grasped the significance of what "Gussie" was doing and planning, he bestowed that credit in full measure upon his son.

The father gave August the benefit of counsel and, with skepticism, advanced the necessary money from time to time, but took no active part in the planning. Adolphus reversed himself completely in his feelings about the venture in June, 1911, when the Interstate Commerce Commission adjudged the railway to be a common carrier. He sent his son this memorandum:

Now, I am really a terminal enthusiast. I mean to say by that, that I shall give you my full support in carrying out your railroad scheme, which you have led very intelligently so far and with untiring perseverance. There is no doubt in my mind any more but that we can safely go on, lay out the most practical plan possible, obtain the best experts in railroad and terminal assistance, then invite the public to subscribe for stocks and bonds such amounts as we may need to carry out our plans eastward and westward.

Naturally, Gussie, of that which we get, I am going to give you a fair share, to which you are undoubtedly entitled. I want to make you satisfied and happy so your further zeal be animated and not diminished.

The inauguration of this railroad is a big thing—an enormous thing—and it must be our intention to hold it forever, i.e., to remain in the lead. . . . This railroad shall be one of the main assets of the Busch family.

Too much emphasis cannot be placed upon the fact that the railway is and always has been an entity unto itself and in no way controlled or directed by Anheuser-Busch. The distinction is important, because the charge that the line was a brewery subsidiary was made repeatedly before the Interstate Commerce Commission and once before the United States Supreme Court. Despite the repeated accusations, the Manufacturers Railway succeeded in proving completely that, although founded by Adolphus Busch, it is not a satellite of Anheuser-Busch.

The Manufacturers Railway Company was organized on April 14, 1887, as a Missouri corporation.

Its original trackage consisted of but a single line running east and west on what was an extension of Pestalozzi Street in those days, east of Broadway, to the river front. By means of the trackage, the Anheuser-Busch Brewing Association and Adolphus Busch, personally, were able to receive from the Missouri Pacific Railroad, which was the only connection at that time, such traffic as the railway handled.

Adolphus did not desire at that time to become engaged in the railroad business, so he leased the property to the old St. Louis-Iron Mountain and

Southern Railroad, now a part of the Missouri Pacific Railroad, for a ten-year period, from 1888 to 1898.

During this first ten-year period the Anheuser-Busch Brewing Association was expanding greatly.

In 1898 a lease of the property was again placed with the Iron Mountain for ten years longer.

During this latter ten years the necessity for adequate railroad service became pressing. It was not forthcoming.

So Adolphus purchased two locomotives from the American Locomotive Company at the conclusion of the World's Fair in 1904. In a formal ceremony, he presented them to officials of the Iron Mountain with the simple statement that no charge would be made for them and no rental would be exacted for the use of them. He requested that they be placed in the service of the Manufacturers Railway Company with the understanding that they be confined to the service of the Anheuser-Busch Brewing Association and one or two other industries which were at that time beginning to function in South St. Louis. The Iron Mountain agreed.

Within six months, the locomotives disappeared from the scene and were never heard of again. No payment was ever made for them.

With the expiration of the lease in 1908, Adolphus determined to operate the property himself.

At that time, George H. Moore, an accounting examiner for the Interstate Commerce Commission, was at work in St. Louis, examining the books of the Terminal Railroad Association. He told Adolphus that he could take charge of the railroad and expand it as an independent property. He became president of the Manufacturers Railway Company.

Shortly after Moore took office, he launched a very extensive newspaper publicity campaign, stating that it was the intention of Adolphus Busch to build a new bridge across the Mississippi River, if necessary, construct and operate ferry service, or in some way or other establish independent, competitive railroad service between St. Louis and East St. Louis to break the Terminal Railroad Association's monopoly of trans-Mississippi River rail traffic.

That was a blunder, because the Manufacturers Railway was not prepared to do any such thing.

In December, 1908, the trunk lines withdrew all payments of switching absorption and revenue to Manufacturers.

For ten years the railway carried on militant struggles before the Interstate Commerce Commission and the Supreme Court, attacking the legality and disputing the right of the trunk lines to take such action.

Several times during those ten years the Cotton Belt agreed to and did absorb Manufacturers' switching rates up to a certain point. But even the support of the Cotton Belt finally failed.

During those years, Adolphus supported the railroad out of his own pocket. He advanced $583,460, for which he was given notes.

In 1918, Manufacturers secured an adjustment of its revenue problems through negotiations with executives of the United States Railroad Administration. From then on, problems began to dissolve so far as revenue was concerned. William Cotter, formerly general manager of the St. Louis-Iron Mountain Railroad, succeeded Moore as president in 1916. He served until 1928, when he left the company, which then elected Arthur E. Wright president.

In the years from 1924 to 1934, the company repaid the principal indebtedness to the Busch Estate in the amount of $583,460, predicated upon the notes which were issued and it likewise paid interest totalling $361,306.76 at the rate of 6 percent, the entire debt thus being liquidated and retired.

Beginning to get on its feet in the early 1920's, the company found it necessary to obtain more revenue.

Negotiations were carried on with St. Louis lines and an agreement was entered into whereby the railway would be given a satisfactory increase in switching rates.

Presumably at the suggestion of a competitive carrier, the Interstate Commerce Commission suspended the tariffs authorizing the increases until it could conduct an investigation and hearing.

The hearing subsequently was held in St. Louis. The company made an excellent showing, with the result that the increases were approved by the Commission and made effective.

Thereafter, the revenue structure began to improve and since that time has formed the basis of what Wright has termed "one of the finest revenue rate structures existing in the United States."

Throughout the years since that time, the railway's charges have been advanced or decreased—mostly increased—in accordance with general rate increases given carriers by the Interstate Commerce Commission.

Beginning in 1925, the company began to exert more influence in South St. Louis. Its traffic materially increased.

It did business with such important industries as the Gaylord Container Corporation, The International Shoe Company, the Lammert Furniture Company, the Rosenthal Paper Company and many others. In fact, the railway was the beneficiary of what was termed in St. Louis then as "a very heavy local migration of industry."

The MacArthur Bridge trackage was idle. It lacked a southern approach. The company finally was able to have the southern approach appropriation authorized by the Bond Issue Supervisory Committee.

A bill which had been introduced in the Board of Aldermen and which would have placed absolute control of the city-owned bridge in the hands of the Terminal Railroad Association was defeated by a vote of 27 to 1.

The company prepared a statement of exceptions and objections to the proposed ordinance and the newspapers gave the statement wide publicity.

A terrific struggle ensued for years, but finally that ordinance was killed.

The railway was supported publicly through an organization known as the Shippers' Conference of St. Louis. A large number of prominent traffic men representing industries in St. Louis and others belonged to it.

The Bond Issue Supervisory Committee finally approved the appropriation of $1,500,000 with which to construct the southern approach.

Following the passage of the ordinance, the Board of Aldermen authorized the southern approach and that was, likewise, bitterly fought by certain interests. The company had one other very serious obstacle to overcome and that was the issuance by the Interstate Commerce Commission of a certificate of public convenience and necessity. That important step involved recognition by the Interstate Commerce Commission that added terminal service was necessary in St. Louis and in the St. Louis terminals.

The very day after the southern approach bill was passed by the Board of Aldermen, by a vote of 27 to 1, Manufacturers started the preparation of exhibits which would reflect the delays to which South St. Louis traffic was being put by the Terminal Association.

The railway prepared data on a year's traffic, which showed where shipments leaving industries on the Manufacturers Railway Company lines were not getting out of East St. Louis on East St. Louis trunk lines for as many as eight days.

Manufacturers used 24 hours as a reasonable period to effect interchange. Anything in excess of 24 hours was considered a delay.

The hearing in Washington upon the application for a certificate of convenience and necessity lasted a week.

It took several trunks to carry the company's data to Washington. The case was won and the certificate issued.

The Nickel Plate, not then a member of the Terminal, and not now a proprietary member, recognized the Manufacturers route, published tariffs and issued division sheets effecting the rates and the revenues, and on September 24, 1930, the Manufacturers Railway ran its first train over the bridge. It was a solid train-load of freight for the Nickel Plate.

From September, 1930, until April, 1931, Manufacturers carried on an incessant campaign of solicitation against all roads except the Nickel Plate.

By letter, by personal contact, by personal solicitation and with the help of a multitude of loyal friends, the company finally won its battle with the other carriers.

The Wabash, under direction of President Taussig, was the first to capitulate.

The other roads soon followed. The company's relations with the other roads in 1952 were very friendly and profitable.

Other properties, the St. Louis & O'Fallon Railway Company and the St. Louis Refrigerator Car Company also went through several test periods.

Those familiar with railroad regulation and financial affairs of the railroads will remember the St. Louis & O'Fallon Railway Company "recapture" case.

The "recapture" clause of the Interstate Commerce Act sought to regain for the government all earnings of common carrier railroads in excess of 5¾ percent.

Because of its prosperity, the simplicity of its operations and other factors, the St. Louis & O'Fallon Railway Company was chosen by the Commission for a test case.

The Commission made the O'Fallon valuation of such liberal proportions that the line could not contest a single item.

That case went to the Supreme Court and the O'Fallon Railway won it.

The trunk lines never offered to pay any of the expenses incurred, which amounted to $100,000—a very substantial burden in those days.

Because of truck competition and some other factors, the traffic handled by the St. Louis & O'Fallon Railway Company declined steadily.

In the late 1920's, it handled a little more than 2,000,000 tons of coal per annum and at that time it was bringing into the St. Louis terminals between 20 and 22 percent of all the coal which arrived at the terminals by rail.

The St. Louis Refrigerator Car Company, too, has been through some hectic struggles. In 1936 it was the butt of an attack by the American Railway Association, to reduce mileage rates on refrigerator cars.

Negotiations were carried on between the company and committees representing the American Railway Association. An ultimatum was served that the rate was to be reduced a certain amount.

The company would not accept it and defeated the carriers. The mileage rate was not disturbed for two years or more, when another effort was made to reduce it. St. Louis Refrigerator objected.

In the first instance, the Interstate Commerce Commission took jurisdiction of the case and rendered the favorable decision. The second time, because of legal reasons, the Commission refused to take jurisdiction. A stalemate followed.

President Wright went to Washington and had a conference with President Pelley of the American Railway Association. Wright told him he was so sure of the soundness and integrity of his position that he would like to have a special committee appointed to review the case. Pelley gave his approval and asked whom Wright would suggest be on the committee.

Wright told him he did not believe that his company needed any representation at all and that he should appoint the committee himself, of his accounting and mechanical officers, for Wright believed they would sustain his position.

Pelley was much surprised. The ensuing negotiations consumed four months.

The rate never was lowered and no further effort was ever made to lower it. On the contrary, it was increased twice.

In 1952, all three companies had an excellent standing before the Interstate Commerce Commission.

In the autumn of 1951, Mr. Wright said:

Present relations with all companies and all individuals are in excellent shape.

We have a wonderful staff. It is efficient, conscientious and loyal. We have one of the cleanest, finest and strongest corporate structures in the country.

In 1952, the Manufacturers Railway was well established as a common carrier and rendered important service to more than 200 industries.

Expedition of traffic to and from industries on the railway had been most important. It ran three trains a day over MacArthur Bridge with outbound traffic and had it out of the terminals in a matter of hours after it got to East St. Louis.

Traffic which was inbound was "on track" at the industry's service on the afternoon of receipt. Prior to the MacArthur Bridge deal, it sometimes took as long as eight days to interchange Manufacturers Railway traffic with the eastern trunk lines.

In December of 1950, the railway was in the enviable position of being able to give the other railroads in the St. Louis terminal 1,350 box cars for which they were very grateful. This is an example of the friendships that have been built up among people who once were bitter enemies.

The St. Louis & O'Fallon Coal Company, like the Manufacturers Railway, was another of Adolphus Busch's successful ventures that was and still is a separate entity having no connection with the Anheuser-Busch Company.

The coal company was licensed under the statutes of Illinois for fifty years on September 16, 1898.

The capital stock was $150,000 with 1,500 shares at $100 each. The shares were subscribed for by:

Edward L. Thomas	1,496 shares
William A. Reiss	1 share
David O. Thomas	1 share
Henry M. Needles	1 share
John T. Taylor	1 share

Thomas was an engineer and promoter. David O. Thomas, his son, was an engineer; Henry M. Needles was an attorney.

The organization was effected in the First National Bank Building, Belleville, Illinois, on October 1, 1898. At this meeting the by-laws were adopted. With minor changes, by amendments, these still are being used.

The original license to do business in Illinois expired September 16, 1948. It was renewed as a perpetual charter.

From the time that the two mines commenced to produce coal, which was about 1905, until the properties were acquired by Adolphus in September, 1913, less than five million tons of coal was mined and sold. This was due primarily to the strong competition of older established mines in the Belleville district cutting prices below the actual cost of production to obtain working time in a saturated market.

The serious situation of that period can be realized when production of more than 400 mines taking the Belleville freight rate is considered. Mines were in operation as far north as Staunton, east to Breese, Nashville and Ashley and south to Pinckneyville and Sparta.

Whether Adolphus had ideas of a reasonable return on his investment in the St. Louis & O'Fallon Coal Company and of the St. Louis & O'Fallon Railway Company is problematical. It seems more likely that the properties were purchased to provide fuel and movement of that fuel to protect the rapidly expanding Busch empire.

In 1913, coal was needed for gas and steam in the three bottle making plants at Belleville, the Dorcas Street glass works in St. Louis, the Manufacturers Railway Company and the rapidly growing boiler plant of Anheuser-Busch, Inc.

Strikes, despite low prices, were common, with plenty of interruptions in fuel deliveries. The deliveries themselves were not too good, due to indifferent rail service.

To purchase the company, 146 bonds at $100 each were issued. These were retired with a $50 each premium prior to 1918 and during the interim (1913-1918) $23,818.19 interest was paid on these bonds.

Adolphus had lent the coal company $25,000, the South Side Bank had lent $25,000, and the trustees under the will of Adolphus Busch had lent $240,000. All of this was repaid prior to January 1, 1927, with interest to the South Side Bank amounting to $4,411.33, Adolphus Busch Trustees $36,753.53 and between 1918 and 1923 both inclusive, $240,000 was paid to the owners in dividends.

From 1917 to 1923 federal taxes in the sum of $499,195.91 were paid.

Between 1917 and 1926 capital stock tax of $9,302.50 also was paid.

Of the money borrowed ($290,000), $130,052.14 was expended to modernize the mine (as of that day) with coal cutting machines, generators, electric locomotives, wash house for men, boilers and water treating plant and loading and picking equipment to clean and load the coal.

About 500 acres of additional coal land was purchased at a cost of $8,113.

The balance was used for corporate purposes due to losses of $204,209 during 1924, 1925 and 1926.

The total coal acreage as of January 1, 1927, was 5,478 acres, of which 2,705 had been mined. The tonnage mined from start of operations was at 13,289,196 tons with 16,635,808 tons still in the ground. Life expectancy was placed at twenty-one years or until 1948.

In 1927 losses amounted to $144,818, in 1928 they were $136,604 and in 1929 they were $150,920. Primarily this was due to antiquated mining methods, trying to compete with strip mines and loading machine shaft mines. About $100,000 was spent for portable conveyors already on the way out in other mines.

In 1929 several engineers conversant with modern practices were employed to prepare studies of the #2 mine (#1 having been abandoned early in 1928) and recommend type of machinery required, its cost, what it would do and what coal so produced would cost.

No plans came close to agreement on what would be possible, but all agreed that either the mine be modernized or losses were inevitable.

Due to the economic situation of 1930, money could not be found to provide the machinery recommended.

The management cut the losses of 1930 to $82,933, compared with $150,-920 of 1929.

With the tools at hand it was out of the question to break even. It became increasingly difficult year after year to find money to carry on. It was being provided by loans to the coal company by the trustees under the will of Adolphus Busch, later by a trustee agreement where money declared as dividends by the St. Louis & O'Fallon Railway Company was diverted for use by the coal company. This resulted in double taxes and as an expedient had little merit.

The sad part about money in the sum of $225,000 advanced immediately following 1929 by the trustees was that it was used to cover the expenses of an ill-advised coke process and other unsuccessful factors. This amounted to $168,000, enough for a substantial part of the machinery to modernize the mine. (Estimates of 1929 were an overall cost of $264,000.)

The losses from 1924 to 1929 were $636,553.59 and from 1924 to 1935 they were $1,222,378.36 and without machinery there was no hope of doing much about reducing them.

In October, 1935, a locally built loading machine, too light to compare with the Myers, Whaley, Joy or Goodman machines commonly in use, was borrowed from the builder who needed a mine in which to try it out. Poor as it was, it produced coal for $0.5774 per ton, as compared with hand loading in adjacent working places at $1.005 per ton.

Not having any money and no chance of getting the amount needed, in 1936 the builder agreed to supply five machines for ten cents a ton out of the saving in production cost.

On June 15, 1936, after a strike, all coal was machine loaded.

Due to wage scale changes the loss of 1936 would have been $137,543 ($104,637 old wage). With these inadequate machines and at the new wage scale the company suffered a loss of $72,378 or it made a saving of $65,165 over what it would have cost had it continued through 1936 with the methods of 1935 at the 1936 wage scale.

Now the losses from 1924 to 1929, both inclusive, were $636,553.59. From 1930 to 1936, losses were $658,203.05, this latter bracket having the benefit of the loading machines which saved $65,165.

The losses from 1937 to 1941 amounted to $339,080.10.

Another engineering report was drafted and submitted to the directors in August, 1941, pointing out the company's inability to remain in business unless adequate tools were provided to meet competitors on a common ground.

The changes (identical except for improvements in design of machines after 1929 and through the years) were approved if the company could get the money from the St. Louis & O'Fallon Railway Company. It got the money, $442,450 of it, including previous loans for corporate uses.

As the mechanization of the mine proceeded the picture changed. In 1942, with few of the changes completed, the property had a loss of $39,128. By the end of 1943 with some changes still to be made the losses were cut to $18,334. This made the over-all losses for 20 years $1,691,299.57. How much of this was spent for mine improvement between 1924 and 1929 is not recorded, but $665,788.01 was used for this purpose from 1930 to 1949.

The president of the St. Louis & O'Fallon Coal Company in 1952 was W. F. Davis and to him went most of the credit for the company's excellent record. In 1952 he submitted the following report on improvements effected since 1943:

> We have loading machines and cutting machines equal to those of any mines using track. Recent developments, however, by mines installing belts to convey the coal in lieu of the track haulage and pit cars, rubber tire loading and cutting machines, roof bolting instead of cross bars and props to support the roofs, shooting the coal with air under high pressures instead of with explosives is rapidly setting us back with respect to some of the more recently opened mines.
>
> These are all matters which will be brought to the attention of the

stockholders from time to time as we become convinced that expenditure of additional money will be justified in an increase in production, or a reduction in cost of the coal mined.

The same thing is true with respect to additional preparation facilities.

We have a washer that is equal to any wet washer and brings the ash content of our coal from approximately 18% as hoisted to 9% as loaded for sale. This washer is inadequate in size and therefore it is wasteful in the quantity of coal in our rejects. Studies are being conducted at the present time with the thought in mind that a future expenditure will be fully justified in the recovery of a substantial tonnage now being wasted to offset this cost.

Among other improvements of the past two years is a very complete plant for the making and oiling of stoker coal. This stoker coal is suitable for either domestic or industrial use, comes from our industrial screenings and sells for roughly $1.50 a ton above the price of our washed screenings. This of course is a seasonal proposition, and we can only figure on the increased revenue during the burning season.

To save labor in the unloading of coal for our local sales we have installed a car shakeout. With frozen coal during the winter months it was necessary for us to have six to eight men to unload coal from the cars. Two men are our normal local sales crew, and since the installation of the car shakeout two men handle all of our coal, winter and summer.

During the past summer we put down two new air shafts using five foot core barrel drill operated from the surface. These shafts were sunk through all strata in about four weeks working time with a crew of three and four men—all working on the surface instead of in the shaft itself as is the custom with hand sinking methods. Some of these cores which were five feet in diameter and fourteen feet high or thick, weighed sixteen tons. These were hoisted out, loaded on a car designed at the mine, and dumped in ravines near the shaft sites.

Both of these fans are now in operation equipped with 175 horsepower electric motors and a 250 horsepower gasoline auxiliary engine. When the power line is broken from any cause, gasoline engines pick up the load within sixteen seconds and without any loss of air being delivered by the fan. When the electrical power comes back on the gasoline engine automatically cuts out in essentially the same period of time. These two installations were steel lined and pressure grouted, and are absolutely dry shafts, which means that all of the water strata through which the shafts are sunk are prevented from flowing into the mine.

With the mine revamped the company was off to a great start. Net profit from 1944 to 1950 amounted to $1,437,509.98, final net profit after taxes being $978,218.85.

The St. Louis & O'Fallon Railway Company had been paid off in full.

The company still owed the Adolphus Busch Estate $225,000. It had $375,-000 in Treasury Certificates and about $240,000 in the bank. Final payment of the debt to Adolphus Busch Estate, Inc., was made on February 27, 1952.

In the northern or unopened part of the property there still was a twenty years' supply of coal. To the south the company bought another block good for eight years. Thus, it seemed that the mine would be carrying out its purpose for another quarter century.

An engineer's report made in 1948 placed a valuation of $1,750,000 on the mine.

After the mine was modernized in 1942, it was producing more than ten tons per seven-hour work day for every man, top and bottom, on the pay roll. That was nearly double the average for the bituminous coal mines of the U. S.

The venture had produced 23,463,818 tons since 1910.

Since the mine was acquired by Adolphus, none of the Busch industries ever had been short of coal.

There had been a number of coal strikes and some rail transportation strikes, but coal had been available at all times.

Storage at the mine and storage at strategic points in St. Louis had insured continuity of delivery up to sixty days.

Facilities at the mine included four bins holding 100 tons each. From each of these bins a truck of twenty tons could be loaded in three minutes.

The feed conveyor could replace this coal by unloading a fifty-ton railroad car in fifteen to twenty minutes.

A diesel powered crane with a ¾ yard bucket, six coal yard conveyors and three under track conveyors handled coal to trucks from cars or storage piles. Each of these conveyors could handle one ton a minute.

More than 600 tons could be moved from the mine to the bins of Anheuser-Busch, Inc. in a single day. A like tonnage could be moved for the protection of other commercial accounts.

Chapter XXVI

HOW THE DIESEL ENGINE

CAME TO AMERICA

THE BUSCH-SULZER Bros. Diesel Engine Company was another of the enterprises founded by Adolphus Busch and carried on independently of the brewery operation. The plant was located at Second and Utah streets in St. Louis.

Adolphus Busch, in 1897, obtained the American rights to build diesels. He retained the inventor, Dr. Rudolph Diesel, as consultant, and the company's first engine was installed in the Anheuser-Busch power plant in 1898.

As now is well known, the diesel engine operates very economically, using crude oil as fuel. It has no ignition system as does the internal combustion engine of the motor car. The oil, after being vaporized, is subjected to such great pressure in the cylinder that the resultant heat reaches intensity enough to explode the compressed gas. In the early days of the diesel, the engine was untried in this country for quite a few years. There was some skepticism as to its efficiency, but as time went on, the diesel demonstrated year after year that it was a formidable competitor of the steam engine.

Busch-Sulzer concentrated on stationary and marine diesels. Many of its engines were installed in ocean-going ships and also large ferry boats. Another big market for Busch-Sulzer diesels was the public utility field. Many municipalities the country over generate electricity with Busch-Sulzer engines. Their record for long life is an enviable one.

As with everything else that he produced, Adolphus was insistent that these engines represent the very best of materials and workmanship.

With the outbreak of World War I, the Navy Department requested Busch-Sulzer to undertake the design of several types and sizes of submarine diesels up to 2,500 horsepower, an assignment which no other firm was qualified by experience to take or cared to undertake. August A. Busch, Sr., immediately acceded to the Navy's request and the entire capacity of the plant was reserved for Navy diesels for the duration of the war.

When the war was over, the diesel was well established in the public mind as a tried and proved prime mover. In the years immediately following World War I, Busch-Sulzer finally began to become a profitable operation and it so continued until the great depression which began in 1929. The president of Busch-Sulzer, Edward B. Pollister, recommended to August A. Busch, Sr., that payment of all dividends cease and available surplus capital be used to finance an extensive development program during the depression years that lay ahead. Large sums were spent during the depression on development and plant projects which held the organization together.

Following the death of August A., Sr., in 1934, Adolphus Busch III became Chairman of the Board of the Busch-Sulzer Company. Five other grandsons of Adolphus served as directors including Leicester Busch Faust, Walter Reisinger, Edward Magnus, August A. Busch, Jr., and Adalbert von Gontard. The latter three also were vice-presidents of the company. In the time between 1928 and the entry of the United States into World War II, the Busch interests received no return from their investment, but by sacrifices in carrying on and keeping the organization intact, the company was again in a position to serve

BUSCH-SULZER BROS. DIESEL ENGINE COMPANY

this country during war. The company responded to a request of the Navy Bureau of Ordnance to undertake the production of some particularly difficult anti-aircraft ordnance. A new machine shop was built in 1941 and after Pearl Harbor, the company operated on a basis of three eight-hour shifts, seven days a week. The production of this ordnance was so accelerated that by March, 1942, deliveries were double the original contract rate. On April 7, 1942, America's oldest builder of diesel engines was awarded the Navy "E" Burgee pennant. In conjunction with the Navy "E" award came the following letter from the Secretary of the Navy, Frank Knox, to Mr. Pollister:

> It is a privilege for me to be able to advise you that the Navy Board for Production Awards has designated Busch-Sulzer Bros. Diesel Engine Company a recipient of the Navy "E" award for production achievements. Since 1906 the "E" has been the traditional Navy symbol for excellence—for a job "well done."
>
> This is an honor not lightly bestowed and one to be cherished by you and your associates.
>
> As the Secretary of the Navy, and as a fellow American, I congratulate you upon the achievement of this honor. And in so doing, let me remind you that your company's contribution, together with that of other of our patriotic countrymen is only the beginning. This production, increased many fold, must and will become the tide of victory.

The nature of the ordnance, for which this award was given, has been described in the Introduction. It might be added here, that with this finely calculated ammunition hoist, it was possible for gunners to pick up enemy planes in a stream of explosives very much like you might bring a bumble bee down with the spray of a garden hose.

In addition to producing this ordnance, Busch-Sulzer also manufactured many types of diesel engines for the Army, the Navy, the Merchant Marine and for our war-time allies.

Upon the conclusion of World War II and with the simultaneous inception of a vast brewery expansion program, the descendants of Adolphus Busch

decided that to continue to direct Busch-Sulzer had become an almost impossible task, and accordingly, the company and its properties and good will were acquired by the Nordberg Manufacturing Company of Milwaukee, Wisconsin. The Nordberg company was an old, established manufacturer of diesels and worthy in every respect of carrying on the Busch-Sulzer traditions.

The deal was closed through the successful negotiations of Horace C. Flanigan, president of the Manufacturers Trust Company of New York and a director of Anheuser-Busch.

Chapter XXVII

ADVERTISE, ADVERTISE
AND ADVERTISE

FOR ITS PRESENT day stature, advertising has many friends to thank. None has been a more loyal friend than Anheuser-Busch—for eighty-seven years.

Truth in advertising was a rule with the company long before members of the advertising fraternity decided to make that the slogan of their craft.

Keeping continuously at it was another conviction of Anheuser-Busch long before agencies had crystallized that sentiment into another slogan.

Adolphus Busch demonstrated that he was advertising minded the moment he joined the old Bavarian Brewery in 1865. He wanted the world to know about the E. Anheuser Co.'s Brewing Association. So, he entertained editors and reporters with the greatest of hospitality and so charmed them with his self-starter approach to business that they wrote copiously about the ever-expanding St. Louis brewery.

In those days, advertising was largely a matter of projecting the personality of the head of the business upon the public mind. Popping with personality, it was inevitable that these projections would lead to Adolphus becoming a full-fledged partner in only eight years. Since what had been a slow-moving business was rocketing along with increasing profit, kindly old Eberhard was content to let his son-in-law have upstage center.

Advertising "themes" and "campaigns" were unknown at the time. Occasionally, you burst into print with proof of superiority—or claims if you didn't have proof. Literally stacks of photostatic copies of Adolphus's advertising reveal that he dealt exclusively in proof.

Meanwhile, he overlooked none of the strategy and none of the gimmicks that generated word-of-mouth advertising. You were told in the Introduction of how he gave gold pieces and pocketknives to people whom he met on his travels and in his business contacts. There were other novelties, too. If you strolled down the avenue, swinging a walking stick topped with a silver boar's head with rubies for eyes, it indicated that "Prince Busch" had counted you among his friends. And, on the heavy gold watch chain that hung from pocket to pocket across your fancy vest was a gold A-and-Eagle sparkling with not too tiny diamonds. In your pocket was a bronze A-and-Eagle fastened to a short leather strap with a slit at the end. The eagle had a spring pincer on the reverse side so that you could clip it to your hat brim and then, with the slitted strap, suspend it from a vest button while you roamed through public buildings bareheaded.

With an eye to home consumption of his beer, Adolphus gave many gifts of fine china and glassware. They did what the donor hoped for—made folks talk about Adolphus, Anheuser-Busch and his beer.

Not content to have merely the brewery be a showplace, he insisted that all horses and wagons that delivered his products be of the finest. Percherons drew red wagons with a green trim through the streets of many cities and those wagons glistened under several coats of varnish. When you saw one of the wagons, horses and sparkling brassed harness you knew that it wasn't just beer that was being delivered; it was Anheuser-Busch beer.

FORERUNNERS OF BUDWEISER ADVERTISING—Adolphus gave fine chinaware to people he believed would generate word-of-mouth advertising. He did the same with charms for watch chains and the now world-famous Adolphus Busch pocketknives containing blades, bottle opener, corkscrew and a peek window that revealed a portrait of the donor.

This, remember, was in the days when advertising was mostly the projection of the personality guiding the business. The time was coming when pictures were to supplement the printed word. Adolphus began to turn to lithography and to distribute the pictures to retailers. Thus, he showed himself to be one of the earliest to recognize the value of what today is called "point of purchase" advertising.

You have only to turn to the moving annual sales total to see that these lithographs helped to do the sales job, yet by comparison with today's items they had their amusing side.

The caption for one had Loreley discovering her favorite brewery. The picture contained a true likeness of the plant over which in a regal fashion hovered Loreley, whose filmy and plunging attire revealed a Teutonic rotundity that indicated that the gentlemen of the time not only preferred blondes, but poundage as well.

Presumably, the implication was that the same skill that had for so long been associated with German brewing methods was present in the St. Louis brewery.

No single advertising idea that Adolphus Busch conceived—or anyone else, for that matter—has enjoyed more sustained popularity through the years than the picture already referred to and entitled, "Custer's Last Fight." It depicted the last few moments of the savage battle between the doomed fire-snorting cavalry general and the Indians in the valley of the Little Big Horn River.

The picture, reproduced on page 334, had an almost uncanny magnetism that stopped pedestrians dead in their tracks when they passed a tavern window that displayed it. After more than fifty years had passed and after more than a million copies had been distributed since it was painted by Cassily Adams, the picture continued to fascinate people.

The original canvas disappeared mysteriously and as mysteriously reappeared. It became the subject of some lengthy newspaper articles.

ALWAYS EXCELLENT PACKAGE DISPLAY—In some of his earliest advertising efforts, Adolphus made no secret of what he was advertising. It was Budweiser, first, last and all the time.

RATHER UNUSUAL, BUT IT SOLD BEER IN ITS DAY

LORELEY? BUDWEISER WAS A GIRL'S BEST FRIEND

BUDWEISER WAS THE BEER
ON TRAINS

BUDWEISER GIRL

WORLD FAMOUS AND NO
QUESTION ABOUT IT

THIS MADE AMERICA PROUD, EUROPE ENVIOUS

A DIRECT APPEAL TO "THE WOMAN MARKET"

PROBABLY THE FIRST COMMERCIAL
CALENDAR GIRL

The El Paso Times of October 25, 1931, reported that "an original painting of historic value is laid away in a storehouse at Fort Bliss, while a correspondence, nationwide in scope, is being carried on in an endeavor to trace the source from which the painting made its way to the rafters of the old storeroom."

The article went on to say that no one at the Army Post knew how the painting got there. It was in poor condition—the canvas cracked and the paint dirty—and funds were needed to restore it. The newspaper recounted a lot of Army red tape, culminating in a departmental request for additional data on the painting. It said that the collection of this data was in the hands of Colonel C. F. Martin, formerly Commander of the historic Seventh Cavalry Regiment, which was Custer's command. It added that Colonel Martin had gleaned the following facts:

From Brigadier General W. J. Nicholson, retired:

> I remember very distinctly its arrival at Fort Riley, Kansas. It was presented to the Seventh Cavalry by the Anheuser-Busch Company of St. Louis. Its value I do not know, but it was a very expensive work.

From Charles Thompson, Junction City, Kansas, formerly an artilleryman, who was present at the presentation:

> The presentation ceremony, I believe, took place in 1892. Mr. Adolphus Busch made the presentation in the Post Mess Hall. The platform was made of mess tables and on it were grouped the Seventh Cavalry officers. Colonel Forsythe accepted the painting in behalf of the regiment. It was about eight or ten feet high and was between forty and sixty feet in length. Mr. Busch said that his firm paid $35,000 for the picture, buying it outright in order to secure the right to re-produce it.

From Anheuser-Busch:

> After buying the picture, we had it in our reception rooms for several years before presenting it to the Seventh Cavalry at Fort Riley. At the outbreak of the Spanish-American War, it was sent elsewhere and we lost all sight of it until we received your letter although we had made inquiry

 CUSTER'S LAST FIGHT.

ANHEUSER BUSCH BREWING ASSOCIATION.

One of the World's Most Famous Pictures

for it through Army publications. To fix the price on the painting would be a hard thing to do because of its subject.

From Brigadier General Ernest A. Garlington, retired, San Diego, California.

I feel that the painting was paid for and presented to the regiment by Anheuser-Busch. I never knew the price and I have forgotten the artist. The work had considerable merit as a work of art, although the portrayal was the idea of the artist, based upon newspaper accounts of the engagement and photographs of the officers represented in the picture.

From Brigadier General Edward S. Godfrey, Cookston, New Jersey:

The artist's name was Adams, but I do not remember the last name.

From the Kansas State Historical Society:

The Custer's Last Fight picture, also known as the Adolphus Busch picture, was the work of an artist, Cassily Adams.

The El Paso Times said that after Colonel Martin had summed up his conclusions, he forwarded his data to the office of the Adjutant General and received this reply:

That the painting was presented to the Seventh Cavalry at Fort Riley, Kansas, sometime near 1890 by the Anheuser-Busch Company; that the original value is unknown, but it was probably several thousands of dollars.

That, oddly enough, is the Army memorandum and what it's supposed to indicate is anybody's guess.

Adolphus later sensed the impact of placing outdoor advertising where traffic was heaviest, and he was one of the first to use the 24-sheet poster.

Another significant thing was his choice of type faces. Display type leaned heavily toward narrow or so-called "condensed" letters. Adolphus elected to have the name Budweiser appear in expanded lower case letters that would contrast sharply with run-of-the-mine printing.

Before the turn of the century, national magazines were few. Adolphus was a big buyer of newspaper advertising. In a time when a dollar a day was a

ANHEUSER-BUSCH BREWING ASS'N

BREW FINE BEER EXCLUSIVELY.

THE MOST PROFITABLE FOR THE DEALER.

THE CHEAPEST FOR THE CONSUMER.

Because IT IS PURE and RELIABLE.

They were the ORIGINATORS of BEER BOTTLING in the United States, and have maintained the lead in the brewing trade on account of the SUPERIOR QUALITY OF THEIR BEER by using ONLY THE BEST MALT and HOPS OBTAINABLE.

NO CORN which is largely used now to reduce the cost of production, is ever used by **ANHEUSER-BUSCH BREWING ASSOCIATION.**

Their Motto is "Not how cheap but how good."

NEW YORK DEPOT,   O. MEYER & CO., 105 BROAD ST.

NHEUSER-BUSCH

BREWING ASS'N,
ST. LOUIS, MO., U. S. A.
The First Brewery to Introduce
PASTEURIZED BOTTLED BEER IN AMERICA.

BREWERS OF FINE BEER EXCLUSIVELY.

Their Beer has never been reached in quality, and has the largest sale of Bottled Beer in the world to-day.

ANHEUSER-BUSCH Brewery never use **Corn** or **Corn** Preparations as a substitute for **Malt** and **Hops**, and its sale to-day is the **Largest** of any Brewery in the World.

Their motto is "Not how cheap but how good."

NEW YORK DEPOT, O. MEYER & CO., 104 BROAD ST.

good wage, most newspapers sold for five cents. They were costly because the paper was made from rags, obtainable in only limited quantities. Wood pulp that was to lower a paper's cost to one cent had not made its appearance.

So, at five cents, a newspaper was something of an investment, not to be read hurriedly and left in the trolley car, but scanned first and later read very carefully by the whole family at home.

As national magazines began to grow in number and importance, Anheuser-Busch advertisements appeared in them regularly and, when color at added cost became available, Adolphus was one of the first to use it for its added attention value.

How the son, August A., Sr., inherited his father's talent for the unusual and beautiful rather than the garish in advertising has been told. He, too, insisted always upon truth in advertising and continuity of advertising. August had seen other national advertisers make the mistake of turning off the advertising pressure when sales were zooming, only to lose their markets to competitors and never regain them.

Nor would August permit any corner-cutting in the company's advertising. He demanded the best artwork available. Before the newspaper matrix had reached its modern state of near-perfection, he insisted that all Anheuser-Busch advertisements be reproduced from expensive electrotypes for the best highlighting and tone quality.

He made a great contribution toward the betterment of poster art when he commissioned Oscar E. Berninghaus to paint a series of oils depicting the romantic growth and expansion of America from pre-Colonial days on. When given this commission, Berninghaus was a struggling young painter in St. Louis, but to August's discerning eye there was a promise of great talent. In the years that followed, Berninghaus justified his first patron's judgment by becoming internationally known as a portrayer of the way of life of the Indians of the Southwest. His canvases brought acclaim over and over again.

August had the frontier day pictures made into posters that were shown all

THE OLD WORLD ASTONISHED!

TRADE MARK.

ANHEUSER, BUSCH BREWING ASSN

ST. LOUIS, MO.

Extract from the Continental Gazette, Paris.

The most surprising triumph for an American product at the Paris Exhibition was the success of the Anheuser - Busch Brewing Association, of St. Louis, which eclipsed Bass, Barclay & Perkins, Alsop & Guinness, the world-renowned English brewers, as well as hundreds of rivals from Austria and Bavaria. It is not surprising that a great sensation was produced when it was understood that the experts reluctantly pronounced the St. Louis beer "superior to any malt liquor ever drank upon the continent," and that all Paris is now seeking to quaff the American nectar.

BUDWEISER

The Standard of Excellence

holds
first place
and has for
28 years.

In that period

1,310,000,000 BOTTLES
have been sold.

More than all other beers combined. It has rightly earned the title, "*King of Bottled Beers.*"

The product of

Anheuser-Busch Brewing Ass'n
St. Louis, U. S. A.

Orders promptly filled by

B. H. HOWARD & CO., Wholesale Dealers, Toronto, Canada.

PLAIN FACTS

Cleanliness is accepted as a rule of self-preservation in every reputable brewery.

AN experienced brewer would no more boast of the purity of his beer than a gentleman would brag of having washed his face.

Purity signifies nothing more than the absence of foreign matter.

For that reason brewers who do not dare to test the substantial merits of beer always harp on purity.

A really first-class beer must, however not alone be free from self-evident defects, but it must combine all the positive excellencies known to the science of brewing.

THE TRUE TEST IS ALL-ROUND QUALITY which cannot be had without SUPERIOR MATERIALS, PERFECT TREATMENT and AMPLE STORING CAPACITY.

Upon this issue of positive superiority we challenge all competitors.

Of materials we use only the most excellent, regardless of cost. Corn, the one important substitute, which, on account of its cheapness, has been extensively adopted, never enters our brewery.

Our facilities for brewing beer are unequaled.

Our storing capacity of 600,000 barrels doubles any other brewery in the United States, and enables us to store our beer from four to five months.

Facts speak louder than words.

Publicity is the demand of the day.

The consumer is entitled to the truth.

Anheuser-Busch Brewing Ass'n
St Louis, U. S. A.
Largest Brewers in the World

THE LADIES' HOME JOURNAL

Endorses
Beer as Opposed to Patent Medicines.

Of course, a pure, wholesome beer
is meant—that is

Budweiser

Mr. Edward Bok, editor of The Ladies' Home
Journal, in a page article in the May issue gives a
list of 36 medicines, with official analysis, asserting
them to contain **12 to 47 per cent. of Alcohol!**

And he adds in black type:

> "In connection with this list, think of beer, which
> contains only from two to five per cent. of
> alcohol, while some of these 'bitters' contain
> ten times as much, making them stronger than
> whisky, far stronger than sherry or port, with
> claret and champagne way behind."

Mr. Bok continues:

> "A mother who would hold up her hands in holy
> horror at the thought of her child drinking a glass
> of beer, which contains from two to five per cent of
> alcohol, gives to that child with her own hands a
> patent medicine that contains from seventeen to
> forty-four per cent of alcohol"

Budweiser contains only $3\frac{80}{100}$ per cent. of
alcohol. It is better than pure water because
of the nourishing qualities of malt and the
tonic properties of hops.

Budweiser is pre-eminently a family beverage; its use promotes the cause of true temperance—it guards the safety of health and
home. Budweiser is

"King of Bottled Beers"
Bottled only at the home plant of the
Anheuser-Busch Brewing Ass'n, St. Louis. U.S.A.

FOR MAY 1904

over America, and they proved so popular with educators and the public, too, that they were published in booklet form for school distribution.

Years later, August prevailed upon Ludwig Holwein, of Munich, one of the greatest poster-technique artists of all time, to make a series for Anheuser-Busch.

Reproductions of the Berninghaus art work are shown on page 342.

A publication called "The Poster," directed at people in the outdoor advertising industry, published an article in September, 1911, which follows and which refers to the Berninghaus posters.

Even ardent prohibitionists have acclaimed the art and excellence in advertising of the series of posters that have been spread broadcast over the face of this country by the Anheuser-Busch Brewing Company of St. Louis, Mo., promulgating the fair fame of its widely familiar product.

Testimonials have come from all quarters praising the pictured scenes and their execution. The posters have, in fact, been the sensation of the year. They have excited more comment than any other designs of this season, and there has been a scramble on the part of collectors to secure copies of them.

These posters were made from sketches by Mr. Oscar E. Berninghaus, a young artist who was born, and who lives, in St. Louis, Mo. He had already established a national reputation for his pictures of western scenes. Much of his success has been due to his intimate knowledge of his subject, for he spends several months each year in different parts of the western country.

The first of this year's series was the Attack Upon a Stagecoach; the second, the so-called Prairie Schooners (immigrants crossing the plains with ox teams); the third, the Mississippi River Steamboat at the St. Louis Wharf, of the type of the early 70's; fourth, the Locomotive and Train of Cars at a Western Railway Station, of the type of some thirty years ago; the fifth will be a typical Erie Canal boat, and will go on the boards in September, and the last of the series will be a scene of New York harbor, showing an up-to-date ocean steamer, loading beer from one of our cars for foreign ports.

A Few of the Famous
Berninghaus Posters

THE HOUSE ORGAN OF ANHEUSER-BUSCH IN THE TWENTIES AND FIFTIES

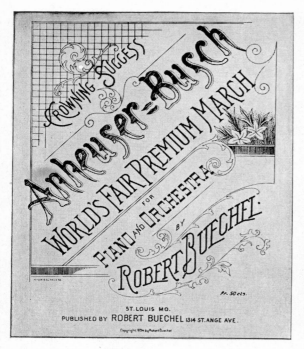

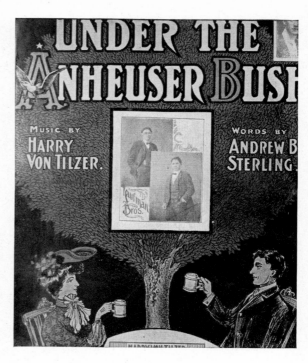

The Song Writers Became Lyrical

When Adolphus III became president, he was thoroughly indoctrinated in his father's and grandfather's ideas of advertising. But The Third had to face a problem that neither his forebears nor more than a very few other advertisers ever had to face. The dilemma was how to advertise Budweiser advantageously when supply not only failed to keep up with demand, but was so inadequate, despite continuing expansion, as to cause year after year of rationing to dealers.

Advertisements with a lot of "sell" in them would be only irritants to consumers who were told by dealers time and again that Budweiser was not available at the moment.

The decision was that, certainly, Budweiser advertising must go on. The name that had been before the public constantly for more than seventy years simply could not be permitted to vanish. Further, the decision was that in magazines and newspapers there would appear what might be called an "association theme." The product was to be associated always with the good things of life and all artwork, text and typography were to be keyed to the good living motif.

The decision proved to be such a good one that it was followed year after year until greatly expanded facilities made it possible to be more aggressive in the advertisements. Reproductions of different treatments of this basic theme appear beginning on page 359 and are amplified by captions.

Anheuser-Busch, as previously noted, had used radio for its malt syrup advertising during prohibition, but never thereafter became a big network user, because opposition to beer advertising entering the home came from many sources during the years immediately after repeal. Wholesalers were provided abundantly with recorded commercials for such air time as they chose to buy at their discretion.

In December of 1941, after the blow at Pearl Harbor and as Adolphus III was preparing to face his wartime business dilemmas and his brother, Gus, was preparing to join the Army, an advertising decision of great strategical importance was made. The plan was to circumvent repetition of World War I experience, when the prohibitionists succeeded in convincing the Congress that one step toward winning the war was to kill the brewing industry.

Early in 1942—and before the federal government asked national advertisers to publicize the war effort—Anheuser-Busch launched a magazine campaign in four colors which proved that the company was an essential industry as well as a brewery. As a prelude to the campaign, The Third issued this statement:

> All America knows Budweiser, but few are aware to what extent endless research in making the world's leading beer has led to the manufacture of many other products. It has been our good fortune over the years to expand our service to the country by the development of many products which contribute to human necessity and progress, thus providing jobs for many workers and economic security for many families.

A few advertisements of this series are reproduced on later pages. The one captioned, "Pinch-hitting for Norway," (p.352) deserves your special attention. Invaded and isolated Norway could not and Japan would not supply America with the fish oils that produced vitamin D so vital to children; the advertisement tells how, from yeast, Anheuser-Busch was able to supply the vitamin D needs of the entire nation if necessary.

The advertisements explained that Anheuser-Busch was the world's biggest single source of B-Complex vitamins and was:

> The biggest supplier of yeast vitamins for livestock and poultry.
> One of the biggest suppliers of yeast and malt syrup for bread.
> The source of millions of pounds of food starches each year.
> The source, also, of millions of pounds of industrial starches.
> The maker of great quantities of syrups for medicines and confections.
> The processor of immense quantities of table syrups.
> The maker of glider fuselages, wing assemblies and parts for gun turrets and military field kitchens.
> The manufacturer of raw materials that went into the production of machine parts, batteries, rubber, textiles, ammunition, inks, gums, glues, flashlights, carpets, twine and many others.

For the reader's convenience, on the following pages, are grouped certain of a series of institutional advertisements just as America got into World War II. Their purpose was twofold—to show the expert skill behind Budweiser and to show that Anheuser-Busch was making an essential contribution to public nutrition and welfare and to thus forestall any attempt by prohibitionists to repeat the "wartime prohibition" of World War I that led to the Eighteenth Amendment and the Volstead Act.

All America Knows Budweiser... but Few Know This

THE STORY OF BREAD
may well be called The Story of Civilization

Bread, the most venerable of prepared foods, has helped man, and man in turn has bettered the quality of his staff of life.

YEAST is the life of bread . . . and the story of yeast is the story of scientific research, uniform quality, mammoth production, modern refrigeration . . . and daily delivery to bakers in every city, town and village throughout the land . . . even by boat, by sled and by plane when other transportation is interrupted by floods and blizzards.

Anheuser-Busch is one of America's biggest sources of baker's yeast.

Year after year, we have striven with research and resources to better the methods and facilities for brewing Budweiser. To do this, a laboratory specializing in fermentology and nutrition was necessary. Discoveries made in the laboratory and in the plant have led to the development of products contributing to human necessity and progress. Some of these products would appear to have only a remote relationship to brewing, yet, they are the result of scientific research into many allied fields.

Endless research in making the world's leading beer has led to other products

VITAMINS, B COMPLEX—Anheuser-Busch is one of the world's biggest sources of natural B Complex vitamins for manufacturers of pharmaceutical and food products.

VITAMIN D—Formerly America depended upon Norway and Japan for fish oils rich in Vitamin D. Today we produce from yeast enough of the basic material for Vitamin D to supply the entire American market.

VITAMINS FOR LIVESTOCK—Anheuser-Busch is the biggest supplier of yeast vitamins to fortify animal feeds, thus improving the quality and propagation of cattle and poultry.

CANDIES—Corn syrup is an essential candy ingredient. Our Corn Products Division, an industry in itself, produces annually many millions of pounds of highest quality corn syrup, rich in food and energy value.

SYRUPS—*(for food—for medicine)*—In addition to fine table and confectionery syrups, Anheuser-Busch produces special syrups used as a basis for medicines.

STARCH—Thousands of food industries all over America choose Anheuser-Busch pure food corn starch for their products—millions of pounds each year. We also supply starch to the textile, paper and many other industries.

FRESHER FOODS—Retailers of frozen foods and ice cream the country over have equipment manufactured until recently by our Refrigeration Division. Today, however, this division is working all out on glider wing and fuselage assemblies for our armed forces.

DIESEL ENGINES—Adolphus Busch, founder of Anheuser-Busch, acquired the first rights to manufacture this revolutionary engine in America and thus started our great Diesel industry on its way.

Budweiser
ANHEUSER · BUSCH · · SAINT LOUIS

FROM GLACIERS TO GLIDERS

Thousands of retailers of ice cream and frozen foods are using equipment made by our Refrigeration Division—a manufacturing activity which was developed from our years of experience in making ice in glacier-like quantities needed for the brewing of Budweiser.

This equipment is helping to keep America's foods fresher and more nutritious.

Today, however, orders for ice cream and food cabinets will have to wait, for this Division is working all-out on glider wing and fuselage assemblies for our Army Air Forces.

Year after year, we have striven with research and resources to better the methods and facilities for brewing Budweiser. To do this, a laboratory specializing in fermentology and nutrition was necessary. Discoveries made in the laboratory and in the plant have led to the development of products contributing to human necessity and progress. Some of these products would appear to have only a remote relationship to brewing, yet, they are the result of scientific research into many allied fields.

Endless research in making the world's leading beer has led to other products

VITAMINS, B COMPLEX—Our plant is one of the world's largest sources for manufacturers of pharmaceutical and food products.

VITAMIN D—Anheuser-Busch produces enough of the basic material for Vitamin D to supply the entire American market.

BAKER'S YEAST—We are one of America's biggest suppliers of standard and enriched yeasts and malt syrup used to make bread.

CORN SYRUP—many millions of pounds annually for America's candy industry.

SYRUPS—for food, table and confectionery uses and special syrups for medicinal purposes.

STARCH—for food, textile, paper and other industries—millions of pounds annually.

VITAMINS FOR LIVESTOCK—We are America's biggest supplier of yeast vitamins used to fortify animal feeds.

DIESEL ENGINES—Adolphus Busch, founder of Anheuser-Busch, acquired the first rights to manufacture this revolutionary engine in America and thus started our great Diesel industry on its way.

Budweiser

A N H E U S E R - B U S C H • • S A I N T   L O U I S

ALL AMERICA KNOWS BUDWEISER... BUT FEW KNOW THIS

...TO GUARD YOUR WELL-BEING

You owe it to yourself and to your country to keep well. Vitamins are an important part of the nation's health program. Did you know that Anheuser-Busch is one of the world's largest sources of natural B Complex Vitamins for manufacturers of pharmaceutical and food products? That it produces yeast vitamin concentrates for civilian and military hospitals?

Year after year, we have striven with research and resources to better the methods and facilities for brewing Budweiser. To do this, a laboratory specializing in fermentology and nutrition was necessary. Discoveries made in the laboratory and in the plant have led to the development of products contributing to human necessity and progress. Some of these products would appear to have only a remote relationship to brewing, yet, they are the result of scientific research into many allied fields.

Endless research in making the world's leading beer has led to other products

In addition to supplying the armed forces with glider assemblies, gun turret parts and foodstuffs, Anheuser-Busch produces materials which go into the manufacture of:

Baby Foods • Bakery Products Confections • Yeasted Peanut Butter Packaged Foods • Ice Cream • Soda Fountain Syrups • Hospital Diets Vitamin Preparations • Food Starches Tonics • Medicines • Animal Feeds Batteries • Rubber • Paper • Soap Machine Parts • Inks • Gums Glues • Textiles • Adhesives • Flashlights • Carpets • Twine

VITAMIN D—Formerly America depended upon Norway and Japan for fish oils rich in Vitamin D. Today we produce from yeast enough of the basic material for Vitamin D to supply the entire American market.

VITAMINS FOR LIVESTOCK—Anheuser-Busch is the biggest supplier of yeast vitamins to fortify animal feeds, thus improving the quality and propagation of cattle and poultry.

CANDIES—Corn syrup is an essential candy ingredient. Our Corn Products Division, an industry in itself, produces annually many millions of pounds of highest quality corn syrup, rich in food and energy value.

SYRUPS—(for food—for medicine)—In addition to fine table and confectionery syrups, Anheuser-Busch produces special syrups used as a basis for medicines.

STARCH—Thousands of food industries all over America choose Anheuser-Busch pure food corn starch for their products—millions of pounds each year. We also supply starch to the textile, paper and many other industries.

FRESHER FOODS—Retailers of frozen foods and ice cream the country over have equipment manufactured until recently by our Refrigeration Division. Today, however, this division is working all out on glider wing and fuselage assemblies for our armed forces.

BREAD—Anheuser-Busch is one of America's biggest suppliers of baker's standard and enriched yeasts and malt syrup to make bread.

DIESEL ENGINES—Adolphus Busch, founder of Anheuser-Busch, acquired the first rights to manufacture this revolutionary engine in America and thus started our great Diesel industry on its way.

ANHEUSER-BUSCH
SAINT LOUIS

Budweiser

TRADE MARK REG.
U. S. PAT. OFF.

*All America Knows
Budweiser...
but Few Know This*

Starch Helps Make Munitions, Batteries..

Everyone knows that corn starch is used in pies, puddings, cakes and other good things to eat. In addition to various household uses, it is necessary, too, for making batteries, cosmetics, paper and textiles, to name a few. Where does Anheuser-Busch fit in this picture? We learned a lot about cereals from constant analysis of barley for Budweiser. With that knowledge we started a Corn Products Division, which now supplies millions of pounds of starches each year to food and other industries.

Year after year, we have striven with research and resources to better the methods and facilities for brewing Budweiser. To do this, a laboratory specializing in fermentology and nutrition was necessary. Discoveries made in the laboratory and in the plant have led to the development of products contributing to human necessity and progress. Some of these products would appear to have only a remote relationship to brewing, yet, they are the result of scientific research into many allied fields.

Endless research in making the world's leading beer has led to other products

VITAMINS, B COMPLEX—Our plant is one of the world's largest sources for manufacturers of pharmaceutical and food products.

VITAMIN D—Anheuser-Busch produces enough of the basic material for Vitamin D to supply the entire American market.

BAKER'S YEAST—We are one of America's biggest suppliers of standard and enriched yeasts and malt syrup used to make bread.

CORN SYRUP—many millions of pounds annually for America's candy industry.

SYRUPS—for food, table and confectionery uses and special syrups for medicinal purposes.

VITAMINS FOR LIVESTOCK—We are America's biggest supplier of yeast vitamins used to fortify animal feeds.

REFRIGERATING EQUIPMENT—for retailers of frozen foods and ice cream the country over. This division is now working all-out on glider wing and fuselage assemblies for our Armed Forces.

DIESEL ENGINES—Adolphus Busch, founder of Anheuser-Busch, acquired the first rights to manufacture this revolutionary engine in America and thus started our great Diesel industry on its way.

Budweiser

A N H E U S E R · B U S C H · · S A I N T   L O U I S

All America Knows Budweiser... but Few Know This

PINCH-HITTING FOR NORWAY

Vitamin D for all the family. Especially for the youngsters. Every mother knows its importance. One vital source was fish oils from Norway,—now unobtainable. But there's no shortage of Vitamin D. Anheuser-Busch is now producing from yeast the basic material from which this essential vitamin is made by pharmaceutical laboratories—enough to supply the entire American market.

Year after year, we have striven with research and resources to better the methods and facilities for brewing Budweiser. To do this, a laboratory specializing in fermentology and nutrition was necessary. Discoveries made in the laboratory and in the plant have led to the development of products contributing to human necessity and progress. Some of these products would appear to have only a remote relationship to brewing, yet, they are the result of scientific research into many allied fields.

Endless research in making the world's leading beer has led to other products

VITAMINS, B COMPLEX—Anheuser-Busch is one of the world's largest sources for manufacturers of pharmaceutical and food products.

BAKER'S YEAST—We are one of America's biggest suppliers of standard and enriched yeasts and malt syrup used to make bread.

CORN SYRUP—many millions of pounds annually for America's candy industry.

SYRUPS—for food, table and confectionery uses and special syrups for medicinal purposes.

STARCH—for food, textile, paper and other industries—millions of pounds annually.

VITAMINS FOR LIVESTOCK—We are America's biggest supplier of yeast vitamins used to fortify animal feeds.

REFRIGERATING EQUIPMENT—for retailers of frozen foods and ice cream the country over. This division is now working all-out on glider wing and fuselage assemblies for our Armed Forces.

DIESEL ENGINES—Adolphus Busch, founder of Anheuser-Busch, acquired the first rights to manufacture this revolutionary engine in America and thus started our great Diesel industry on its way.

Budweiser

ANHEUSER · BUSCH · · SAINT LOUIS

All America Knows Budweiser... but Few Know This

THEY'VE PASSED THEIR 'PHYSICAL'—TOO

America's feathered and four-legged armies are very much on their toes these days. Yeast vitamins used in fortifying animal feeds have done wonders in recent years to better the quality and propagation of livestock and poultry. Did you know that the Home of Budweiser is America's biggest single source of these vitamins?

Year after year, we have striven with research and resources to better the methods and facilities for brewing Budweiser. To do this, a laboratory specializing in fermentology and nutrition was necessary. Discoveries made in the laboratory and in the plant have led to the development of products contributing to human necessity and progress. Some of these products would appear to have only a remote relationship to brewing, yet, they are the result of scientific research into many allied fields.

Endless research in making the world's leading beer has led to other products

VITAMINS, B COMPLEX—Our plant is one of the world's largest sources for manufacturers of pharmaceutical and food products.

VITAMIN D—Anheuser-Busch produces enough of the basic material for Vitamin D to supply the entire American market.

BAKER'S YEAST—We are one of America's biggest suppliers of standard and enriched yeasts and malt syrup used to make bread.

CORN SYRUP—many millions of pounds annually for America's candy industry.

SYRUPS—for food, table and confectionery uses and special syrups for medicinal purposes.

STARCH—for food, textile, paper and other industries—millions of pounds annually.

REFRIGERATING EQUIPMENT—for retailers of frozen foods and ice cream the country over. This division is now working all-out on glider wing and fuselage assemblies for our Armed Forces.

DIESEL ENGINES—Adolphus Busch, founder of Anheuser-Busch, acquired the first rights to manufacture this revolutionary engine in America and thus started our great Diesel industry on its way.

 # Budweiser

ANHEUSER-BUSCH · · · SAINT LOUIS

...To Help a Child's Dream Come True

A candy castle...snowdrifts of marshmallow! What youngster hasn't seen them in his dreams?

To the great candy industry of America, corn syrup is a necessary ingredient. Used in other foods as well as candy, it contributes much to the energy and nutrition of the nation. Many millions of pounds of corn syrup are produced each year by Anheuser-Busch for manufacturers of many essential products. Our Corn Products Division is an industry in itself.

Year after year, we have striven with research and resources to better the methods and facilities for brewing Budweiser. To do this, a laboratory specializing in fermentology and nutrition was necessary. Discoveries made in the laboratory and in the plant have led to the development of products contributing to human necessity and progress. Some of these products would appear to have only a remote relationship to brewing, yet, they are the result of scientific research into many allied fields.

Endless research in making the world's leading beer has led to other products

In addition to supplying the armed forces with glider assemblies, gun turret parts and foodstuffs, Anheuser-Busch produces materials which go into the manufacture of:

Baby Foods • Bakery Products
Confections • Yeasted Peanut Butter
Packaged Foods • Ice Cream • Soda
Fountain Syrups • Hospital Diets
Vitamin Preparations • Food Starches
Tonics • Medicines • Animal Feeds
Batteries • Rubber • Paper • Soap
Machine Parts • Inks • Gums
Glues • Textiles • Adhesives • Flashlights • Carpets • Twine

VITAMINS, B COMPLEX—Anheuser-Busch is one of the world's biggest sources of natural B Complex vitamins for manufacturers of pharmaceutical and food products.

VITAMIN D—Formerly America depended upon Norway and Japan for fish oils rich in Vitamin D. Today we produce from yeast enough of the basic material for Vitamin D to supply the entire American market.

VITAMINS FOR LIVESTOCK—Anheuser-Busch is the biggest supplier of yeast vitamins to fortify animal feeds, thus improving the quality and propagation of cattle and poultry.

SYRUPS—*(for food—for medicine)*—In addition to fine table and confectionery syrups, Anheuser-Busch produces special syrups used as a basis for medicines.

STARCH—Thousands of food industries all over America choose Anheuser-Busch pure food corn starch for their products—millions of pounds each year. We also supply starch to the textile, paper and many other industries.

FRESHER FOODS—Retailers of frozen foods and ice cream the country over have equipment manufactured until recently by our Refrigeration Division. Today, however, this division is working all out on glider wing and fuselage assemblies for our armed forces.

BREAD—Anheuser-Busch is one of America's biggest suppliers of baker's standard and enriched yeasts and malt syrup to make bread.

DIESEL ENGINES—Adolphus Busch, founder of Anheuser-Busch, acquired the first rights to manufacture this revolutionary engine in America and thus started our great Diesel industry on its way.

**ANHEUSER-BUSCH
SAINT LOUIS**

Budweiser

HORSEPOWER
FOR VICTORY

The first American-made Diesel engine was built to create more and better power for the brewing of Budweiser. • Adolphus Busch, founder of Anheuser-Busch, acquired the first rights to manufacture this revolutionary engine in America and thus started our great Diesel industry on its way.

He also founded Busch-Sulzer Bros.-Diesel Engine Company which made submarine engines in World War I, and today holds the Navy E Award for excellence in the production of Navy ordnance and Diesel engines essential to the war effort.

Year after year, we have striven with research and resources to better the methods and facilities for brewing Budweiser. To do this, a laboratory specializing in fermentology and nutrition was necessary. Discoveries made in the laboratory and in the plant have led to the development of products contributing to human necessity and progress. Some of these products would appear to have only a remote relationship to brewing, yet, they are the result of scientific research into many allied fields.

Endless research in making the world's leading beer has led to other products

VITAMINS, B COMPLEX—Our plant is one of the world's largest sources for manufacturers of pharmaceutical and food products.

VITAMIN D—Anheuser-Busch produces enough of the basic material for Vitamin D to supply the entire American market.

BAKER'S YEAST—We are one of America's biggest suppliers of standard and enriched yeasts and malt syrup used to make bread.

CORN SYRUP—many millions of pounds annually for America's candy industry.

SYRUPS—for food, table and confectionery uses and special syrups for medicinal purposes.

STARCH—for food, textile, paper and other industries—millions of pounds annually.

VITAMINS FOR LIVESTOCK—We are America's biggest supplier of yeast vitamins used to fortify animal feeds.

REFRIGERATING EQUIPMENT—for retailers of frozen foods and ice cream the country over. This division is now working all-out on glider wing and fuselage assemblies for our Armed Forces.

Budweiser

ANHEUSER · BUSCH · · SAINT LOUIS

As the war progressed, Anheuser-Busch received gratis much favorable publicity on its help in perfecting a water-tight package for the armed services. Into these packages went food, medicines, other supplies and enough air to keep the sealed packet from sinking in water. Supply ships thus were able to stand off-shore from invaded enemy territory and, with the help of incoming tides, float the essentials to the armed forces on land without the necessity of ferrying them in by boat.

In World War II, no one tried to suggest that Anheuser-Busch be jettisoned as it had been in the first world conflict.

When the suggestion came from the federal government that advertisers publicize at their own expense wartime directives, activities and needs, the company responded instantly. The first advertisement had for its headline, "The Minuteman Is Still the Man of the Hour," and its sequel bore the caption, "You Know the Minuteman—Now Meet the Missus." Both are reproduced on pages 360 and 361.

With the launching of this campaign, Adolphus III issued another widely quoted statement, which follows:

THE SPIRIT OF THE MINUTEMAN had been slumbering for decades when the news of America's worst blow exploded into a peaceful Sunday afternoon. Then, as if by magic, that spirit was quickly revived. Our people took a horse sense look at the mess they were in . . . and went to work—on battle front and home front.

The way in which our Nation agreed to suspend hard-won personal rights and privileges considered inalienable in our democracy—to defeat the powers of tyranny and autocracy—has been inspiring to our Allies and confounding to our enemies. Business and industry have given new glory to America's treasured free enterprise.

Our despotically regimented foes can never forget what our voluntary and efficient Civilian Defense, our breath-taking war production and our overpowering fighting forces recruited from peaceful civilians have accomplished. And all this with free speech still at liberty to be just as free, just as noisy—or just as purposeful—as it pleased.

The pages that follow show one phase of free speech in action . . . reminding people of the tasks to be done . . . persuading . . . and, above all, getting results. Yet, Anheuser-Busch claims to have done no more than hundreds of other National advertisers whose printed words about themselves and their products have been minimized so that their advertising columns could give wider circulation to messages helpful to our country in its hour of need.

Some of these wartime advertisements are reproduced on pages 360-374. They resulted in the Certificate of Merit Award (p.358) and a special award for the advertisement entitled "Not an A Card in Ye Group" (p.362).

At its own expense, the War Advertising Council sent reprints of the Anheuser-Busch advertisements to other advertisers as examples of how the war effort could be helped. The Council gave its reactions in the following letter:

WAR ADVERTISING COUNCIL, INC.

A NON-PROFIT ORGANIZATION, REPRESENTING ALL PHASES OF ADVERTISING, CREATED TO ENLIST THE POWER OF ADVERTISING FOR VICTORY

1010 Vermont Avenue, N.W.
Washington 5, D. C.

60 East 42nd Street
New York 17, N. Y.
Washington, D. C.
May 10, 1944

Mr. P. J. Orthwein, Vice President
D'Arcy Advertising Company
Missouri Pacific Building
St. Louis 3, Missouri

Dear Mr. Orthwein:

I am taking the liberty of answering your letter of May 8, addressed to Mr. LaRoche, to which was attached proofs of your new series of magazine advertisements.

I don't believe it is an overstatement to say that this new series ranks as one of the most important contributions to the war made by any advertiser. The fact that this series has continuity with a circulation of 60,000,000, that it is supplemented by a 5-months showing of 24 sheet posters exposed

1944
WARTIME ADVERTISING AWARDS
CERTIFICATE OF MERIT TO

ANHEUSER-BUSCH, INC.

AND

D'ARCY ADVERTISING COMPANY, INC.

FOR A CAMPAIGN CONTRIBUTING TO THE WELFARE, SECURITY
AND ACTIVITY OF THE NATION AT WAR

WARTIME ADVERTISING AWARDS JURY

H. W. RODEN, *Chairman*

WILLIAM REYDEL	GORDON COLE	ALLEN BILLINGSLEY
CHARLES MORTIMER	L. STANFORD BRIGGS	C. C. CARR
LEO BURNETT	JAMES W. YOUNG	DAVID FREDERICK

CHAIRMAN

ADMINISTRATIVE BOARD

Chairman: STUART PEABODY, *Advertising Director, The Borden Company;* ALLEN L. BILLINGSLEY, *President, Fuller & Smith & Ross, Inc.;* EARNEST ELMO CALKINS, *Director, Calkins & Holden;* GEORGE T. EAGLE, *Philadelphia Bulletin;* EBEN GRIFFITHS, *Advertising Manager, Socony-Vacuum Oil Co., Inc.;* WILLIAM A. HART, *Director of Advertising, E. I. du Pont de Nemours & Company, Inc.;* GEORGE BURTON HOTCHKISS, *Professor of Marketing,* *New York University;* ROY LARSEN, *President, Time, Inc.;* MRS. OGDEN REID, *Vice President, N. Y. Herald Tribune;* H. W. RODEN, *President, American Home Foods, Inc.;* G. LYNN SUMNER, *President, The G. Lynn Sumner Co., Inc.;* P. L. THOMSON, *President, Audit Bureau of Circulations.*

to 70,000,000 people, plus the excellence of the material, itself—combine to make us extremely enthusiastic over the job you are doing.

The Council would like to inform a good many people, both here in Washington and throughout the country, of your new program, and I will appreciate your rushing me ten sets of proofs as a starter. If you have no objection, we will undoubtedly ask you to supply a larger number of proofs at a later date.

I am sure your client may feel that he has not only made an important contribution to the war, but that he will win a measure of good-will that could not be secured by purely product advertising.

Very sincerely,

T. S. Repplier
Executive Director

*On the following pages are shown magazine adver-
tisements and posters published during World
War II. Hardly any promotion of the product was
made in these advertisements. They are confined
to messages which the Federal Government wanted
put across to the American people to increase
everyone's contribution to the war effort.*

The Minuteman *is Still the Man of the Hour*

The Minuteman was a most resourceful civilian who worked hard for his family and home and was quick to fight when their security was threatened.

He did the very things we are asked to do today. He made things last. He wore things out and did without. He was one of the first to stretch food and fuel.

Farmers, fishermen, sailmakers, smiths or cobblers—all were Minutemen—all were dreamers who loved their America—all were doers who fought and saved and sacrificed. They showed us the way to win.

Americans, since the days of the Minuteman, have welcomed their opportunity to earn security for themselves and their families in a better world.

Today, when wartime trials provoke us, America is recapturing the spirit of '76—America's fighting spirit, so perfectly symbolized by the Minuteman—the spirit that will hasten Victory by hours, by days, perhaps even months.

* * *

In addition to supplying the armed forces with glider and bomber fuselage frames, wing parts, gun turret parts and foodstuffs, Anheuser-Busch produces materials which go into the manufacture of: Rubber · Aluminum · Munitions · Medicines · B Complex Vitamins · Hospital Diets · Baby Foods · Bread and other Bakery products · Vitamin-fortified cattle feeds · Batteries · Paper · Soap and textiles—to name a few.

Americans have always been neighborly. It is quite natural then for Budweiser to be America's favorite beer—for, when good friends get together, Budweiser is a friend that needs no introduction.

Budweiser

ANHEUSER-BUSCH · · SAINT LOUIS

For Freedom's Sake
BUY WAR BONDS AND STAMPS

You Know the Minuteman...
Now...Meet the Missus

The hand that rocked the cradle had to have a good trigger finger, because the Minuteman's wife often did her "marketing" in the forest with a gun. She was a Jill of all trades, too—cook, spinner, weaver, pork salter, candle maker, baker, laundress and gardener.

How are her great, great granddaughters doing? Very well, thank you. Some are serving with our armed forces. Some work in war plants. Others grow Victory Gardens, preserve fruits and vegetables, cook, serve, sew...save fats, cans and paper ...make things last, wear them out and do without. They carry their own bundles, keep the family cheerful—in a word, they are doing their share to win the war by taking over on the home front—for their husbands and sons.

*   *   *

In addition to supplying the armed forces with glider and bomber fuselage frames, wing parts, gun turret parts and foodstuffs, Anheuser-Busch produces materials which go into the manufacture of: Rubber · Aluminum · Munitions · Medicines · B Complex Vitamins · Hospital Diets · Baby Foods · Bread and other Bakery products Vitamin-fortified cattle feeds · Batteries · Paper · Soap and Textiles—to name a few.

The women of America have proved their resourcefulness in the kitchen in countless ways. Many have discovered that a glass of cold, golden Budweiser makes their simple wartime meals taste better.

Budweiser

A N H E U S E R - B U S C H · · · S A I N T   L O U I S

SAVE GASOLINE
SAVE TIRES

Not an A Card in Ye Group

Wherever they went, they walked . . . on guard at every step. Hardships taught our forefathers the virtue of self-reliance and the need for cooperation. Thus, in the humble cradle of privation the spirit of our Democracy was born.

Our enemies foolishly ignored the enduring influence of our Nation's heritage when they jeered that we were too soft to fight. Little did they dream that, almost overnight, free men could perfect the finest and best-equipped fighting forces the world has ever seen.

So, today when good citizens see an A card on a windshield, they recognize it as a symbol of what people can accomplish who have learned from experience to work together to attain a common objective.

That same spirit will win this war— and in peacetime that same unity of effort will keep America strong and prosperous for our men and women now on the fighting front.

Most folks are more tired than usual when they finish each wartime day. A bottle of golden, foaming Budweiser is a welcome companion in a moment of relaxation—and it makes simple, wartime meals taste better.

* * *

In addition to supplying the armed forces with glider and bomber fuselage frames, wing parts, gun turret parts and foodstuffs, Anheuser-Busch produces materials which go into the manufacture of: Rubber · Aluminum · Munitions · Medicines · B Complex Vitamins · Hospital Diets · Baby Foods · Bread and other Bakery products Vitamin-fortified cattle feeds · Batteries · Paper · Soap and textiles—to name a few.

Budweiser

ANHEUSER-BUSCH · · SAINT LOUIS

If it's harmful to our war effort, don't repeat it

Thinking Americans Today...
Are Not Too Free With Free Speech

Since our republic was founded, no privilege has been guarded more jealously than the right to talk things over—a right for which men had fought in vain for centuries. The more viewpoints discussed, the clearer our national vision and the stronger our national unity.

Today, public opinion in America asks us all to protect our privilege. It warns, us against spreading rumors thoughtlessly or circulating information helpful to the enemy. It urges us to challenge the person with "inside information on the war" by asking him, "Where did you get your facts?" It reminds us that the enemy lays important plans by piecing together little scraps of offhand information. *There is no such thing as unimportant gossip.*

When a product maintains the character that people respect, they are quick to demand it. Generations ago, the makers of Budweiser set a standard—distinctive in taste, pure, good and distinguished for its uniform quality. That's why people everywhere have agreed that Budweiser is "something more than beer". No wonder it is the most popular beer in history.

In addition to supplying the armed forces with glider and bomber fuselage frames, wing parts, gun turret, parts and foodstuffs, Anheuser-Busch produces materials which go into the manufacture of: Rubber • Aluminum • Munitions • Medicines • B Complex Vitamins • Hospital Diets • Baby Foods • Bread and other Bakery products Vitamin-fortified cattle feeds • Batteries • Paper • Soap and Textiles—to name a few.

Budweiser

ANHEUSER-BUSCH • • SAINT LOUIS

EAT PLENTY OF BREAD

More came *Out* of that
Old Lunch Pail than went *In*

Big sandwiches with thick slices of bread helped to build the brawn that built America's industrial might.

Wartime demands upon men and women, young and old, have brought us as a nation to a stern realization of the need for an adequate diet for all.

So today—in homes, in plant cafeterias and in restaurants-large and small—America is wisely recognizing the nutritive importance of bread. Now enriched, it is the finest bread ever set before the human race . . . so good that our ancestors would have called it cake.

When you eat plenty of enriched bread, you improve your diet besides saving ration points for other good foods.

In your own family circle or on evenings when good friends surround you, simple sandwiches become delicacies when served with golden, bubbling Budweiser . . . which accents the flavors of all good foods, yet never loses the identity of its own distinctive taste.

In addition to supplying the bakers of America with yeast, Anheuser-Busch manufactures glider and bomber fuselage frames, wing parts, gun turret parts and foodstuffs for the government, and produces other materials which go into the manufacture of: Rubber • Aluminum • Munitions • Medicines • B Complex Vitamins • Hospital Diets • Baby Foods • Bread and other Bakery products Vitamin-fortified cattle feeds • Batteries • Paper • Soap and Textiles to name a few.

Budweiser

A N H E U S E R - B U S C H • • S A I N T L O U I S

Grandma Knew Just What To Do
...AND WHAT TO DO WITHOUT

Scraps, nails and string . . . paper, fats and fuel . . . anything and everything that could serve another time or another purpose was saved by our ancestors as a matter of dire necessity. The frugality of America's rugged pioneers helped to win battle after battle in our nation's history.

Today, our country asks us to practice that same frugality to help win the war, to save our way of life and to protect our freedom of opportunity for every American family.

Peace and the change-over from war-stimulated activity will pose many problems to challenge the ingenuity of every one of us. Fortune will favor the family that has learned to save and has bolstered its future by the purchase of War Bonds. It's so much sounder to save than to wait to be saved.

* * *

In addition to supplying the armed forces with glider and bomber fuselage frames, wing parts, gun turret parts and foodstuffs, Anheuser-Busch produces materials which go into the manufacture of: Rubber • Aluminum • Munitions • Medicines • B Complex Vitamins • Hospital Diets • Baby Foods • Bread and other Bakery products Vitamin-fortified cattle feeds • Batteries • Paper • Soap and Textiles—to name a few.

REMINDER FOR THRIFTY HOUSEWIVES: *There's nourishment in simple, wartime meals, but, to make them taste better—simply serve the world's most popular beer—cold, bubbling Budweiser.*

Budweiser

A N H E U S E R - B U S C H • • • S A I N T   L O U I S

SHARE THE RIDE *TODAY*

...and *You Give Uncle Sam a Lift*

Where would we be today if our forefathers had gone their separate ways at their own convenience? When this nation was in its infancy, neighbor gave neighbor a helping hand. That spirit expanded 13 struggling colonies into a vast, united nation.

Today our country is calling upon every one of us to enlist in a great awakening of that early American creed of helping ourselves by helping our neighbors. Sharing our automobiles is as easy as it is helpful. Wherever we go, there's somebody going our way. When we give him a lift, we give Uncle Sam a lift on the way to Victory.

* * *

In addition to supplying the armed forces with glider and bomber fuselage frames, wing parts, gun turret parts and foodstuffs, Anheuser-Busch produces materials which go into the manufacture of: Rubber • Aluminum • Munitions • Medicines • B Complex Vitamins • Hospital Diets • Baby Foods • Bread and other Bakery products Vitamin-fortified cattle feeds • Batteries • Paper • Soap and Textiles—to name a few.

It is in those moments of well-earned relaxation that a beverage of moderation proves a welcome companion. Budweiser matches your mood for a friendly chat or your mood for repose. It is considerate of tomorrow's obligations.

Budweiser

A N H E U S E R - B U S C H • • S A I N T L O U I S

TRAVEL ONLY WHEN NECESSARY

When Buffaloes Stopped the Iron Horse
...TRAVELERS WERE PATIENT

Remembering the hardships of the stagecoach and covered wagon days, travelers once looked upon the new woodburner trains as solid luxury . . .

Despite choking smoke, bumpy roadbeds; no electric lights, no berths or dining cars . . . despite delays of hours on end when great herds of migrating buffaloes marooned them in the middle of an endless prairie, travelers were cheerful and understanding.

Today, if the train, plane or bus is late, if reservations are hard to get or we can't squeeze into the dining car,

we can still take comfort in the fact that America is moving at a pace that has astounded the world.

When this war is won, the transportation facilities of our country will have hung up an incredible record for efficient movement of fighting men and freight—and civilians, too. Meanwhile, public opinion is agreed that we should not travel unless absolutely necessary and, if we must go, take inconveniences cheerfully and patiently—like good soldiers.

Like so many other worthwhile products, Budweiser may not be available every time you call for it. People everywhere have discovered that only Budweiser tastes like Budweiser. That is why they continue to ask for it. That is why it is the world's most popular beer.

* * *

In addition to supplying the armed forces with glider and bomber fuselage frames, wing parts, gun turret parts and foodstuffs, Anheuser-Busch produces materials which go into the manufacture of: Rubber · Aluminum · Munitions · Medicines · B Complex Vitamins · Hospital Diets · Baby Foods · Bread and other Bakery products Vitamin-fortified cattle feeds · Batteries · Paper · Soap and Textiles—to name a few.

Budweiser

ANHEUSER-BUSCH · · SAINT LOUIS

INVEST IN AMERICA

Stake YOUR Claim NOW with War Bonds

It took a lot of grit for a man and wife to stow their children into a prairie schooner with a few bare necessities and fight it out with all the hardships the frontier had to offer. Yet, these self-reliant pioneers proved their ability to win the finest reward a family can have —security in a land of growing opportunities.

Today, solid citizens are staking their claim in America's future by buying and keeping War Bonds. They know Bonds help to win battle after battle. They know, too, that Bonds will provide security and opportunity for personal initiative when war-supported activity ceases.

Do you know of anything that offers you as much for your money as a War Bond? INVEST IN AMERICA.

*   *   *

A journey's end is the beginning of relaxation. In such a moment, Budweiser will prove a welcome companion. Count on Budweiser to make your simple wartime meals taste better. Every sip will tell you why.

In addition to supplying the armed forces with glider and bomber fuselage frames, wing parts, gun turret parts and foodstuffs, Anheuser-Busch produces materials which go into the manufacture of Rubber • Aluminum • Munitions • Medicines • B Complex Vitamins • Hospital Diets • Baby Foods • Bread and other Bakery products Vitamin-fortified cattle feeds • Batteries • Paper • Soap and textiles—to name a few.

Budweiser

ANHEUSER-BUSCH • • SAINT LOUIS

HELP YOUR NEIGHBOR...
AND YOU HELP YOUR COUNTRY

They Builded Better Than They Knew

With the help of the neighbors, many a little red schoolhouse was built. That readiness to help the folks down the road and the family across the square was the strength of our early America, the foundation for our democracy. Because of it, we have a greater heritage to defend than any other people on Earth.

In these wartime days, the spirit of neighborliness so characteristic of our people is again paying dividends. Did you ever dream ten years ago that today you would pull up to the curb and offer a ride to a stranger? That you would have a bundle of salvaged paper ready when the Boy Scouts called? That you would walk home with awkward packages because your dealers have difficulty making deliveries? When you aid your neighbor, you aid your country. Isn't it surprising how many things one person can do to help win a war?

*   *   *

In addition to supplying the armed forces with glider and bomber fuselage frames, wing parts, gun turret parts and foodstuffs, Anheuser-Busch produces materials which go into the manufacture of: Rubber • Aluminum • Munitions • Medicines • B Complex Vitamins • Hospital Diets • Baby Foods • Bread and other Bakery products Vitamin-fortified cattle feeds • Batteries • Paper • Soap and Textiles—to name a few.

People who get results agree that there is no substitute for hard work and also that recreation and relaxation are essential to accomplishment. In your well-earned leisure, select a beverage of moderation. A tall, stately glass of Budweiser is a standing invitation to make your moments of relaxation complete.

Budweiser

A N H E U S E R - B U S C H • • S A I N T   L O U I S

Ye Olde
Melting
Pot

EARLY AMERICA
SHOWED US HOW

HELP YOUR COMMUNITY DRIVES
...and You Help America

In Colonial days when a family faced misfortune, kindly neighbors set up a melting pot before the door. The community was quick to contribute, because lean and perilous years taught our forefathers that only by helping one another could all survive and earn security in a land of growing opportunities.

Today, when this hard-won security is in jeopardy, our country and many of its citizens need a helping hand. The Red Cross, the War Chest, the scrap and salvage drives and other calls on each community are realistic reminders of the pioneer spirit that bound our nation together ... that gave us the highest standard of living the world has ever known. When we help our neighbors we help our country.

*   *   *

In addition to supplying the armed forces with glider and bomber fuselage frames, wing parts, gun turret parts and foodstuffs, Anheuser-Busch produces materials which go into the manufacture of: Rubber • Aluminum Munitions • Medicines • B Complex Vitamins • Hospital Diets • Baby Foods • Bread and other Bakery products • Vitamin-fortified cattle feeds • Batteries • Paper • Soap and textiles — to name a few.

In every community, Budweiser is known as the Perfect Host to a host of friends. To serve your neighbors beer is simple hospitality, but to serve them Budweiser is a gracious compliment ... and, it makes your simple wartime meals taste better.

Budweiser

ANHEUSER-BUSCH • • SAINT LOUIS

RATIONING
came over on The Mayflower

THEY RATIONED EVERYTHING

The Pilgrims knew they were ill-prepared for one of the cruelest winters that resolute men, women and children ever had to face. Foreseeing trials that would challenge their endurance, they treasured their scanty store of food and rationed every helping.

But, when a Spring and Summer of strenuous labor rewarded them with an abundant harvest, the Pilgrims were grateful—but not alone for food. They felt they were well on their way toward an established home in a new world, bright with freedom, security and a promising future for their children. America's goal has never changed. And for such a goal rationing is a small price to contribute.

"Food Fights For Freedom".

* * *

In addition to supplying the armed forces with glider and bomber fuselage frames, wing parts, gun turret parts and foodstuffs, Anheuser-Busch produces materials which go into the manufacture of: Rubber • Aluminum Munitions • Medicines • B Complex Vitamins • Hospital Diets • Baby Foods • Bread and other Bakery products • Vitamin-fortified cattle feeds • Batteries • Paper • Soap and textiles—to name a few.

What ration points bring to our tables today would have seemed like banquets to generations of our forefathers—but you have Budweiser, too, to make simple wartime meals taste better.

Budweiser

ANHEUSER - BUSCH • • • SAINT LOUIS

FOUR OF AMERICA'S MOST POPULAR POSTERS—
The fortune teller poster was judged the poster of the year by a committee of artists, advertisers and advertising agencies. The Christmas poster was so popular that it was repeated for ten consecutive years.

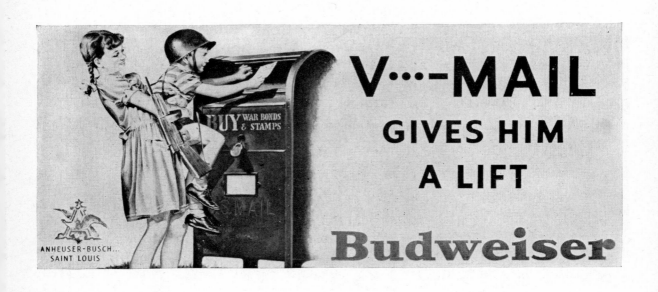

Chapter XXVIII

MORE PRODUCTION,
MORE ADVERTISING

WITH THE WAR won, Anheuser-Busch again found itself in the position of being unable to meet the demand for Budweiser beer. What in other times would have been an expected, normal situation was aggravated further by an order from the federal government, which still was exercising certain wartime powers. The order established a grain conservation program, limiting domestic consumption of cereals so that more grain could be shipped to populations of countries in need of rehabilitation.

This situation existed for about six months and affected the entire brewing industry. Some brewers used a substitute, manioc, in place of barley malt. Manioc was obtained from the root of a plant found in the tropics.

Anheuser-Busch refused, of course, to use any substitutes whatsoever and the rationing of Budweiser went on. So, the company's pre-war advertising policy of "low pressure selling" to avoid further irritating of national dealers and consumers was revived. Again, the product was associated pictorially and in

375

headline and text with the good things of life. Reproductions of some of these advertisements appear on pages 382-387.

Meanwhile, a great post-war expansion program went steadily on—and the demand for Budweiser increased as steadily. Certain competitors found it expedient to try to persuade dealers to "push" their brands, suggesting that there was little profit in stocking a beer that could be obtained only in ration quantities. Dealers were led to believe that matters always would be that way.

So, in 1948, the D'Arcy Advertising Company, agency for Anheuser-Busch, prepared a four-page, newspaper-size announcement for distribution among the retail trade. The announcement simulated the rotogravure section of a Sunday newspaper and was composed almost entirely of pictures.

The photographs told the story of the great tidal wave of Budweiser that was to come in the not too distant future. Completed lagering cellars were shown. Other photographs depicted more cellars nearly complete. There were rows upon rows of new, glass-lined lagering tanks. There was a new power generating plant, and a third tremendous chimney flanked the two that for three generations had been a landmark in St. Louis.

Thousands of copies of this "newspaper" were printed and distributed. It served to impress upon the retailer that such a gigantic building program was being carried out for only one reason, i.e., because a very great number of people wanted to enjoy Budweiser. Nearly all dealers went along patiently and, in due time, saw their patience rewarded with ever increasing allotments of Budweiser. By the end of December, 1950, production reached an all-time high for Anheuser-Busch with five million barrels for the year.

With the new Newark, New Jersey, brewery set to begin production in 1951, Anheuser-Busch had reason enough to shift from low-pressure to a more aggressive type of advertising. This was accomplished without sacrifice of the dignity that long, long ago had placed Budweiser on a pedestal in the public's estimation.

The full-page, four-color magazine advertisements were smartly styled and pictured the many occasions, both day and night, when Budweiser contributed to companionship, contentment and well-being. Through them ran a competitive undercurrent, with stress placed upon the fact that Budweiser was one of America's very few true lager beers. By that time, 93 percent of the beer produced in America was a single fermentation product. The brewers of such beer long before had abandoned the two-fermentation lagering process as too expensive. Budweiser advertisements stressed the point that it was brewed and aged by the most expensive process known.

A powerful impact was delivered all over America through a startling change in poster design. Each poster, with a scene-in-miniature apropos to beer enjoyment, bore a giant reproduction of the Budweiser bottle placed at such an angle that it went from edge to edge of the poster. Vivid coloring made the bottle appear crispy-cold.

In January, 1950, Anheuser-Busch became the first brewing company to sponsor a big-time network television show. It was an hour-long variety show starring Ken Murray, who also was its producer. Murray had just completed a seven-year run at El Capitan Theater in Hollywood and his T.V. offering was built around the format developed in California.

The Ken Murray Show quickly climbed to a top audience rating and held it and increased it despite the efforts of rival networks to attract audiences with costly talent. The Ken Murray Show appeared over the entire Columbia Broadcasting System's T.V. network of 51 stations.

Television, after floundering around for several years immediately after the end of World War II, suddenly had lost its amateur standing and, with better programming, the number of T.V. receivers increased by the millions in a matter of months. So great was its impact that the motion picture industry suffered great losses in both audiences and revenue.

On the average, the rate of increase in sales of Budweiser beer was twice as much in the areas having television as it was in the non-T.V. areas. When contract renewal time came at the end of a year, Anheuser-Busch promptly took up its option on time and talent and, in the spring of 1952, exercised its option for the second time with the show then costing approximately $65,000 per week.

The year of 1951 saw Anheuser-Busch's greatest outdoor advertising effort. One of the very largest animated electrical "spectaculars" in Times Square was featuring Budweiser, as it had done for several years. This one spectacular was being maintained at an annual cost of $100,000.

There was another huge spectacular commanding the attention of all who trod the famous Boardwalk of Atlantic City, New Jersey. And, atop the new brewery in Newark was another great electrically lighted and animated display.

Motorists crossing the great Bay Bridge linking San Francisco and Oakland, California, were seeing a Budweiser spectacular high in the sky at the span's level.

The outdoor advertising industry calls a combination of painted panel and animated lighting a "semi-spectacular." In 1951 there were several of these in Los Angeles and Pittsburgh, two in Philadelphia, three in Chicago, and one each in St. Louis, Peoria, Atlanta, Dallas, Houston, New Orleans and Miami.

Times Square saw a new and greater Budweiser spectacular go into action in November, 1952. The unit, a hundred feet long and eighty-five feet high, was atop the Brill Building at Forty-ninth Street and Broadway. It was so brilliantly lighted that it could be seen from Thirty-fourth Street.

Two things were featured in the spectacular—the A-and-eagle trademark and the brewery's famous Clydesdale horses. The trademark was faithfully produced in color. The edges of the "A" were outlined with gold leaf. The eagle was fifty-five feet tall—approximately the height of a five-story building —and had a wing spread of sixty-five feet.

By means of changing lights, the eagle simulated the flight of a real bird. To achieve this effect, six different eagles were mounted on the sign and illuminated in cycles.

When the flight of the eagle was completed, the Clydesdales went into motion. Prior to the sign's erection, an animated cartoon of the horses was made in order to depict the motion faithfully. This called for forty-eight individual horses to be lighted in cycles and thus give the illusion of an eight-horse hitch going at a trot.

The horses on the spectacular were nine times actual size. Neon tubing ten miles long defined them.

The name Budweiser appeared in three-dimensional lettering. The B was fifteen feet high and the lower-case letters ten feet high. The dot over the "i" in Budweiser was four feet in diameter.

Finally, there was a motograph which sent advertising and public interest messages across the spectacular in a ribbon of lighted letters ten feet tall.

The electric wiring in the huge sign was long enough to reach from New York to Boston.

Putting the spectacular into action occasioned quite a ceremony. The Sixty-fourth National Horse Show was being held at Madison Square Garden and the famous Clydesdales were appearing there. August A. Busch, Jr., president, drove the hitch from the garden to the Astor Hotel in Times Square, where he was greeted by Mayor Impelliteri. The mayor threw a remote control switch on the hotel roof top to put the spectacular into action.

Into Times Square each day came 1,098,000 persons—approximately 400,000,000 annually—comprising the largest single outdoor advertising audience in the United States.

The huge Budweiser spectacular in Times Square faced the spot where before prohibition one of the most attractive and ambitious Budweiser spectaculars of that time was situated. The pre-prohibition sign was 96 feet long and 59 feet high and located on a building top west of the Times Building on Forty-second Street. It was brightly lighted and also contained a motograph. The city government publicly thanked Anheuser-Busch for making the motograph available for important civic messages and charity drives. The sign was seen by millions of people who at one time or another visited Times and Longacre Squares at night.

BUDWEISER'S GREATEST SPECTACULAR
ON TIMES SQUARE

SPECTACULAR AT ATLANTIC CITY—
It works day and night for Budweiser.

The magazine advertisements shown on pages 382 to 387, inclusive, were published after the war. At that time the demand for Budweiser was the greatest in all its history, and dealers as well as wholesalers were rationed. These advertisements, therefore, could not emphasize selling of the product so much but sought rather to associate the product with wholesome and historical circumstances.

GREAT CONTRIBUTIONS
TO GOOD TASTE

Oysters and Lobsters
gave the Trail its Start

When Henry Wells started what was to become Wells, Fargo & Co., few people could see any need for express service. He finally sold his idea by delivering fresh oysters and lobsters far inland where such delicacies never before had been seen. His express company went beyond Buffalo to St. Louis and Chicago and then fanned out through the hazardous West to the Coast.

Today, railway and air express deliver whatever you want anywhere and fast. Tables all over America are enriched by delicacies from everywhere which combined with Budweiser make that notable difference between eating and really dining. Every sip tells you why Budweiser has become something more than beer ... a tradition in hospitality.

*It lives with good taste
everywhere*

TRADE MARK REG. U. S. PAT. OFF.

ANHEUSER-BUSCH
SAINT LOUIS

GREAT CONTRIBUTIONS
TO GOOD TASTE

Ice Gave All 48 States
a Seashore...

America's early fishermen little dreamed that ice, which drove them off the
Atlantic in winter, would some day bring to your table, wherever you dined,
all the delicacies of the sea the year 'round.

Today, thanks to refrigeration and fast transportation, a great industry
supplies all America with seafood in great and appetizing variety—fresh
lobsters, crabs, tender scrod and pompano, shrimp, oysters on
the half shell, whatever your favorite may be. Each is delicious—
especially when served with golden, brilliant Budweiser. This world-
famous beer brings out the flavor of fine food, yet it never loses
the distinctive taste that makes it preferred wherever you go.

*It lives with good taste
everywhere*

Budweiser

ANHEUSER-BUSCH...SAINT·LOUIS

GREAT CONTRIBUTIONS
TO GOOD TASTE

Our Third President was Our First Spaghetti Maker

Most of us know that Thomas Jefferson expressed America's idea of freedom by writing the Declaration of Independence, but few know that he guided our forefathers to better living by also writing an excellent cookbook.

From Naples he got a mould to form spaghetti and introduced what today is one of our most important and popular foods. He did the marketing for the White House and presided genially over its inviting table. Jefferson earnestly believed that good food and drink temperately enjoyed each day with good friends were essential to a worthwhile lifetime.

Live life, every golden minute of it.
Enjoy Budweiser, every golden drop of it.

It lives with good taste everywhere

Budweiser
TRADE MARK REG. U. S. PAT. OFF.

ANHEUSER-BUSCH · · SAINT LOUI

GREAT CONTRIBUTIONS
TO GOOD TASTE

FRED HARVEY

He made the Frontier
a Good place to Eat

On time or late, travelers in the '70's could count upon one thing with absolute
certainty. Their meals along the way would be the worst imaginable. In 1876,
young Fred Harvey opened his first restaurant in Topeka and astounded
patrons with tempting dishes excellently cooked and superbly served. Soon
Harvey hotels and restaurants followed Santa Fe rails across half a
continent. Then came the dining car making train passengers in America
the best fed on Earth.

In that same year of 1876, Budweiser came into being and quickly
took its rightful place beside the best that cooking skill had to offer.
As yesterday, so today, every sip tells you why it is something more
than beer—a tradition in hospitality.

*It lives with good taste
everywhere*

Budweiser
TRADE MARK REG. U. S. PAT. OFF.

ANHEUSER-BUSCH · · · SAINT LOUIS

GREAT CONTRIBUTIONS
TO GOOD TASTE

He Started Your Country Club

James VI saw the mistake of Scotland's earlier kings, who forbade golf as a time-waster. James made it a popular recreation. Suddenly and deservedly in good taste, the game quickly found its way 'round the world. It promoted the country club idea, where whole families could enjoy good sport, good fellowship, good food . . . and where Budweiser usually is the oldest member. Every sip tells you why.

It lives with good taste everywhere

Budweiser

TRADE MARK REG. U. S. PAT OFF.

ANHEUSER-BUSCH · · SAINT LOUIS

GREAT CONTRIBUTIONS
TO GOOD TASTE

He gave Nature
100,000 New Ideas

Most of the fruits, flowers, grains, vegetables and nuts that come to your table today are superior to those that grew before Luther Burbank's time. Most people know of his fame, but few know that his genius in cross-breeding plants produced more than a hundred thousand new varieties. His California home was a mecca for Nature lovers and each mail brought him letters and rare specimens of plants and flowers from admirers the world over.

But before Burbank, Anheuser-Busch in 1876 had made a great contribution to the American table—the distinctive taste of Budweiser. It quickly won national and then international fame as a complement to fine food and a compliment to good company.

It lives with good taste everywhere

TRADE MARK REG U S PAT OFF

ANHEUSER · BUSCH · · · SAINT LOUIS

Top—Huge Illuminated Message on the Newark Brewery. Bottom—An Example of How Budweiser Bulletins Are Spotted Around the Country to Reap the Best Results from Traffic Circulation.

In the year of 1952, every wholesaler's territory had a 12-month poster showing with the exception of a few northern states, where cold weather made seasonable declines in sales inevitable. No market was without at least a 50 percent showing and, in highly competitive areas, the showings were 100 percent.

The 1951 outdoor advertising of Budweiser cost the company 2½ million dollars.

Wholesalers who had sweated and grumbled through the rationing years responded enthusiastically to the increased supplies of Budweiser and the advertising and sales effort put behind it by the company.

Not a few wholesalers began buying radio time on their own. Prejudice against beer advertising over the air, prevalent in the early days of radio, had virtually vanished, largely because sectional brewers sponsored broadcasts of major and minor league ball games and other sports events of interest to thousands of listeners.

The wholesalers who bought radio time began writing to the D'Arcy Advertising Company for scripts to be read by station announcers chosen for the commercials. The number of these requests grew so rapidly that Anheuser-Busch decided to make "platters," or recorded commercials available at no cost to wholesalers needing them. This policy worked so well that soon the regular provision of new platters was a part of the advertising program and resulted in tens of thousands of dollars' worth of air time being bought by the wholesalers to augment the national advertising of Anheuser-Busch.

In its hundredth year, Anheuser-Busch had the satisfaction of knowing that the name Budweiser was a household word all over America, even among people who did not drink beer, and of knowing that the name was a by-word in many foreign countries. Best of all, it was a name that commanded respect among all people everywhere.

Since the earliest, successful days of Adolphus Busch, Anheuser-Busch has been a constant user of "point-of-sale" advertising—the illuminated signs, the

SOME OF THE NOSTALGIC POSTERS CELEBRATING THE ONE HUNDREDTH ANNIVERSARY

of Anheuser-Busch, and One Appearing Just before the 1952 Election

metal signs, the window valances, and other material designed to complete the sale started by the consumer's exposure to Budweiser advertising in magazines, in newspapers, on posters and, in more recent years, on television.

This merchandising function and the point-of-sale material that goes with it have become big business.

Unlike media such as newspapers and periodicals, which have established circulation departments organized to bring the publication to the consumer, point-of-sale material must depend upon the thousands of Anheuser-Busch wholesaler employees who place signs in stores daily. They constitute the "circulation department" for these signs—and training these men to use this material wisely and effectively is a never-ending responsibility.

To help focus attention on effective use of this material, Anheuser-Busch, in 1951, resolved its point-of-sale material into two classifications: material designed for the precise point-of-sale in an outlet—and from which definite sales returns were expected—and material designed for general identification. Into this latter classification falls miscellaneous cardboard and other signs which are installed wherever they are greatly exposed to traffic.

The company's policy is not to distribute this costly advertising with a view to obtaining greatest distribution but rather to concentrate it in such places as promise the greatest sales potential.

Salesmen have been instructed that their efforts toward installing point-of-sale material should be concentrated in outlets specializing in premium-priced beers where Budweiser is not getting its fair share of turnover. They have been taught that it is useless and pointless and expensive to place more material in an outlet where Budweiser already accounts for fifty or sixty percent of the total volume.

Another point on which sales personnel have been well schooled is that advertising material placed in a prestige outlet often has more value than the same material placed in an outlet on a lower level but doing a greater volume of business.

Budweiser point-of-sale advertising avoids complicated artwork and anything else that militates against getting over quickly the name Budweiser. Budweiser material has a rich look in that the finest of colors and metal are employed. Another reason for avoiding artwork that involves people and situations is that the picture after a while tends to lose its interest, whereas an artistically designed Budweiser reminder is always certain of permanence in the outlet in which it is installed.

Anheuser-Busch, except on rare, worthwhile occasions, avoids special displays of packages in favor of constant display where sales of packaged beer normally are made. In the matter of grocery stores, it has been proved over and over again that when Budweiser is displayed with foods in the higher profit brackets, the beer not only sells itself but actually helps to sell high-profit items such as anchovies, olives, pickles, potted meats, cheeses and other foods that are natural accompaniments to good beer. The company has hundreds of letters from grocers telling how they took the advice of the Anheuser-Busch salesman and increased Budweiser and food sales tremendously.

The company is a firm believer in a merchandising organization and, in addition to its own personnel in branches, it has helped to train merchandising men for seventy leading wholesalers in the year 1951 with every promise of this number being greatly increased. The program of the merchandising department encompasses the following: (1) To know, outlet by outlet, the interior and exterior point-of-sale position. (2) How these positions compare with those of competitors. (3) To know the key outlets in a market specifically and what is the point-of-sale position in these outlets. (4) To know the prestige outlets in a market specifically and to know the point-of-sale position in them. (5) To know geographically where Budweiser point-of-sale is weak or strong and to correct where correction is indicated. (6) To have regular organized routine coverage of the market. This requires complete precise records of installations, outlet by outlet, and records of competitive activities. (7) Inventory is based upon requirements indicated by all the foregoing—by knowledge of the market as opposed

One of the Prohibition Era Spectaculars Erected in Major Cities

to guesswork. Thus provision is made for inventory control and a clean storage room. To have consistent maintenance of point-of-sale material, signs are checked to be sure that they have not been removed, that they are functioning properly, that they are kept clean and that they are not deteriorating to the disadvantage of Budweiser.

Some episodes in the Budweiser advertising effort seem worthy of recounting. For example, a famous man named Charles A. Lindbergh might have slipped into oblivion as just another stunt man had he not tried to get a sponsor for an idea he long had had in mind. He wanted to fly a silvery little airplane called The Spirit of St. Louis across the Atlantic to Paris. This west-to-east crossing never had been attempted because weather conditions were considered too hazardous to make the flight.

Lindbergh called upon the D'Arcy Advertising Company and explained that, needing money to finance his venture, he thought it might be a good idea for one of the agency's clients, possibly Anheuser-Busch, to provide the funds and advertise its products. P. J. Orthwein, vice-president of the D'Arcy Company, pointed out—and Lindbergh agreed—that if commercialized his flight would be cheated of its glory.

The Lone Eagle, backed by contributions from close friends, made his trip without commercial tinge and was greeted at Le Bourget Field outside of Paris by Ambassador Herrick and thousands of screaming Frenchmen whose trumpeting gave a clue to the great fame that the St. Louisan was to enjoy.

Another anecdote concerns an "original" idea that pops up as regularly as the sunrise. Had a tab been kept, it probably would reveal in the year 1952 that fifty thousand persons have offered as a slogan, "Drink Bud and be wiser." Each volunteer always has emphasized that he would like to be handsomely rewarded and one Oklahoman concluded his letter with the sentence, "Please send me a check for $5,000 at once." He got the same polite letter that the others received.

When a company spends the sort of money on advertising that Anheuser-Busch has spent, it is understandable that its officers often ask, "How effective is our advertising? How many people read it?" Of course, one answer comes when sales go up and another when sales go down. Nonetheless, advertisers and agencies each year spend large sums on surveys. Then again you get a pretty conclusive answer for free. For example . . .

In 1934 a Budweiser magazine advertisement pictured a roof top garden. There were many dancing couples shown in a down-shot perspective. Somehow, the artist had the man's right hand in each instance holding the woman's left hand instead of having it on her back. Nobody in either Anheuser-Busch or the D'Arcy Company noticed the error, but the number of somebodies among magazine readers who observed it and wrote in to tell of the discovery was staggering—and very convincing.

On another occasion, a magazine advertisement mentioned that George Washington "sent to the faraway Mediterranean for his favorite wine, Madeira." Washington's wine merchant stored his wares on the island of Malta. Again came a flood of letters from readers pointing out proudly that the island of Madeira was in the Atlantic, not the Mediterranean.

Another flood of letters resulted from a newspaper advertisement which mentioned that the planet Jupiter had nine moons. The information was taken from the Encyclopaedia Brittanica—an edition which went to press the year before two additional moons were discovered. One of the letters came from a professor of mathematics and associate professor of astronomy in a Louisiana university. He wrote facetiously that the advertisement was badly in error in saying that Jupiter had nine moons when it really had eleven.

When asked as a professor of mathematics if he would not concede that the whole was greater than any of its parts and, if Jupiter had eleven moons, it must have nine, he wrote such a jolly retraction that Adolphus Busch III sent him a goodly supply of Budweiser beer with a letter of thanks.

One of the methods of promoting the sale of Budweiser was unique in the brewing industry. It began in 1933 when August A. Busch, Sr., conceived the idea of sending an eight-horse hitch of Clydesdales from city to city. The best of breed available were bought and equipped with a huge wagon and appropriate trappings.

One of the first assignments of the new team was to parade up Fifth Avenue in New York City to the Empire State Building and there deliver one of the first cases of relegalized Budweiser to former Governor Al Smith, a tireless opponent of prohibition, who had his offices there.

The New York police cheerfully granted the necessary parade permit, little suspecting the traffic jam that was to follow. Al Smith came down to the street and graciously accepted the carton of bottled beer. Thousands of pedestrians gathered 'round and spilled from the sidewalks into the thoroughfare itself until they were packed so tight that traffic came to a stop. Police reserves were called to untangle the snarl.

Newspaper photographers were very much on the job and before long the whole metropolitan area knew that Anheuser-Busch and its famous Budweiser had made a considerable impact.

The Clydesdales attracted such crowds wherever they went after their New York debut that it was decided to acquire a second team and route it, too, around the country.

Following is some descriptive matter from a booklet distributed among those who came to see the Clydesdales:

> Human beings and horses have been partners for so many thousands of years that today in a motor age the humans' love for the horses has not waned. Anheuser-Busch has been showing champion draft horses for over 35 years at fairs and horse shows throughout the United States.
>
> In 1933 the late August A. Busch, Sr., while witnessing the six-horse hitch classes at the International Livestock Exposition at Chicago conceived the idea of a draft horse hitch to advertise his famous beers BUDWEISER and MICHELOB. However, he wanted something more spectacular and

selected an eight-horse hitch of Champion Clydesdales. It is easy to admire any good horse, but when people look at a Clydesdale they fairly gasp.

The Anheuser-Busch Champion Clydesdales have made people gasp in big cities and small towns—from coast to coast. The thunder of their hooves on the pavement attracts attention more than a motor horn. Their immense size makes average horses appear as dwarfs by comparison. Their brass-trimmed harness sparkles in the sunlight. The huge, red, 6,000 pound brass-trimmed wagon which they pull rumbles over the street like thunder.

Hundreds of thousands of persons all over the United States have seen these beautiful Clydesdales. They have captured one trophy after another in horse shows throughout the United States. One of the things that never fails to thrill spectators is the ease and agility with which these animals move about despite their size and weight of approximately a ton each. When giving an exhibition drive at horse shows and fairs they pull their heavy wagon around in a series of breath-taking maneuvers and go through intricate paces while the wagon virtually stands still. Another thing that amazes spectators is the intelligence with which the Clydesdales respond to directions. The driver holds four reins laced through his fingers on each hand, thereby giving him individual control of each horse.

Scotch by ancestry, Clydesdales are purchased in Scotland, Canada, Illinois and Iowa. They are usually three to four years old when purchased. It is quite difficult to find Champion Clydesdales to match into our teams, therefore, we are only able to purchase two or three horses each year. Every one of the Anheuser-Busch Champion Clydesdales is a direct descendant of Baron Buchlyvie who was foaled in 1900 and who at three years of age commanded a price of $3,750.00, but who in 1911 was sold at Ayr, Scotland, for $47,500.00—the highest price ever paid for a draft horse.

The horses answer to their names just like a well trained dog does—but only when the driver or someone closely connected with them calls them. When they are in the stalls, the driver can call the roll—and each horse will lift his head as his name is called. People often wonder if there isn't danger of these Clydesdales getting out of hand, because of their immense size and the fact that the lead pair are so far from the driver's seat. The driver has no trouble at all in guiding them with the reins, and their behavior, even in the thickest traffic, has been perfect. Fire sirens can blow all around them,

Top—THE FAMOUS BUDWEISER CLYDESDALES. Middle—THE STABLE. Bottom—INTERIOR OF STABLE

and while they show annoyance at the commotion by perking up their ears and exhibiting a little nervousness, they never once have tried to bolt, kick or plunge.

The BUDWEISER Champion Clydesdales are the most widely-traveled horses in the United States. The BUDWEISER Caravan is transported in five large special built vans, 38′ long x 8′ wide. Three horse vans—four horses to a van, with all stalls facing forward and so arranged that they cannot be pushed off their balance, one van for the huge brass-trimmed wagon, and one van for the portable stalls and other miscellaneous equipment. The average mileage traveled by one caravan in a year is approximately 10,000 miles and showings in approximately 50 cities. When the horses hear the harness being packed and other preparations being made for a journey, they show eagerness to get going and the driver and grooms encounter little difficulty getting them into the vans.

People think traveling with a BUDWEISER Caravan is a perfect circus. In some respects it is, especially when we arrive in a city, the work involved —setting up the portable stalls for the horses, tack room for the harness and getting the showroom ready for the many thousands of visitors. The schedules for the Caravans are prepared in St. Louis for tours of 4 to 5 months in advance, thus enabling all preparations to be ready when the Caravan arrives in a city. Most important, a good, large, well-ventilated building must be secured, usually an automobile showroom or garage, since these horses are too valuable to expose them to ailments from neighboring horses in big stables. While on exhibit, the driver and grooms watch carefully to keep visitors from offering tidbits to the horses, as these Clydesdales would eat all the sugar you would offer them, but it would be very bad for them. And the same goes for candy, apples and similar offerings. It is also necessary to politely ask the visitors not to pat the horses' noses. Rubbing a horse's nose is one of the most widespread errors kind-hearted people make. It has a tendency to irritate the animal's nose and make him uncomfortable in harness. Incidentally, the horses' harness is always checked to be sure that it fits properly and does not cause any irritation. The harness for one eight-horse team costs $5,000.

The average weight of these Clydesdales is 2,000 pounds each. The average age is 8 years. The average height 17 hands. (A hand is four inches.)

Horses are purchased in Scotland, Canada, Illinois and Iowa. Most of our horses are imported. Horses raised in this country don't usually grow to be as large as the horses imported from Scotland and Canada.

The shoes worn by these horses are all handmade by a horseshoer in St. Louis. It requires a piece of steel 22″ x 1½″ x ½″ to make one shoe. No machine made shoe is large enough to fit these Clydesdales.

These Clydesdales are exhibited at various horse shows and fairs throughout the United States.

St. Louis is their home city, and while in St. Louis they are kept in the old private stable of the Busch family, where they kept their own personal driving horses and carriages before the motor age.

Each Caravan has a personnel of nine men: supervisor, driver, four grooms (take care of the horses), two tack men (take care of the harness) and one man takes care of the wagon and trucks.

Another advertising medium, unknown before prohibition, was the sound-motion picture.

It became apparent soon after repeal that the public at large had only vague ideas about the brewing of beer. Thanks to happy-go-lucky, hit-or-miss home-brewers of the dry era, the impression was prevalent that making beer was a comparatively simple process with no demand for great skill.

The technical staff of Anheuser-Busch cooperated with the D'Arcy Advertising Company and the Jam Handy Motion Picture Company in the making of a sound-motion film called "Something More Than Beer." Beginning on an entertainment level, the picture soon modulated into an educational sphere. It proved that to make good, palatable beer in general was no easy undertaking and that to make Budweiser in particular was a time-consuming, painstaking operation requiring the finest of skill and the costliest of ingredients and facilities.

Truckloads of cameras, floodlights, cables and other equipment were brought to the brewery and every phase of the brewing process was covered.

Through clubs, civic, business and fraternal organizations, "Something More Than Beer" was seen and heard by 35 million persons within fewer than fifteen years.

In 1949, the technical staff, the advertising department and the advertising agency and The Wilding Motion Picture Company of Chicago produced an even more ambitious sound-motion picture entitled "The House That Faith Built." It began with young Adolphus Busch taking over management of the Bavarian Brewery, pictured the sensational steps he took to build it into the world's largest brewery, the blow dealt by prohibition, the diversification of operations and products that saved the property and the final triumph with repeal.

"The House That Faith Built" proved to be a magnificent documentary film that portrayed faithfully the reasons for the stature and influence of Anheuser-Busch. The principals in the cast were brought from Hollywood to the Chicago studios for the filming. So were a director, a make-up expert and other technicians. All costuming was of Hollywood origin.

In less time than two years, the picture had been seen and heard by nearly half a million persons in group and auditorium showings and by uncounted millions via the Columbia Broadcasting System's television network.

Another motion picture called "Give Us This Day" chronicled the history of bread from civilization's beginning to the spic-and-span bakeries of modern times and it showed the important part that yeast plays in achieving the perfect loaf. Needless to say, this effort won many new friends in the baking industry for the Yeast, Malt and Corn Products Division, which sponsored it.

The same division in 1951 produced a sound-motion drama called "The Mark of 'C'," built around the heroic exploits of the baker-in-chief of Washington's Continental Armies, Christopher Ludwick. (It was Chris's custom to mark his loaves with his initial, "C.") After unfolding this drama, which concerned itself with the important part that Chris's bread played in leading to the surrender of Cornwallis, the picture moved into historical sequences that empha-

The former Lilly Anheuser tells a young Army officer of her father's hopes for the success of her new husband, Adolphus Busch.

Adolphus tells a group of bankers of his plans for building the first successful refrigerated railroad car.

The photographs on pages 403-406 are "stills" made during the filming of the sound-motion picture "The House That Faith Built."

Adolphus tells his son of his dream to have a bottle of perfectly pasteurized Budweiser.

Adolphus tells his staff of his friendliness toward union labor.

The Hollywood actor, Lyle Talbot, who
portrayed August A., Sr.

August A., Sr., tells the rest of management that prohibition will not close their
doors and throw men out of work—that they will build anew.

St. Louisans in the seventies arriving at Conrad's restaurant to taste Budweiser.

Adolphus Busch and Carl Conrad in an old-world taproom where Adolphus conceives the idea of an entirely new kind of beer for America.

sized the many improvements in baking techniques and ingredients that resulted in bread becoming more than ever the keystone of human nutrition.

Still another sound-motion picture was made—this one in 1937, when a sudden business recession threatened to bring back the great depression of the early thirties.

The picture reflected Anheuser-Busch's confidence in America, its institutions and its people and gave example after example of how our forefathers survived one disheartening setback after another. It had wide circulation and inspired many fine compliments from distinguished persons.

Filming of various happenings at American Legion conventions became quite a large operation. It began with a national convention in St. Louis in 1935, where, over a bar several hundred feet long, Anheuser-Busch played host to the thirsty delegates. They were served copious quantities of Budweiser beer gratuitously and escorted through the plant. The hospitality proved more costly than anticipated, since most of the legionnaires sentimentally kept the glasses after they had been drained. However, priceless goodwill resulted.

The filming of Legion national conventions in Chicago, Boston and Kansas City added to the picture library and provided entertainment and gained friendships in Legion posts everywhere.

When the Benevolent and Protective Order of Elks had a national convention in Chicago, it, too, was filmed and the pictures shown in the many Elks Clubs in America.

What with a $65,000 weekly, hour-long show on television, two caravans of horses touring the country and motion pictures being shown constantly, the Home of Budweiser beer in 1952 found itself very much in "show business" as one phase of advertising and selling. Indeed, it was a far cry from the days when Grandfather Adolphus began his advertising activities modestly by giving away pocketknives, canes and other souvenirs.

Anheuser-Busch can be proud of one among many things. Its whole advertising career leaned strongly toward good taste. Nor did it ever lose sight of the fact that in advertising influence flows downward. It has appealed always to the sort of people that other people look up to.

Beginning with the first Eberhard Anheuser and continuing through a century, each successive head of the enterprise that became Anheuser-Busch, Inc. has understood the importance of a trade-mark, especially to a business relying on sales to individual members of the public, and the importance of keeping that trade-mark in the public's consciousness.

The first trade-mark adopted by the E. Anheuser Co.'s Brewing Association comprised the representation of an eagle with raised wings, in association with a capital A, and a shield constituting a perch for the eagle. This trade-mark has always been known as the A & EAGLE mark.

The E. Anheuser Co.'s Brewing Association was one of the first businesses to recognize the value of a United States Patent Office trade-mark registration and obtained certificate of registration No. 4623 on May 8, 1877, for the A & EAGLE trade-mark. When a new trade-mark law supplanted that under which the 1877 registration was issued, a new registration, No. 28,866, was obtained September 8, 1896, to take the place of the earlier registration under the obsolete law.

Like many design trade-marks, the A & EAGLE mark has varied in minor details from time to time and in the mode of presentation. For instance, it is sometimes used in plain black and white and at other times in red, gold and black. The positions of the wings and body of the eagle have been varied occasionally, but always it has remained the same trade-mark.

Thus the A & EAGLE may be regarded as the institutional or family trade-mark of Anheuser-Busch, Inc., being used on substantially all of the established products sold by the company. New products are normally put through a period of market testing without the A & EAGLE trade-mark appearing on them, but after the preliminary period has been passed success-fully, the new product is almost always given the accolade of the A & EAGLE trade-mark.

Inspection of the A & EAGLE mark shows that the design has artistic beauty adapting it for many publicity and advertising purposes. Thus, its presence in colors on letterheads, in much publicity matter, on the covers of annual reports and elsewhere, adds greatly to the artistic appearance and appeal of such materials. The A & EAGLE also has been the characteristic feature of many advertising novelties, such as knives, watch fobs, drinking glasses and tumblers. It has also been used as an architectural ornament in various buildings of Anheuser-Busch, Inc.

The standard A & EAGLE design, with such changes as are necessitated by limitations of size, color and material, was developed in 1903, and the original stone for producing decalcomanias is still in use and constitutes a reference for checking the accuracy of any new design.

In addition to the A & EAGLE design mark, Anheuser-Busch, Inc., and its predecessor companies have featured the brands or word trade-marks appearing on their several products. The first and most important word mark was the BUDWEISER mark which was first used on beer in 1876, being applied by C. Conrad & Co., to beer produced for it by the E. Anheuser Co.'s Brewing Association. The BUDWEISER mark was also registered in the United States Patent Office, No. 6376, dated July 16, 1878. This registration showed not merely the word BUDWEISER, but also other words and features of the label used at that time. It is of interest to note that the present day label still follows so closely the make-up of the original label that the two actually constitute one and the same trade-mark. As in the case of the A & EAGLE mark, the passage of a new trade-mark law was followed by the obtaining of a new BUDWEISER registration, No. 13,064, dated March 2, 1886. The BUDWEISER trade-mark and label, along with the goodwill of the business, passed to the Anheuser-Busch Brewing Association January 27, 1891.

Following the practice of registering all trade-marks, a separate registration, No. 64,125, of the word BUDWEISER alone as a trade-mark for beer was obtained July 23, 1907.

The trade-mark BUDWEISER has been used on many products other than beer, and additional registrations of the mark have been obtained from time to time.

An appreciative and friendly public has naturally made frequent use of the familiar diminutive BUD in asking for BUDWEISER beer and other BUDWEISER products. So much has this been the case that BUD has itself been recognized as an Anheuser-Busch trade-mark for beer and other products. In the case of certain products, where the short form seemed more appropriate than the long form, the labels themselves bear the mark BUD, and it has been so registered.

Another important beer trade-mark of Anheuser-Busch, Inc., is the FAUST mark. Because the Tony Faust restaurant was one of the world's renowned eating places, and members of the Faust family have been active in the Anheuser-Busch brewery, it was only natural that the word FAUST would be selected as a trade-mark for beer. For the most part, the FAUST mark has been used in association with a representation of the character, Mephistopheles, from the opera Faust.

As has been discussed elsewhere, MICHELOB draft beer has been recognized by connoisseurs and experts wherever the beer is sold. This trade-mark is also one of the important assets of Anheuser-Busch, Inc. It was first used April 15, 1896. MICHELOB, like BUDWEISER, has also been used as a trade-mark for other products of Anheuser-Busch, Inc., particularly barley-malt syrup.

It was inevitable that a company making and selling so many diverse products, would, over the course of years, use numerous trade-marks. Among such trade-marks are A-B, MALT-NUTRINE, BEVO, CAR-CHO, KAFFO, SWEET MOMENTS, DELTA, ZEET, BASAMIN-BUSCH and ABINCO. In the design trade-mark category, along with the A & EAGLE design mark and the BUDWEISER label mark, are such marks as the CLAW design used on various beer packages and the zig-zag design used on yeast packages.

In presenting all of its products to the purchasing public, Anheuser-Busch, Inc., has always endeavored to have the package, by its attractive appearance and effective presentation of the company's trade-marks, inform the purchaser in advance of the high quality of the product to be found in the package.

Moreover, the company's advertising has made the trade-marks, Budweiser and Bud, known the world over.

As a firm believer in trade-marks, Anheuser-Busch has been zealous in demanding recognition of its trade-marks, even to the extent of resorting to litigation when negotiations have failed to stop infringement. In the case of the trade-mark Budweiser, for instance, one attempted infringement after another has been stopped and the company's ownership of the trade-mark has been thoroughly established.

Chapter XXIX

THE WAGONS KEEP

THINGS ROLLING ALONG

WHEN THE ADVENT of prohibition prompted August A., Sr., to try to find some kind of activity for different Anheuser-Busch departments and their workmen, one of the first to swing into productive and profitable operation was the Vehicle Department.

For thirty-five years, this department had taken care of the vehicles of all brewery branches, maintaining them in the traditional spic-and-span condition that was insisted upon by Adolphus Busch. And, traditionally, the vehicle shops had only the finest of facilities and the most skilled workmen that could be hired.

August A. decided that bodies to fit the chassis of standard trucks were to be the department's output and he was insistent that nothing but top quality go into these bodies. All lumber used was air-dried for greater tensile strength. Forged and hand-wrought bracings supported all points of strain.

The department's catalogue was prepared with August's guidance. With

412

his customary flair for the unusual, he had pictured on the cover not a snappy, shining truck, but a huge ox cart of Mexican design, which had been built for advertising purposes. The cover was eye arresting and smacked of experience and tradition. The ox, Tom, was reputed to be the largest of his kind on earth, being six feet six inches high, nine feet eight inches from nose to tail and weighing 3,000 pounds. His driver was six feet six inches tall.

On the first inside pages were shown, as a demonstration of construction versatility, a miniature wagon drawn by six beautiful ponies to advertise Bevo, a prairie schooner pulled by four oxen and the "Bevo Victory Boat," which actually was an ornate boat mounted on an automobile chassis and put at the government's disposal for recruiting and war bond drives for two years.

The department was proudest of its refrigerator truck bodies. They were of superior materials and construction and proved popular for the transportation of ice cream, milk, meats, dairy products and other perishable foods. It took but a glance at the unit's specifications to see that no skimping was permitted.

Other vehicle bodies were for general utility and heavy hauling, armored car bodies for banks and other movers of large sums of money, a "Kampkar" containing built-in beds and cooking equipment for campers and tourists, a model called "The Rancher," which very much resembled the modern day station wagon, and elaborate stables-on-wheels for the transportation of racing and show horses. Finally, there were massive bus bodies for the use of passenger lines and for schools.

The buyers of these units were promised vehicles of much longer-than-average life and that is just what the equipment delivered.

Through this Vehicle Department, August A. and his staff were able to whittle down overhead and bring in a profit. It was in excellent shape to handle the brewery's delivery equipment when repeal brought beer back.

A BUS BODY

Shown here are various types of bodies produced by the Vehicle Department.

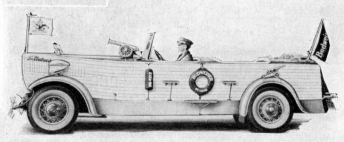

"THE BEVO BOAT" WHICH WAS TO TOUR THE COUNTRY ON RECRUITING DRIVES IN WAR TIME

A BIGGER AND BETTER "BEVO BOAT."

HORSE VAN

A SUPERIOR REFRIGERATED TRUCK BODY

Chapter XXX

ANHEUSER-BUSCH

BUILDS FOR KEEPS

WHEN ONE remembers that the Anheuser-Busch brewery in St. Louis is the world's largest single source of beer, a brief study of its building and engineering factors seems desirable.

Brewery buildings, like other industrial buildings, are designed and constructed to meet various production requirements. The brewing process requires the use of large and heavy equipment, such as brewing kettles and beer storage tanks, cooling equipment, and bottling and canning equipment.

Refrigerated areas must be provided for the product in process and storage. Because of high standards of sanitation required in breweries, large quantities of water are used for cleaning purposes. Therefore, buildings must be protected from water damage. Interiors and exteriors must be aesthetically pleasing, and structural stability is of course essential.

Adolphus Busch, the founder, worked with his architects and builders to produce such buildings between 1878 and 1913. Because of the heavy floor

415

loads, all the foundations for supporting walls and columns were placed on solid rock. As reinforced concrete had not come into regular use in those years, massive concrete arches supported on iron beams and columns were used for floor construction.

Double brick walls with hollow air spaces were used for insulation of refrigerated areas, because no suitable insulating materials were available. In this era the German rococo style was prominent among brewery buildings and, as was the custom of the architects of that period, certain distinctive features were developed which were characteristic of buildings belonging to one organization. The Anheuser-Busch buildings can be distinguished by the *Eselohren* (mule ears) which the architects used as much as possible for embellishment. This feature had become so prominent that it was used on the branch buildings in other cities as well.

When the bottling plant was built in 1917, the *Eselohren* were not included, because the trend in building was toward more modern design.

Adolphus always built his buildings strong enough to carry additional stories, which proved sound planning as the brewery grew before prohibition. It was definitely helpful after the prohibition era, when many of the old buildings were rehabilitated.

The architecture of the buildings constructed during the expansion program in the years just before the company's centennial had a new look, being of functional design. Careful planning blended the modern buildings in with the old buildings and accentuated them rather than taking away the traditional characteristics.

Structural steel, reinforced concrete, insulation and many modern materials were used to the best advantage.

Simplicity characterized operations in the early days.

There was a time when there were no centralized engineering and utilities services for brewery operations. Buildings were heated by stoves. Mash cookers and brew kettles were direct-fired vessels using wood and coal. Natural ice and well water supplied a little cooling. Caves housed beer storage vats, since mechanical refrigeration was unknown. Power was measured in terms of men and horses, and the principal machinery available for plant operations was as simple as the hammer, the shovel and the wheelbarrow. That was in the days of the Bavarian Brewery.

It has been the consistent policy of Anheuser-Busch management to invest in the best available production facilities. By keeping in step with technical progress in all problems affecting efficiency of operation and quality of product, the firm set the pace for the brewing industry.

Anheuser-Busch was one of the earliest users of steam power. Steam was still new as a source of industrial motive power and the first steam railroad to span the continent was just being constructed when steam driven machinery started to work at Anheuser-Busch. The first unit of mechanical power equipment to be acquired by the brewery was a 25-horsepower reciprocating steam engine, installed in the old brew house to operate an agitator in the mash cooker. In 1866 it was the finest available and its use marked an important step forward in process control.

The first steam boilers were small, low pressure units located in the plant buildings where needed. When the use of steam became more general, a central boiler house was constructed on Eleventh Street between Pestalozzi and Lynch Streets. Then a larger plant was built in 1898, near Second and Dorcas Streets. The new plant first housed seven boilers of 350 horsepower each, operating at a pressure of 150 pounds per square inch. The boilers supplied steam for a 500-ton distilled water ice plant, live steam for cookers and isolated steam engines and for two 500-kilowatt direct current generators. This plant was operated until 1930, when the first of the high pressure boilers was installed in the Ninth Street plant.

Three years after the Second Street plant was completed, another boiler house was built to meet the rapidly growing demands for steam. Located on the west side of Ninth Street between Arsenal and Pestalozzi Streets, the new building housed ten 350-horsepower boilers, with room for four more which were added in 1906. The Ninth Street boiler house supplied steam for cookers, engines and pumps in the brew house area. Steam for refrigeration compressors and for the big steam engines in the old power house also came from the Ninth Street plant.

Boilers were equipped with mechanical stokers to supplant hand firing in 1908, within a few years after the first commercial stokers were developed. The plant represented the last word in boiler plant practice in its day, but progress was so rapid that the new boilers were replaced by still newer units of more efficient type within about twenty years.

During the 1920's the more economical higher steam pressures for power generation were incorporated in the newer boiler designs. In 1930 Adalbert von Gontard, the chief of the Engineering Department, installed three large boilers, each capable of generating 120,000 pounds of steam per hour at a pressure of 500 pounds per square inch. These three new boilers replaced all of the old units, which had been built to operate at pressures up to 150 pounds per square inch. The fourteen old-timers at Ninth Street, as well as the eleven at Second Street, were scrapped.

The new boilers were fired with pulverized coal, a relatively new development at the time of installation. A fourth unit was installed in 1934, increasing the capacity of the plant to 480,000 pounds of steam per hour. An additional pulverized coal boiler of advanced design was installed in 1947, increasing the plant capacity to 660,000 pounds of steam per hour.

All boilers were equipped with mechanical fly ash collectors. In 1952 the installation of electrostatic precipitators in addition to the mechanical collectors was completed. By thus utilizing the most recent developments in industrial equipment for the prevention of air pollution, ash emission from the stacks was reduced to such a small amount that it had to be measured in fractions of a grain per cubic foot of stack gas. Virtually 100 per cent of the ash was disposed of as mud.

The brewery's centennial was marked by the completion of No. 6 boiler, a newer and larger unit fired with natural gas. It increased the capacity of the plant to 860,000 pounds of steam per hour, which could be increased to more than a million pounds per hour for short term peak loads. Besides a considerable amount of natural gas fuel, the plant consumed fourteen carloads of coal per day.

Within two years after Thomas Edison built the first electric light plant, having a single generator at the New York Pearl Street Station in 1882, a similar generator was installed by Anheuser-Busch. The company's original installation was a direct current generator of 125-kilowatt capacity driven by a steam engine. Newer and larger engines and generators were installed from time to time and by 1907 the installed capacity was over 2,000 kilowatts.

During the period 1909 to 1917, six diesel-driven generators having a capacity of over 1,700 kilowatts were installed in the Eleventh Street area. With a combined capacity of more than 4,000 kilowatts, the steam- and diesel-driven power plants were operated until 1930, when the first two of the modern turbogenerators were installed at the Ninth Street plant. Since then the use of alternating current power increased steadily while direct current usage diminished.

In 1952, power requirements were supplied by five modern turbogenerators having a total capacity of 23,500 kilowatts. Exhaust steam from the turbines was utilized throughout the plant for cooking, pasteurizing and other processes, as well as for heating.

In the early days, a brewery's output was limited by the necessity of maintaining a cool, uniform temperature during the fermentation and ageing processes. The caves which housed the vats in which beer was stored were not very satisfactory for a large operation.

The development of mechanical refrigeration in the early 1870's seemed to offer an answer and in 1875 Anheuser-Busch installed two of the very first ammonia compressors ever built. These machines proved to be highly successful.

They provided perfect temperature control and, with the pasteurization process developed during the same period, opened up brewery operations to vast rates of production.

During the St. Louis World's Fair in 1904, an ammonia compressor of 500 tons' capacity was exhibited by the Ball Ice Machine Company as one of the scientific wonders of the day. Adolphus Busch purchased this machine in 1905 and installed it in the Second Street plant. Two years later he installed a similar but larger machine having a capacity of 800 tons. This was followed by a giant 900-ton machine, which increased the total installed capacity to nearly 4,000 tons and carried the brewery's refrigeration needs until the Second Street plant was abandoned during the prohibition era.

When beer was relegalized, rehabilitation of refrigeration facilities already had begun with the installation of a 450-ton compressor that increased the capacity of the Ninth Street plant to over 2,000 tons. The new machine was driven by a synchronous motor, more compact and more efficient than the old steam engine drives. Within a few years synchronous motors had replaced all of the old steam engine drives in the refrigeration plant. The 1952 system capacity of nearly 7,000 tons was supplied by eight units varying in capacity from 450 to 1,800 tons.

Until near the end of the nineteenth century, natural ice was of vital importance as a source of refrigeration for a brewery. A considerable tonnage was harvested from the Mississippi River at St. Louis. Some was shipped by barge from the north. The ice was stored in huge sheds where it was buried in sawdust. With the advent of mechanical refrigeration the use of natural ice was discontinued because the "artificial" ice was cleaner, more easily handled and its source more reliable.

By 1900 the Anheuser-Busch plants had an ice making capacity of 700 tons daily. Many other plants were built along the railroad routes for re-icing carload shipments of draught beer. The outlying plants were not needed during prohibition and all were sold or abandoned. Increasing use of direct mechanical refrigeration resulted in further reduction of ice requirements. In consequence, 1952 ice manufacturing facilities, although modern, were reduced in capacity to 150 tons per day. Ice still was unexcelled as a cooling medium for protecting shipments of draft beer.

Chapter XXXI

THE FINANCIAL
STRUCTURE IS STRONG, TOO

FOLLOWING IS a condensed outline of the Anheuser-Busch financial structure through the years.

The company operated as a partnership until it was incorporated on July 7, 1875, as the E. Anheuser Co.'s Brewing Association, with a capital of $240,000 represented by 480 shares of $500 each. The original shareholders were:

Adolphus Busch	238 shares
H. A. Hauessler, Trustee for Mrs. Lilly Busch	100 shares
Eberhard Anheuser	140 shares
Erwin Spraul (qualifying shares)	2 shares
	Total . . . . 480 shares

On April 29, 1879, the name was changed to Anheuser-Busch Brewing Association, and on May 16, 1895, its charter was extended to July 7, 1925.

The corporate name was again changed on November 22, 1919, to Anheuser-Busch, Incorporated. No change in its authorized capital was made until 1925, and all outstanding capital stock was still held by the Busch and Anheuser families.

On June 20, 1925, just prior to the expiration of its charter, the present corporation was organized for the purpose of continuing the business of its predecessor. The name was not changed, but its capitalization was increased from $240,000, represented by 480 shares of $500 each, to $18,000,000, represented by 180,000 shares of $100 each. The increase in capital was accomplished by a stock dividend of $17,760,000. The capitalization of the new corporation, on the date it commenced business, was . . .

> 180,000 shares of capital stock of $100 par value. . .$18,000,000
> Surplus 13,837,667
>
> Total. $31,837,667
> Book value per share. $176.88

All the new stock was still owned by the Busch and Anheuser families.

Stock Splits

In January 1938, the stockholders authorized a five for one split in the number of shares outstanding and the reduction in the par value to $20 per share. The capitalization, immediately prior to increase in number of shares, was . . .

> 900,000 shares of capital stock of $20 par value. . . .$18,000,000
> Surplus 13,276,280
>
> Total. $31,276,280
> Book value per share. $34.75

In August 1947, the stockholders again authorized a five for one split in the number of shares outstanding and the reduction in the par values to $4 per share. The capitalization, immediately prior to increase in number of shares, was . . .

4,500,000 shares of capital stock of $4 par value. . . .$18,000,000

Surplus 46,083,839
_____

Total $64,083,839

Book value per share. $14.24

The present capitalization remains at 4,500,000 shares with the Anheuser and Busch families owning slightly more than 70 percent.

The corporate records have been audited by Haskins & Sells, certified public accountants, since 1933, and annual reports have been distributed to stockholders, banks, brokers, investment houses, and other interested persons. In September 1950, the company started issuing unaudited quarterly reports to its stockholders and others.

Dividend Record

The dividend record of its predecessor corporation is not complete, but since July 7, 1925, the present corporation has a most enviable dividend record, having passed only one dividend in 26 years, and that one in 1932. Since 1925, it has paid cash dividends aggregating $61,303,731, which is equivalent to $13.62 per share, or 3.41 times the par value of its stock. By five year periods, the record stands . . .

1926 through 1930. . . . .$ 2,736,000

1931 through 1935 (dividend passed in 1932) 3,127,731

1936 through 1940. 11,790,000

1941 through 1945. 19,350,000

1946 through 1950. 24,300,000
_____

Total $61,303,731

On October 7, 1952, a public offering was made of the company's

$35,000,000 in principal amount of $3\frac{3}{8}\%$ debentures, due October 1, 1977. Out of the proceeds derived from the sale of the debentures, the company prepaid the principal of its long term bank loan in the amount of $15,000,000.

The company through the years enjoyed excellent public relations. It was a generous donor to charitable and civic enterprises, as the following example of contributions indicates.

St. Louis Community Chest

Pledge	Year Paid	Amount
1946	1945	$135,000
1947	1946	100,000
1948	1947	100,000
1949	1948	110,000
1950	1949	125,000
1951	1951	125,000

American Red Cross

Pledge	Year Paid	Amount
1946	1945	$60,000
1947	1946	36,000
1948	1947	20,000
1949	1949	17,000
1950	1950	15,000
1951	1951	15,000

(In addition to regular contribution, in August, 1951, $2,500 was given to Red Cross Flood Relief Campaign.)

CONTRIBUTIONS OVER $2,500.00

	Year 1946	Year 1947	Year 1948	Year 1949	Year 1950	9 Mos. 1951
American Legion			$ 5,954.85			
Boy Scouts of America		$5,000.00				
Boys Town of Missouri				$20,000.00		
Columbia University						$25,000.00
Cardinal Glennon Memorial Children's Hospital Fund					$25,000.00	
Institute of Human Nutrition			10,000.00			
Jefferson National Expansion Memorial Assn.	$5,000.00					
Jewish Federation of St. Louis		15,000.00			20,000.00	7,500.00
Jewish Welfare Fund		5,000.00	10,000.00	10,000.00		
Mine Disaster in Centralia, Ill.				5,000.00		
Ryder, Mrs. Mary E. (Home)					25,015.00	
St. Louis Children's Hospital Expansion Fund		25,000.00				
Texas City Relief Fund		4,100.00				
Underprivileged Children of France and Italy		25,000.00				
Washington University						
Total	$ 5,000.00	$79,100.00	$25,954.85	$35,000.00	$70,015.00	$32,500.00

General Accounting Dept.
11/14/51

The name of the company after Eberhard Anheuser took over the Bavarian Brewery was E. Anheuser Co.'s Brewing Association, later changed to The Anheuser-Busch Brewing Association, and later changed to Anheuser-Busch, Inc.

The following corporate changes were made through the years from 1875 to 1920:

DATE AUTHORIZED	DATE FILED	CHARTER AND AMENDMENTS
	July 7, 1875	Certificate of Incorporation was issued by Secretary of State of the State of Missouri.
April 25, 1879	April 29, 1879	Change of name from E. Anheuser Co.'s Brewing Association to Anheuser-Busch Brewing Association.
April 24, 1895	May 16, 1895	Extending term of corporation 30 years from July 7, 1895.
May 29, 1909	June 3, 1909	Increasing Number of Directors from 3 to 5.
January 26, 1911	January 30, 1911	Increasing Number of Directors from 5 to 7.
December 3, 1912	December 10, 1912	Increasing Number of Directors from 7 to 9.
December 22, 1914	January 14, 1915	Decreasing Number of Directors from 9 to 7.
March 27, 1918	April 4, 1918	Business purposes extended.
May 29, 1919	July 28, 1919	Business purposes extended.
November 12, 1919	November 22, 1919	Business purposes extended.
November 12, 1919	November 22, 1919	Change of name from Anheuser-Busch Brewing Association to Anheuser-Busch, Incorporated.
January 28, 1920	January 30, 1920	Number of Directors increased from 7 to 11.

Chapter *XXXII*

THE BUSINESS OF

REFRIGERATION IS BIG

WHEN PROHIBITION forced Anheuser-Busch in desperation to turn to other endeavors and products, management decided to guide a portion of the company's facilities into two fields that were to prove profitable . . . the manufacture of refrigerator cabinets and the manufacture of ice cream.

With the many scattered ice plants that were needed to pioneer the shipping of chilled draught beer long before the turn of the century, Anheuser-Busch people had become expert in artificial refrigeration. Obviously, an important part of this sort of work concerns itself with insulation.

Moreover, the company had a large department with many skilled workers for the purpose of keeping wagons in repair. Why not use these skilled wood and metal fabricators to make insulated refrigerator cabinets and sell them to food and ice cream dealers?

The venture was started and once more the traditional insistence upon top quality in every detail paid off. The early stages of the new venture were attended

428

by the expected feeling the way, fumbling, floundering and, finally, finishing in the money. News of the excellence of material and workmanship in the Anheuser-Busch mechanically refrigerated cabinets got around steadily and created demand, but the biggest source of demand stemmed from the long life of the equipment.

There is no need here to expound to those not vitally concerned with the business of refrigerating ice cream and food the virtues of the equipment that the Cabinet Division produced. A glance at the yearly catalogues is an eyeful of revealing data on the excellence of material, construction and service.

The new business grew and grew. The trend in the industry toward beauty of design and the incorporation of baked enamel and stainless steel were not overlooked. Soon Anheuser-Busch cabinets and storage boxes were as good to look at as they were good in point of service.

What once had been "the wagon shop" was a hefty new industry in St. Louis, too important and too profitable to think of abandoning when repeal brought beer back. Indeed, the division was so efficient that, as noted elsewhere in this history, the federal government in World War II asked Anheuser-Busch to turn all facilities over to the making of glider fuselages, wing assemblies and other war materials. It was, of course, done. When peace permitted the plant's returning to its original production schedule, Anheuser-Busch cabinets and storage boxes soon were back in the running, thanks to their excellent reputations.

When the company decided to turn to production of equipment for ice cream dealers, it was only natural that the idea of actually getting into the ice cream business itself should fit hand in glove with plans for rejuvenation and rehabilitation.

The trial balloon went up in New Orleans on February 15, 1920, when a part of the company's ice plant in that city was turned over to producing ice cream. One of the reasons for the success of the venture was that Anheuser-Busch chose to use powdered milk as one of the ingredients. The reason for this decision was based on the fact that the run-of-the-mine milk in many southern

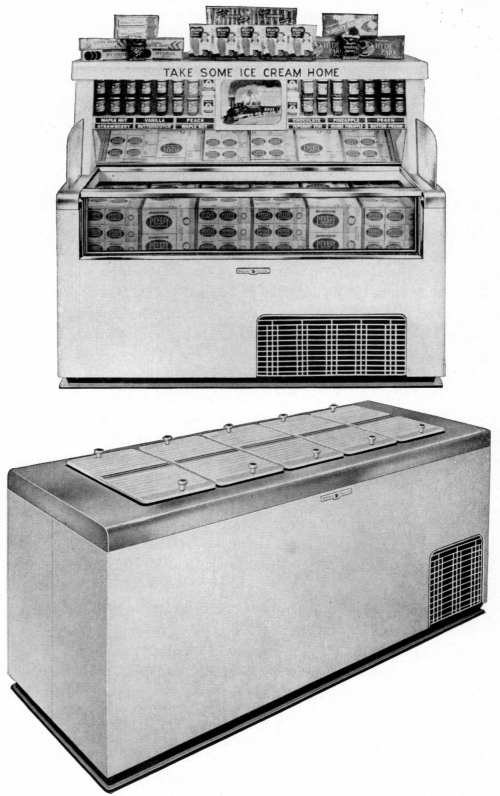

REFRIGERATED CABINETS ARE BIG BUSINESS—When August A., Sr., put idle hands and idle plant to work on different products in prohibition years, the Cabinet Division became one of the most successful ventures.

dairies at the time was far from reliable in quality, a circumstance that was often reflected in the ice cream made with it.

Another factor that made the superior quality of A-B Ice Cream, as it was called, apparent to the consumer was the holding down of the "over-run." That expression has to do with the amount of air permitted to get into the finished product. Anheuser-Busch held the over-run to a minimum in its mix and the result was a creamy, smooth-textured delicacy rather than the icy, frothy type so common in retail outlets.

In the first year of operation in New Orleans, 114,000 gallons of A-B Ice Cream were sold and that year gave encouragement to proceed with an operation that no brewer would have even considered just a few years earlier.

Among the innovations brought out by the New Orleans ice cream venture was a chocolate coated ice cream bar called "Smack." It was the forerunner of a similar product called "Eskimo Pie" produced by local manufacturers all over the country. Another product that caught on was frozen eggnog containing a small, legal quantity of bourbon whisky.

Production and sales grew nicely and, finally, in January, 1924, the ice cream business of the ice plant was incorporated as the Anheuser-Busch Ice Cream & Beverage Company. By 1927, the company was selling 387,000 gallons a year. This was accomplished by virtually nothing but sheer quality, since there was hardly any advertising and only one roving salesman to supplement the work of seven driver-salesmen.

The successful first year of the New Orleans project led Anheuser-Busch in the following year, 1921, to begin producing ice cream in Oklahoma City. This, too, proved a profitable undertaking.

In 1922, the decision to break into the big leagues was made. One of the company's thirty subsidiary ice plants was located on One Hundred Sixty-fourth Street in the Bronx, New York. It was expanded and converted to the manufacture of ice cream. The new product was so instantly successful in the metropolitan area that a second plant was erected at Woodhaven, Long Island, under the supervision of G. G. Kindervater, who had been in charge of the thirty refrigeration properties.

The new brand in the New York area was strictly a price and quality product, which made no effort at all to compete with cheaper brands. It was so popular that within eight years sales had soared to a million and a half gallons a year.

By 1930, Anheuser-Busch ice cream had become such a big factor around New York that a big competitor, the Borden Company, eager to attain the lead in the business, made overtures looking toward a purchase. St. Louis authorized Gus Kindervater to negotiate, because signs of repeal were growing more encouraging all the time.

The deal was consummated and "Kindy" found that he had made the bargain for his company by parting with it. The Borden Company insisted that he and his staff become a part of the acquisition. Accordingly, he signed a five year contract with Borden and was a part of its management until the pact expired, when he returned to Anheuser-Busch as manager of the branches. He was made a vice-president on March 27, 1947, and continued in that capacity until his retirement on December 31, 1951.

Almost simultaneously the Oklahoma business was sold to the Commonwealth Utilities Company and the New Orleans business was sold to the Brownlee Cream Company, maker of a popular brand called Velvet Freeze.

Budweiser's return was little more than two years away.

Thus, the Anheuser-Busch people proved once more that they possessed a goodly share of business acumen as well as brewing skill.

One sidelight of the ice cream venture in New Orleans is interesting enough to merit mention. Anyone who has visited that city knows that many miles of its streets are paved with flat stones brought back as ballast many years ago by ships that had taken cargoes abroad.

For those unfamiliar with the city it might be said that most of the metropolis lies on marshy, almost soggy land. Pile-driving is the first step in erecting even residence buildings. The flat stones brought in as ballast were several square feet in area and less likely to sink down as far as the conventional cobblestone. But, sink they did, with the result that many New Orleans streets have a sort of hill-and-dale topography.

The Anheuser-Busch trucks bumping over these surfaces took a thorough pounding that showed up with rattles, squeaks and looseness, particularly in the bodies. So the Vehicle Department (whose story is told in another chapter) in St. Louis was asked to do something about it.

A new type of cushioned body was developed and tried out. It proved so successful that soon the plant in St. Louis was building those bodies on an assembly line scale for other operators of trucks and fleets . . . another bit of good business for the company that refused to get out of business when prohibition moved in.

Chapter XXXIII

THIS IS THE STORY
OF MALT-NUTRINE

A STEP TAKEN in 1895 was to prove an anchor to windward when prohibition struck. It was the decision to produce a tonic called Malt-Nutrine. Although this new product suffered, too, from prohibition, because of its alcoholic content, it had had the good effect of causing Anheuser-Busch to set up a separate sales department for the wholesale drug field since Malt-Nutrine was retailed almost entirely in drugstores.

Certain Anheuser-Busch personnel became more and more familiar with a type of market previously unexplored and formed the nucleus of the organization which in the twenties and thirties was to be so important in the company's varied pharmaceutical activities.

In order to tell just what Malt-Nutrine was, it is better to begin by telling what it was not. It was not a tonic in the sense that that word is understood today. That is, it was not a patent medicine hawked about with extravagant claims. Actually, it was highly esteemed by the medical profession and its great

434

popularity resulted mainly from the fact that doctors prescribed it for patients in need of building up.

Nor was Malt-Nutrine a form of beer, although its principal ingredients were barley malt and hops.

When introducing the new product, Anheuser-Busch traced its origin to a dramatic moment in the life of Maria Theresa (1717-1780), Empress of Austria-Hungary and Queen of Bohemia. The story was that a month after Maria Theresa had given birth to Marie Antoinette, who was later to die on the guillotine, she lay desperately ill.

Although Maria Theresa was of sound constitution, she failed to rally after being delivered and failed to respond to her physicians' treatment. News of her plight got around among the Bohemian peasantry and a woman in the gaily colored costume of her kind came to the palace with a bottle of medicine. She explained to the doctors that at childbirth the Bohemian women relied upon it for strength, for appetite stimulation and for an increase in mother's milk.

The medicine proved to be an extract obtained by boiling down a mixture of barley malt and hops until it reached a near-syrup consistency. The doctors prescribed regular dosages and, the story goes, the Empress's recovery was rapid and complete.

Anheuser-Busch's original Malt-Nutrine never contained less than 14.5 percent of solids by volume nor more than 1.9 percent of alcohol.

Year after year, the sales of Malt-Nutrine climbed higher and higher. It was virtually a standard remedy in childbirth and during breast feeding. Pleased by results, doctors began prescribing it for convalescents, for sickly children, for the anemic and for the aged. There probably was not a drugstore in the United States that did not carry Malt-Nutrine in stock at all times.

The fact that Malt-Nutrine had improved the health of many, many persons and carried the approval of physicians in general did not save it from prohibition's ax. It was guilty of the great sin of containing more than half of one percent of alcohol. Management was too concerned with the staggering blow of seeing Budweiser wiped out to give too much thought immediately to Malt-Nutrine.

Eventually the laboratory got around to seeing what could be done to salvage this once prosperous property. There was a mountain range of new and confusing regulations that had to be crossed. Perhaps the strangest part of the dilemma was that Malt-Nutrine never had been offered as a beverage. Your author, who was given the tonic by his physician during a childhood convalescence, remembers it as a pleasant-tasting liquid whose dosage was a wineglassful and one which would have been unpleasant and unpalatable in larger quantities. But, medicine, tonic or what-have-you, it contained more than half of one percent of alcohol.

So, in the prohibition twenties, a new Malt-Nutrine emerged. Anyway that you looked at it—and particularly when you drank it—it just wasn't the same old Malt-Nutrine. Changing formulae incident to changing laws and regulations made any product containing alcohol one of uncertainty and physicians no longer felt that they could prescribe the tonic without qualification. Malt-Nutrine as a medicinal product was on the way out but on the way in with a new role on the burlesque stage of prohibition.

Word got around that it was a palatable substitute for beer either when spiked with grain alcohol or mixed with near-beer and alky. So for a while the revamped tonic enjoyed a healthy sale, but as bootlegging efficiency increased sales receded.

Anheuser-Busch continued through the early part of the thirties to manufacture Malt-Nutrine with the vague hope that some sort of miracle some day would restore it to prestige and popularity. One puzzling development was that the product, which always had enjoyed a healthy sales curve in the Latin-American countries, suddenly took on boom proportions in Cuba and particularly in Puerto Rico.

A marketing investigation revealed that the women of those countries, rightly or wrongly, had concluded that Malt-Nutrine was conducive to curvaceousness. Their male admirers liked the opposite sex with more figuration than frailty—not fat, mind you, but curvy. The ladies were led to believe that beer was fattening, but Malt-Nutrine would bring on a nicely worked out roundness sans fat.

Needless to say, Anheuser-Busch did not foster or promote this idea. It finally died out of its own delusion.

In the middle thirties, management decided to continue to produce Malt-Nutrine and protect the trademark but not to attempt at once to restore it to its former big volume sales.

Moreover, Anheuser-Busch faced a gigantic task in rehabilitating its property for the return of Budweiser beer without trying to budget too much money for Malt-Nutrine.

One thing certainly can be said of Malt-Nutrine: The company had every reason to be very proud of its first product in the pharmaceutical industry.

The Luxurious Adolphus Hotel in Dallas, Built by Adolphus Busch as a Tribute to Texas

Chapter XXXIV

ADOLPHUS REMEMBERS
TEXAS WITH A HOTEL

THIS SHORT chapter is included in the history of Anheuser-Busch not because the subject matter has any relation to the company itself, but because it concerns another of the enterprises of Adolphus Busch, co-founder of the company. It is a short story of the Hotel Adolphus in Dallas, Texas.

Adolphus, who had volunteered for service in the Army to preserve the Union, found in more pleasant times a great love for the Lone Star State that had fought the Union. He had every good reason to like Texas, because Texas was very kind to him.

It, you will remember, was the first state into which he decided to ship beer in his newfangled refrigerator cars that were re-iced at sidings along the way. The way in which the tall-hatted and booted Texans took to that cold, golden, foaming beer from St. Louis was heart-warming, indeed. Adolphus never ceased to be sentimental about Texas and what it had done to help him in his dream of national expansion.

So, in 1910, when the city of Dallas was sure it was on the way to greatness and wanted a hotel commensurate with its new stature, Adolphus decided to do something about it. After a series of meetings with leading citizens of the community, he agreed in the next year to form a corporation to build a very modern hotel, provided that local people would take a minor portion of the shares as a token of their interest.

The result was that Adolphus bought about 90 percent of the shares at par and the others were subscribed to by people who virtually represented the Who's Who of Dallas.

He delegated the task of supervising this entire venture to his son-in-law, Edward A. Faust, vice-president of Anheuser-Busch in charge of all grain and raw material purchases. Adolphus was lavish in his praise for the job that was done.

The structure, completed in the autumn of 1912, was the tallest and handsomest structure in the state. It was in architecture and detail much like the famous Blackstone Hotel of Chicago. Its initial cost was $1,870,000. Adolphus brought a group of representative St. Louisans to Dallas in his private railroad car for the dedication ceremonies.

By 1917, four years after the founder's death, the hotel was inadequate for the stepped-up activities of Dallas. The discovery of new oil fields and the presence of troops and visiting kin at nearby Army cantonments presented an urgent need for more rooms. The heirs of Adolphus elected to spend $1,300,000 on a second building to be annexed to the original hotel. This increased the number of rooms to 482. On top of the new edifice was the first roof garden in Dallas for dining and dancing.

The Hotel Adolphus continued year in and year out to be a show place. In March, 1919, during a cattlemen's convention, it had its all-time peak of 1,126 guests.

The fabulous expansion of Dallas now was in full swing. The Adolphus perpetually had demands for accommodations far in excess of its ability to meet them. The owners decided that another addition to the hotel group was needed and, at a cost of $800,000, the second annex was erected, this one between the other two so that now all three were a single unit. This occurred in 1926, the year in which radio station KRLD opened studios in the hotel.

In subsequent years, the Busch interests spent approximately $750,000 on improvements, including air-conditioning, a revamp of "the roof" (which was dedicated with a performance by Theodore Kasloff and his ballet) and the inclusion of the beautiful Century Room. In this room, President Roosevelt was the guest of honor at a luncheon in connection with the Texas Centennial Exposition.

The Century Room gave Dallas its first ice show. Ingenious construction permits a polished hardwood floor to be slid over the ice in a trice to make room for dancing by guests.

After repeal, the heirs of Adolphus found that the problems incident to almost constant brewery expansion gave them less and less time to devote to the hotel and, in 1949, reluctantly decided to sell the property to L. F. Corrigan, one of the city's leading citizens. The new owner immediately added a third annex to the building.

The Hotel Adolphus in 1952 still was upholding its traditional reputation for hospitality and excellence of accommodations and service.

Chapter XXXV

A PRIVATE GARDEN
DEVOTED TO CHARITY

MENTION WAS made in an earlier chapter of the beautiful and famous Pasadena Gardens which Adolphus Busch and his wife, Mrs. Lilly Busch, created on their California estate. A little more detailed description follows.

Adolphus and his wife for some time had been visiting their magnificent home on Orange Grove Avenue in Pasadena, when in 1903 he conceived the idea of transforming the neighboring land into a beautiful garden. He commissioned Robert G. Fraser, landscape architect, to create the beautiful spot out of the adjoining thirty acres. After Fraser's original start, the gardens were improved from time to time and were, within a few years after 1903, reputed to be worth $3,000,000.

Photographs indicate that the gardens were comparable to the Missouri Botanical Gardens in St. Louis created originally by Henry Shaw. Magnificent palms and other types of trees grew profusely and there were many flower beds embellished with statues.

After Mr. and Mrs. Busch had enjoyed their gardens in the company of friends, they decided to open them to the public. Thus the acreage became a show place for natives of Pasadena and visitors to the city. The gardens continued their public-private aspect until 1921 when Mrs. Busch, now a widow, decided that since so many people visited the place, it could be made into a source of profit for charity. Accordingly, she set up the Busch Gardens Fund for Disabled and Needy Veterans and turned the management over to the American Legion. Thereafter, each visitor paid 25 cents to go through the gardens. Altogether more than $144,000 was collected and given to the Disabled Veterans. When the California department of the American Legion asked what was to be its share of maintenance of the place, Mrs. Busch said that she intended to pay every cent of the maintenance cost. Sometimes when the number of visitors was not as great as others, she made up the difference in receipts with her own money. A conservative estimate would be that several hundred thousand persons visited the gardens.

When Mrs. Busch died on February 25, 1928, it was necessary to take steps to liquidate the property in order to avoid many court complications in handling her estate. These involvements were such that it was not until 1941 that sale of the property could be made. In the period between 1941 and 1946, the land was subdivided and parcels of it sold to individuals.

In later years, Mrs. Busch's daughter-in-law, Mrs. August A. Busch, Sr., was to help to create an entirely different kind of garden spot.

After World War II ended, the Federal War Assets Administration found itself with seven thousand acres of land in St. Charles County, Missouri, on its hands. On the tract had been a very important munitions plant that was needed no longer. Since most of the tract was in its original primitive condition, the Missouri Wildlife Conservation Commission was eager to acquire it for development of a wildlife area. The price was $225,750, but the commission lacked $70,000 of that sum to consummate the deal.

The widow of August A. Busch, Sr., volunteered to supply the needed sum,

CHILDREN'S PLAYHOUSE IN BUSCH GARDENS, PASADENA, CALIFORNIA

MRS. ADOLPHUS BUSCH, SOLDIERS' BENEFACTRESS—She gave to disabled service men and their dependents all of the admission money collected from visitors to the famous Busch Gardens.

the purchase was made and the place named the August A. Busch Wildlife Area. With the exception of a few shelters for visitors, the tract was left just as Nature designed it. Fishing was permitted but hunting prohibited. The Conservation Commission was anxious to determine just what could be expected if wildlife were given an opportunity to choose its own destiny in an area undisturbed by man.

BIG NEWS BREAKS

IN THE 101ST YEAR

In the one hundred and first year of Anheuser-Busch—specifically on February 20, 1953—a step was taken that virtually caused dancing in the streets among St. Louis baseball fans. The company bought the St. Louis Cardinals, the famous "Redbirds" who made the winning of pennants and world championships a habit.

What brought the greatest joy to Cardinal rooters was that Anheuser-Busch made certain that St. Louis would keep its favorite team. Newspaper stories for weeks had hinted that the team might be moved to another city. Note the St. Louis Globe-Democrat headline reproduced here.

To Keep Your SYMPHONY— Back It!

St. Louis Globe-Democrat.

Over Hundred Years Old This Year

For Quicker WANT AD RESULTS Dial GA. 1212 The Result Number

Vol. 78—No. 255—Section A   St. Louis, Saturday Morning, February 21, 1953—2 Sections—18 Pages   FIVE CENTS IN GREATER ST. LOUIS | TEN CENTS ELSEWHERE

BUSCH SAVES CARDS FOR ST. LOUIS
Buys Baseball Club From Fred Saigh for $3,750,000

The news was published in newspapers and news magazines the country over and, of course, brought thousands of telegrams and much new goodwill to Anheuser-Busch.

Included in the purchase were the Cardinals' farm teams in Houston, Texas; Columbus, Ohio; Rochester, New York; Omaha, Nebraska; Fresno, California; Columbus, Georgia; Albany, Georgia, and Winston-Salem, North Carolina. The total price was $3,750,000.

Thus August A. Busch, Jr., president of Anheuser-Busch, became president of the Cardinals club, too. He laid great emphasis upon the fact that the purchase had been consummated as a sports venture "and not as a sales weapon."

Roscoe C. Hobbs, chairman of the board of the Chamber of Commerce of Metropolitan St. Louis sent this message to Mr. Busch:

All St. Louisans heartily applaud the purchase of the St. Louis Cardinals by Anheuser-Busch, Inc. This is but another instance of the many fine contributions you have made to the civic and business welfare of St. Louis over the years. On behalf of the Chamber of Commerce, we wish to be among the first to express our warmest appreciation and best wishes for the success of the club.

Finis? Certainly not!

As Anheuser-Busch begins the second century of its life, there is evidence in abundance that future historians will lack neither facts nor color to spread upon their pages.

The men and management in 1953 are well schooled to carry on the traditions that are Anheuser-Busch—to be better, to produce better.

To them, a salute!

I see you have

excellent taste